NIGHTWING
THE NEW ORDER

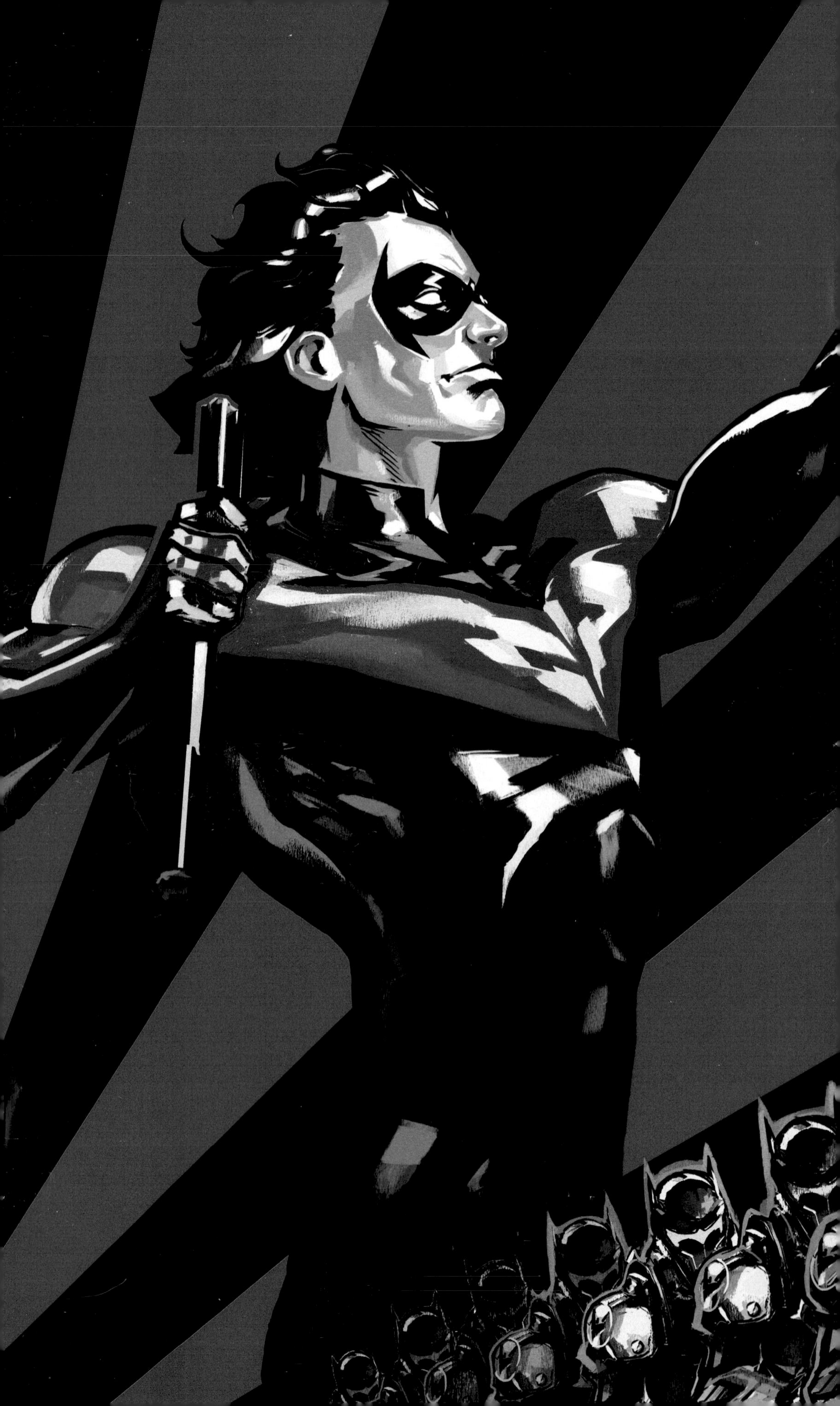

KYLE HIGGINS writer

TREVOR McCARTHY artist

DEAN WHITE colorist

CLAYTON COWLES letterer

TREVOR McCARTHY cover art & original series covers

NIGHTWING
THE NEW ORDER

MARV WOLFMAN and GEORGE PÉREZ

NIGHTWING created by MARV WOLFMAN and GEORGE PÉREZ

SUPERMAN created by JERRY SIEGEL and JOE SHUSTER
By special arrangement with the Jerry Siegel Family

ALEX ANTONE Editor – Original Series
DIEGO LOPEZ Assistant Editor – Original Series
JEB WOODARD Group Editor – Collected Editions
SCOTT NYBAKKEN Editor – Collected Edition
STEVE COOK Design Director – Books
MONIQUE NARBONETA Publication Design

BOB HARRAS Senior VP – Editor-in-Chief, DC Comics
PAT McCALLUM Executive Editor, DC Comics

DIANE NELSON President
DAN DiDIO Publisher
JIM LEE Publisher
GEOFF JOHNS President & Chief Creative Officer
AMIT DESAI Executive VP – Business & Marketing Strategy,
Direct to Consumer & Global Franchise Management
SAM ADES Senior VP & General Manager, Digital Services
BOBBIE CHASE VP & Executive Editor, Young Reader & Talent Development
MARK CHIARELLO Senior VP – Art, Design & Collected Editions
JOHN CUNNINGHAM Senior VP – Sales & Trade Marketing
ANNE DePIES Senior VP – Business Strategy, Finance & Administration
DON FALLETTI VP – Manufacturing Operations
LAWRENCE GANEM VP – Editorial Administration & Talent Relations
ALISON GILL Senior VP – Manufacturing & Operations
HANK KANALZ Senior VP – Editorial Strategy & Administration
JAY KOGAN VP – Legal Affairs
JACK MAHAN VP – Business Affairs
NICK J. NAPOLITANO VP – Manufacturing Administration
EDDIE SCANNELL VP – Consumer Marketing
COURTNEY SIMMONS Senior VP – Publicity & Communications
JIM (SKI) SOKOLOWSKI VP – Comic Book Specialty Sales
& Trade Marketing
NANCY SPEARS VP – Mass, Book, Digital Sales & Trade Marketing
MICHELE R. WELLS VP – Content Strategy

NIGHTWING: THE NEW ORDER

DC Comics, 2900 West Alameda Ave., Burbank, CA 91505
Printed by LSC Communications, Kendallville, IN, USA. 3/30/18. First Printing.
ISBN: 978-1-4012-7499-3

Library of Congress Cataloging-in-Publication Data is available.

PEFC Certified

Printed on paper from
sustainably managed
forests, controlled
sources

PEFC/29-31-337   www.pefc.org

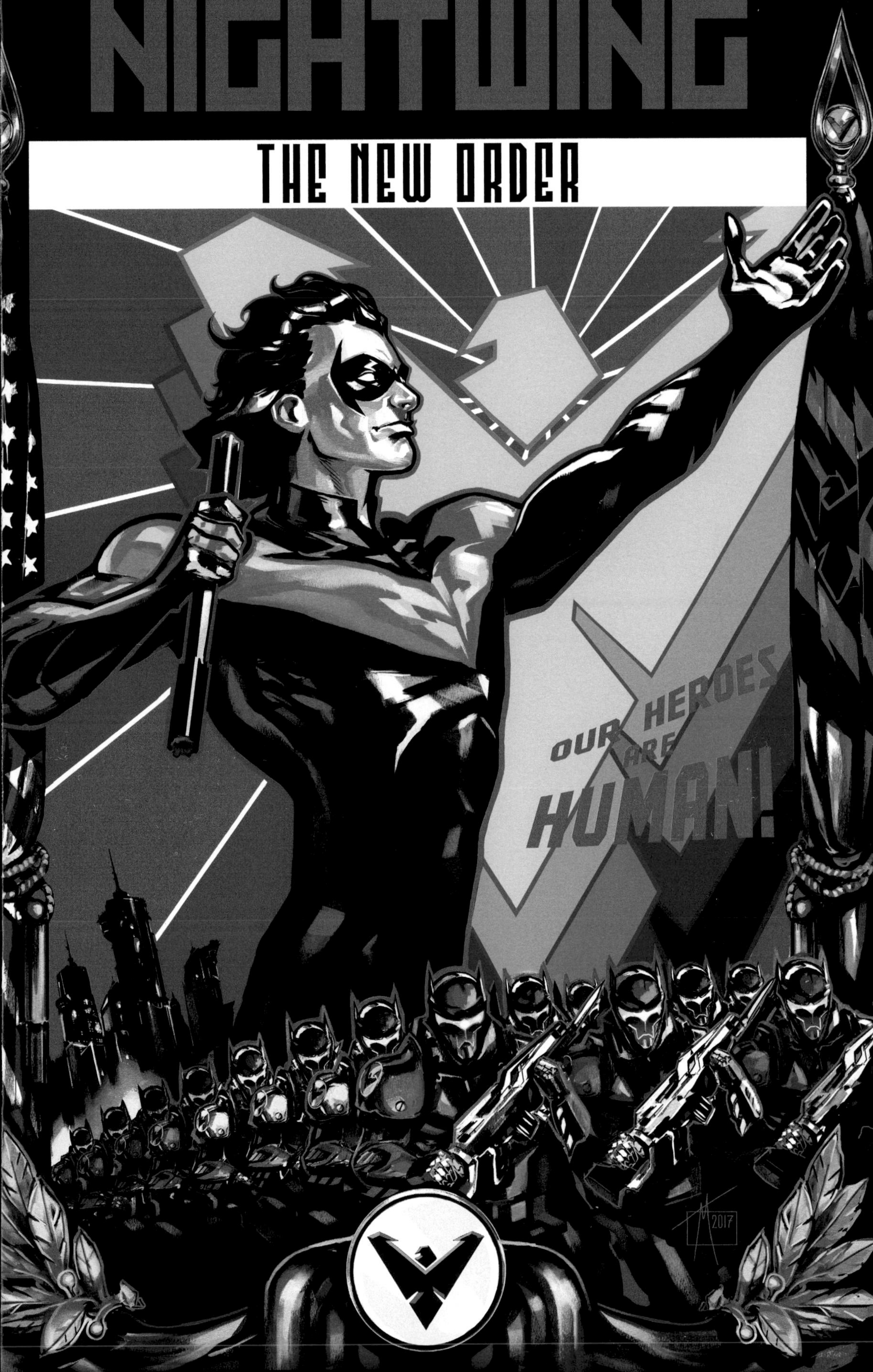
NIGHTWING
THE NEW ORDER
OUR HEROES ARE HUMAN!
2017

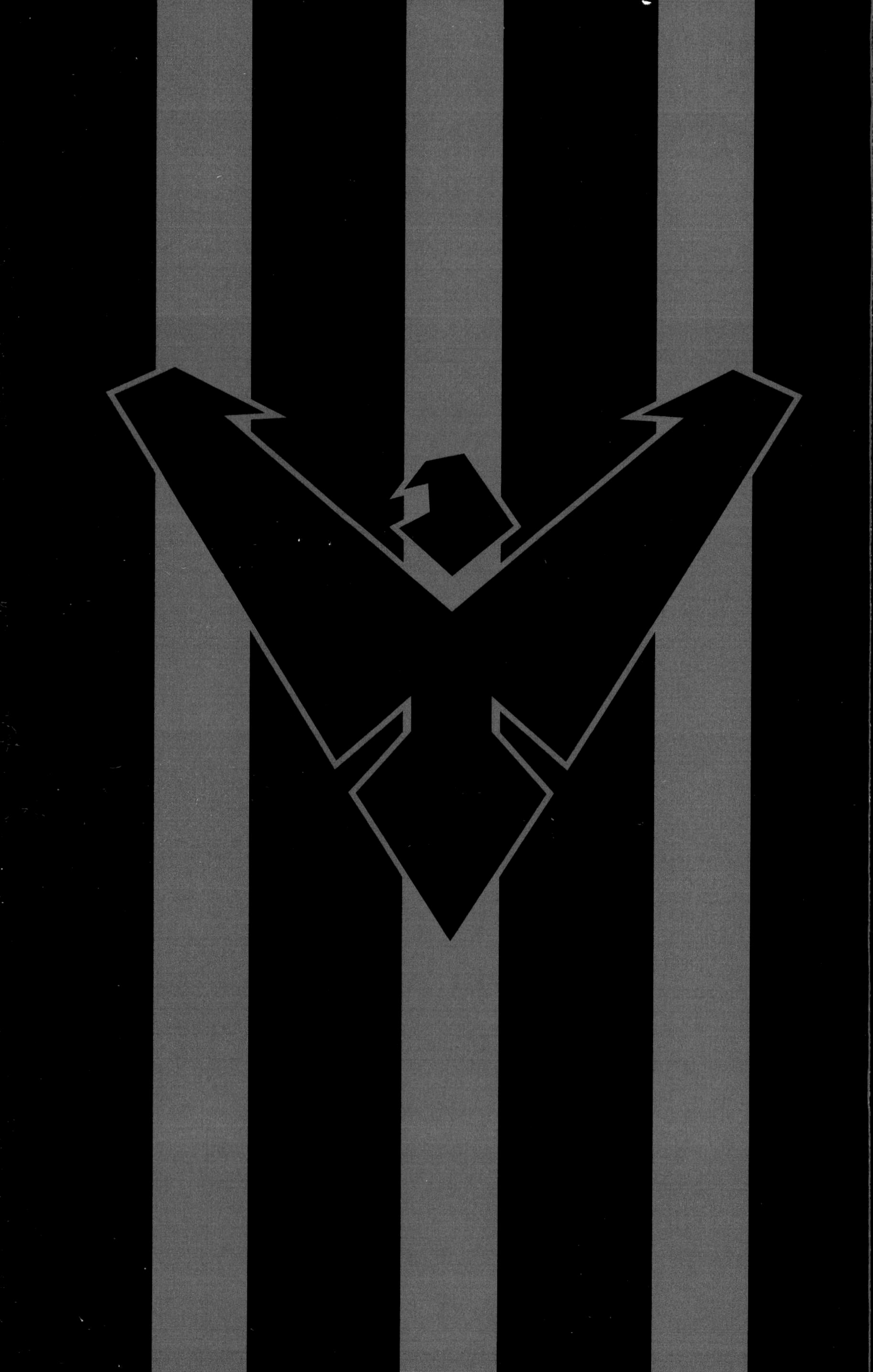

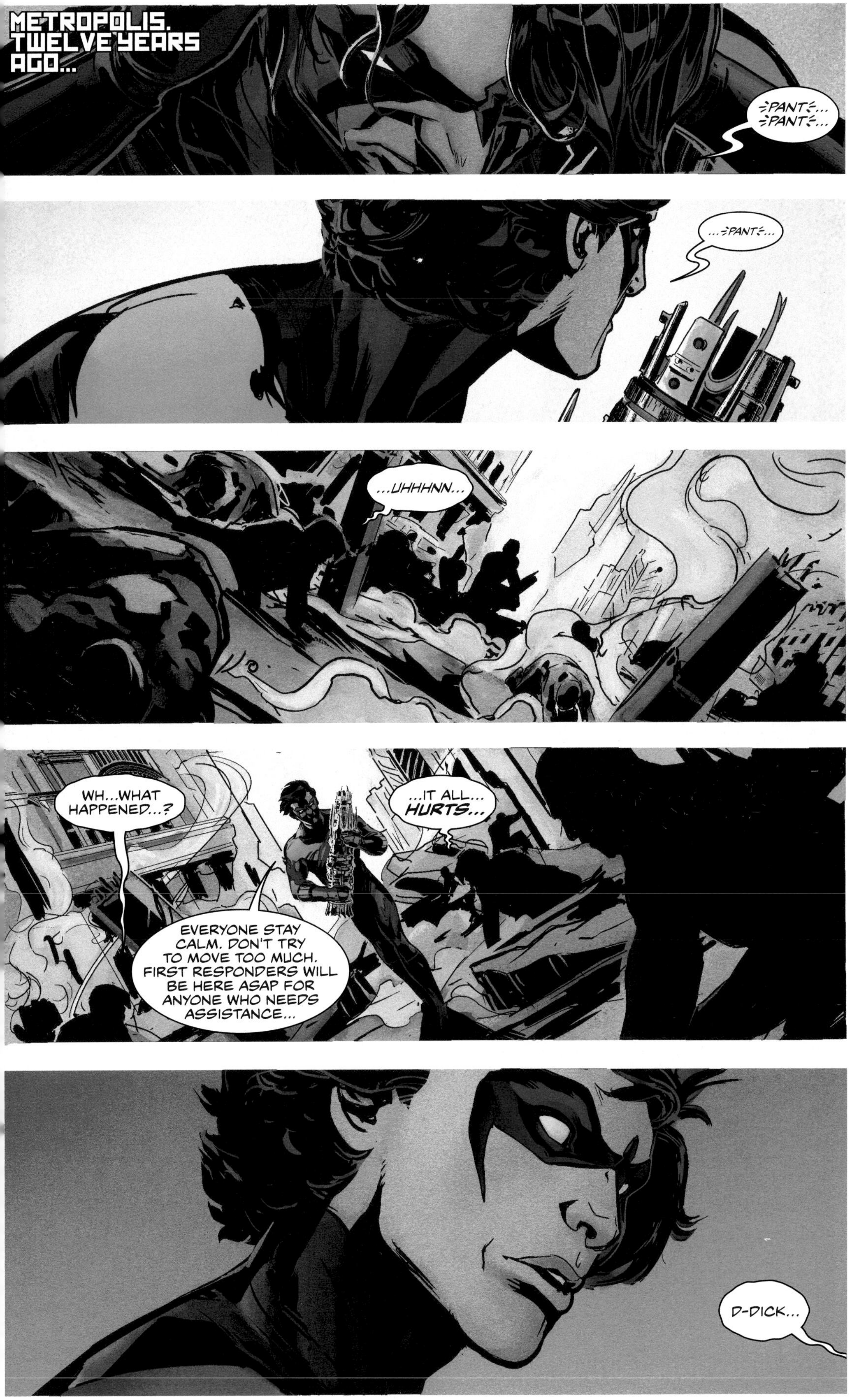

METROPOLIS. TWELVE YEARS AGO...
≈PANT≈... ≈PANT≈...
...≈PANT≈...
...UHHHNN...
WH...WHAT HAPPENED...?
...IT ALL... HURTS...
EVERYONE STAY CALM. DON'T TRY TO MOVE TOO MUCH. FIRST RESPONDERS WILL BE HERE ASAP FOR ANYONE WHO NEEDS ASSISTANCE...
D-DICK...

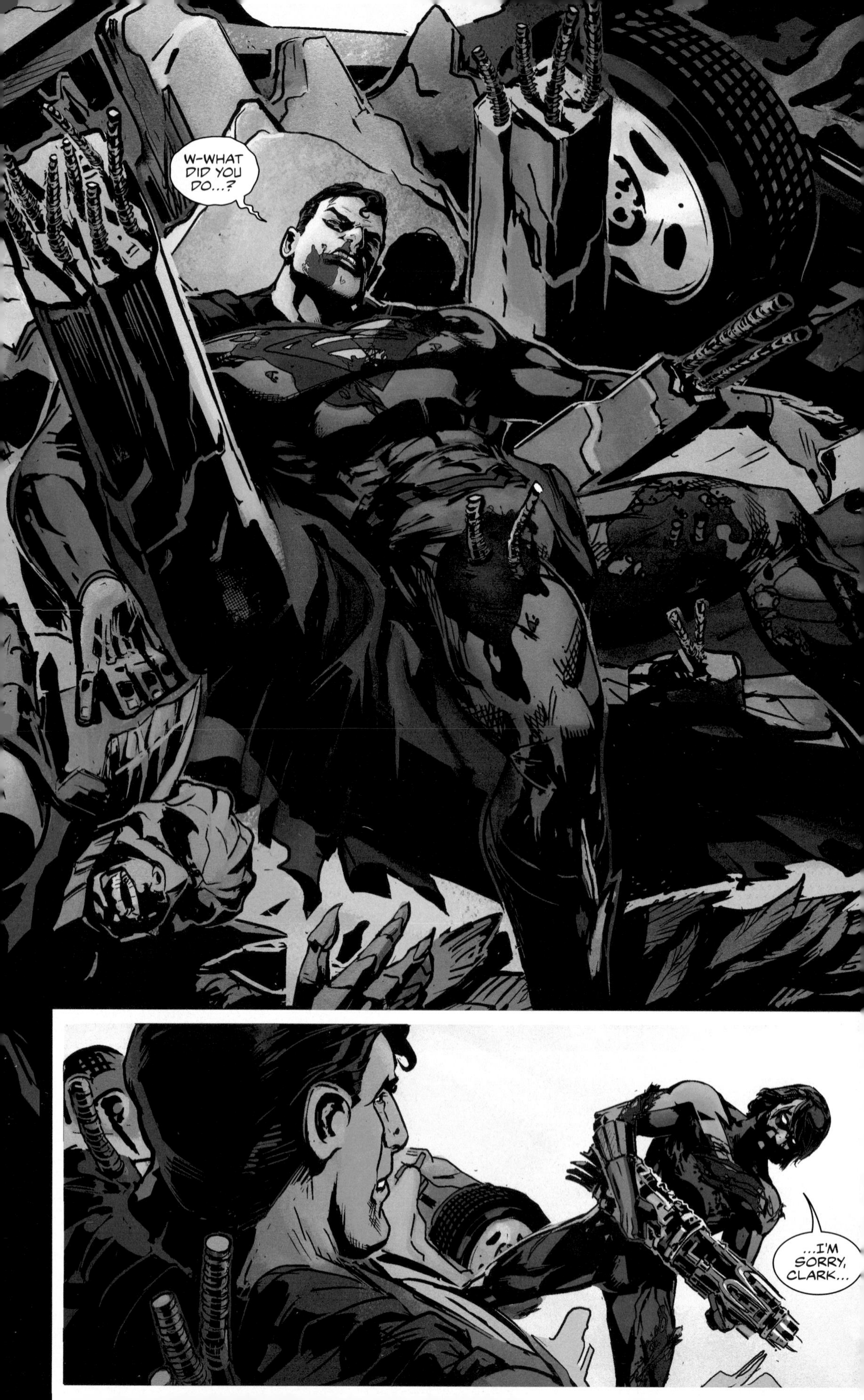
W-WHAT DID YOU DO...?
...I'M SORRY, CLARK...

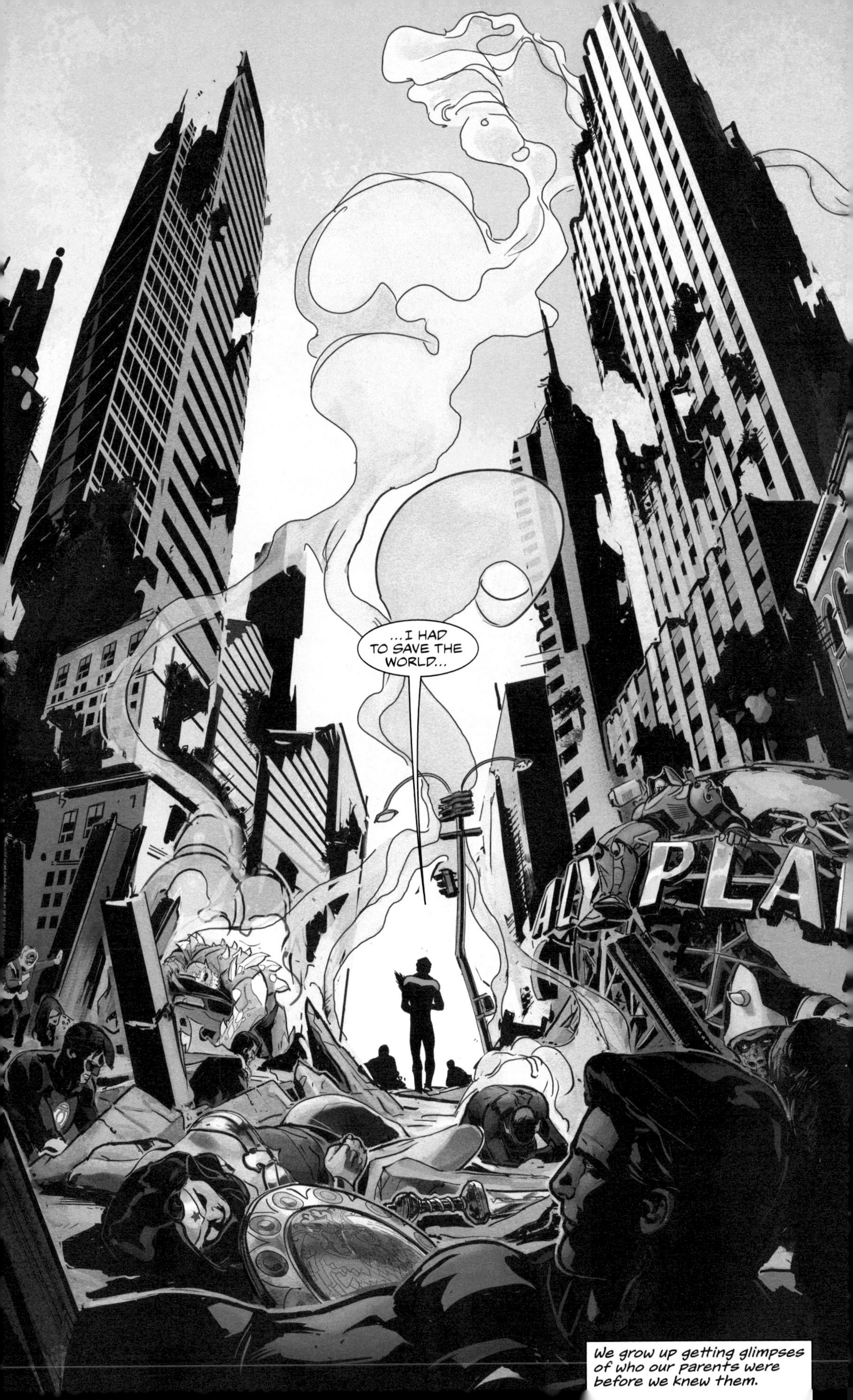
...I HAD TO SAVE THE WORLD...
PLA
We grow up getting glimpses of who our parents were before we knew them.

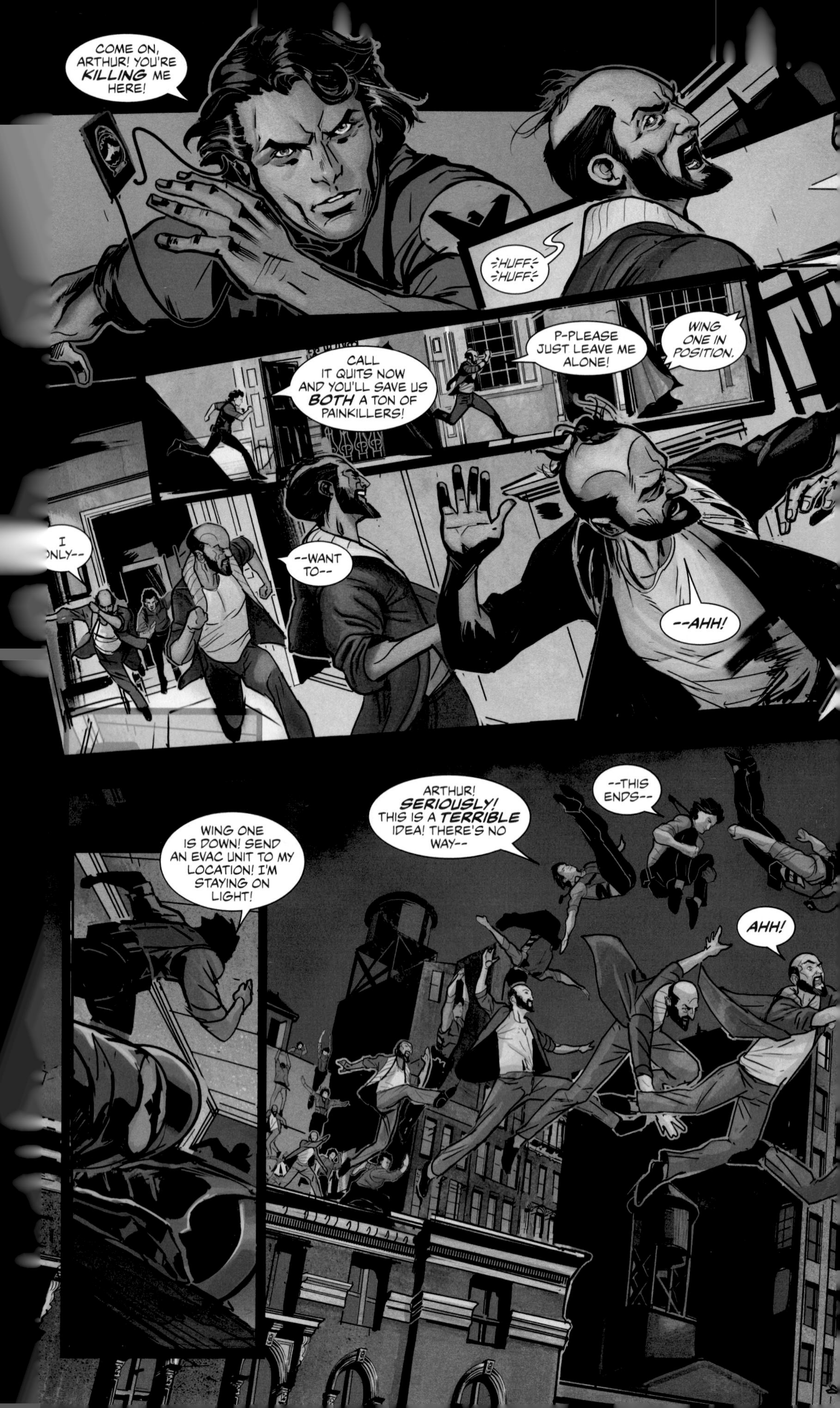
COME ON, ARTHUR! YOU'RE KILLING ME HERE!
HUFF HUFF
CALL IT QUITS NOW AND YOU'LL SAVE US BOTH A TON OF PAINKILLERS!
P-PLEASE JUST LEAVE ME ALONE!
WING ONE IN POSITION.
I ONLY--
--WANT TO--
--AHH!
WING ONE IS DOWN! SEND AN EVAC UNIT TO MY LOCATION! I'M STAYING ON LIGHT!
ARTHUR! SERIOUSLY! THIS IS A TERRIBLE IDEA! THERE'S NO WAY--
--THIS ENDS--
AHH!

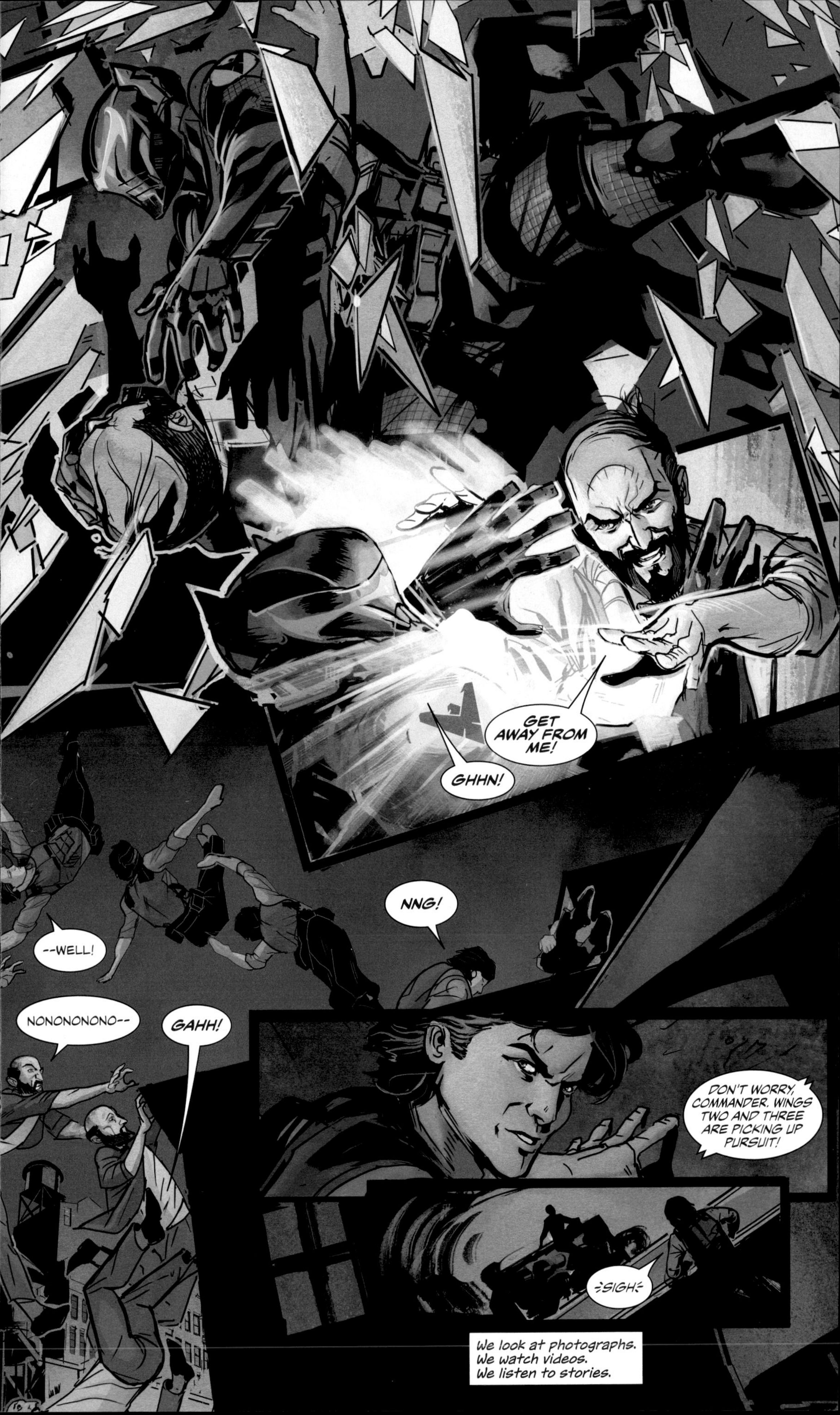
GET AWAY FROM ME!
GHHN!
NNG!
--WELL!
NONONONONO--
GAHH!
DON'T WORRY, COMMANDER. WINGS TWO AND THREE ARE PICKING UP PURSUIT!
=SIGH=
We look at photographs.
We watch videos.
We listen to stories.

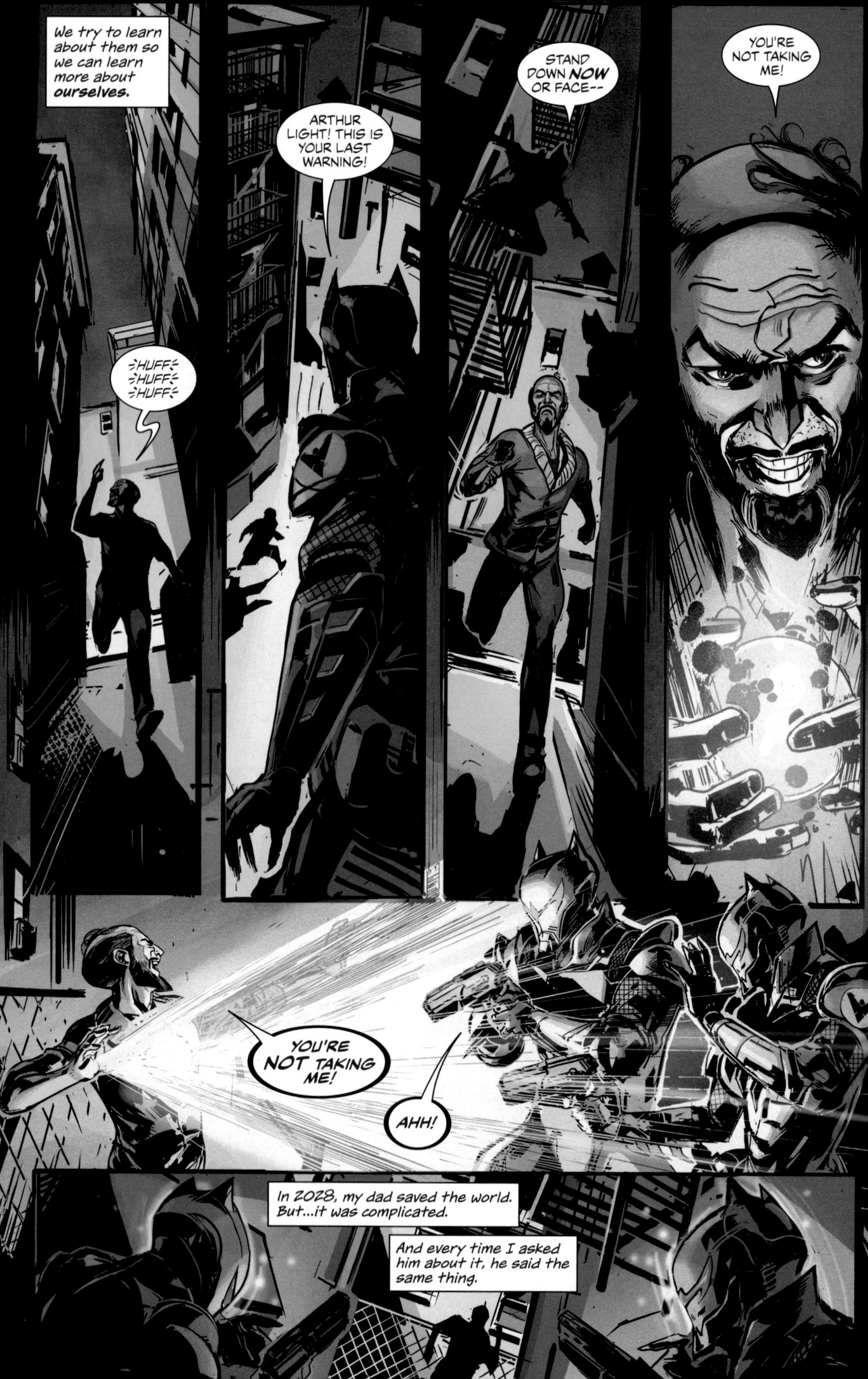

We try to learn about them so we can learn more about **ourselves.**
HUFF HUFF HUFF
ARTHUR LIGHT! THIS IS YOUR LAST WARNING!
STAND DOWN **NOW** OR FACE--
YOU'RE NOT TAKING ME!
YOU'RE **NOT** TAKING ME!
AHH!
In 2028, my dad saved the world. But...it was complicated.
And every time I asked him about it, he said the same thing.

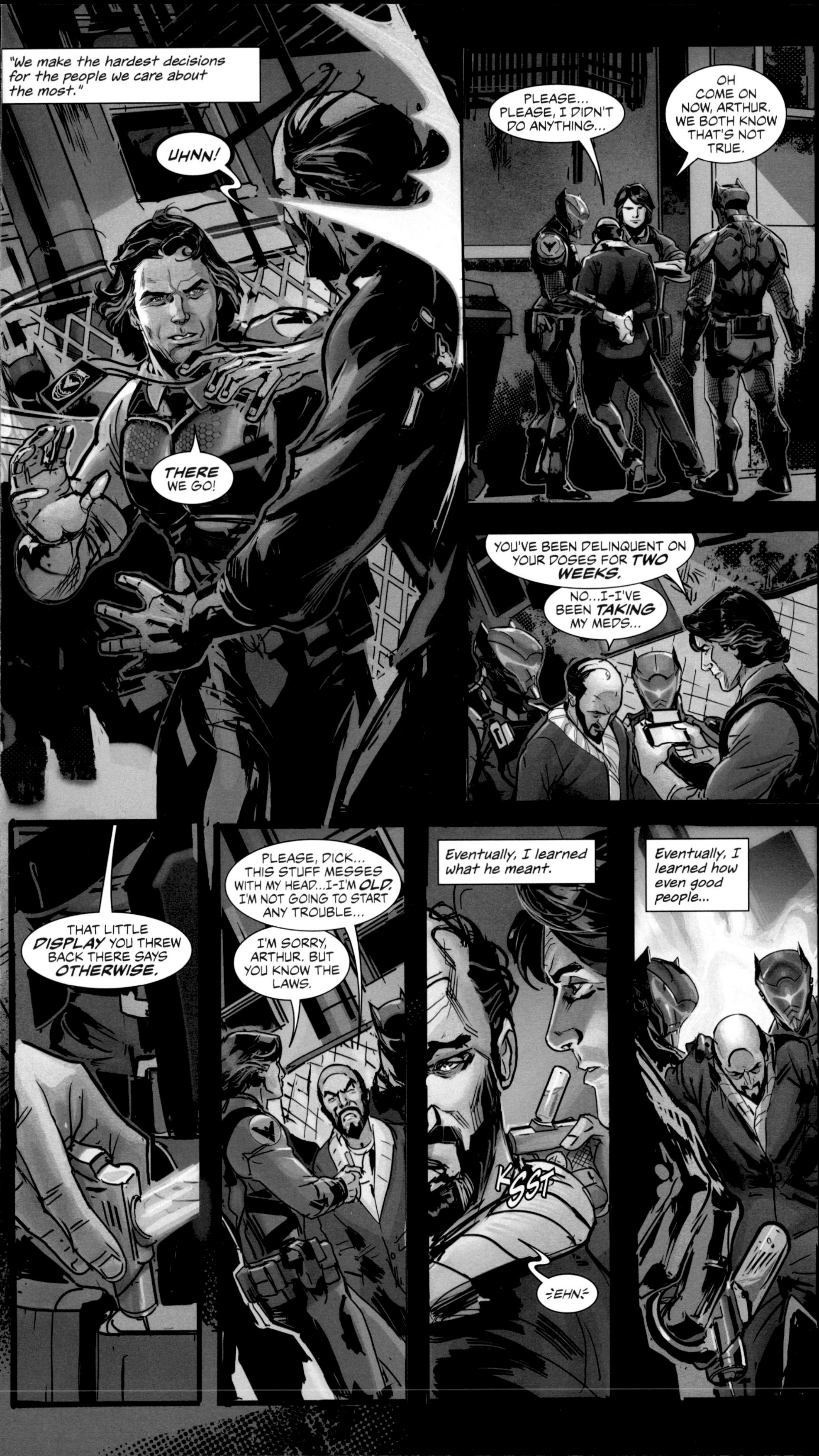
"We make the hardest decisions for the people we care about the most."
UHNN!
THERE WE GO!
PLEASE... PLEASE, I DIDN'T DO ANYTHING...
OH COME ON NOW, ARTHUR. WE BOTH KNOW THAT'S NOT TRUE.
YOU'VE BEEN DELINQUENT ON YOUR DOSES FOR TWO WEEKS.
NO...I-I'VE BEEN TAKING MY MEDS...
THAT LITTLE DISPLAY YOU THREW BACK THERE SAYS OTHERWISE.
PLEASE, DICK... THIS STUFF MESSES WITH MY HEAD...I-I'M OLD. I'M NOT GOING TO START ANY TROUBLE...
I'M SORRY, ARTHUR. BUT YOU KNOW THE LAWS.
Eventually, I learned what he meant.
KSST
EHN
Eventually, I learned how even good people...

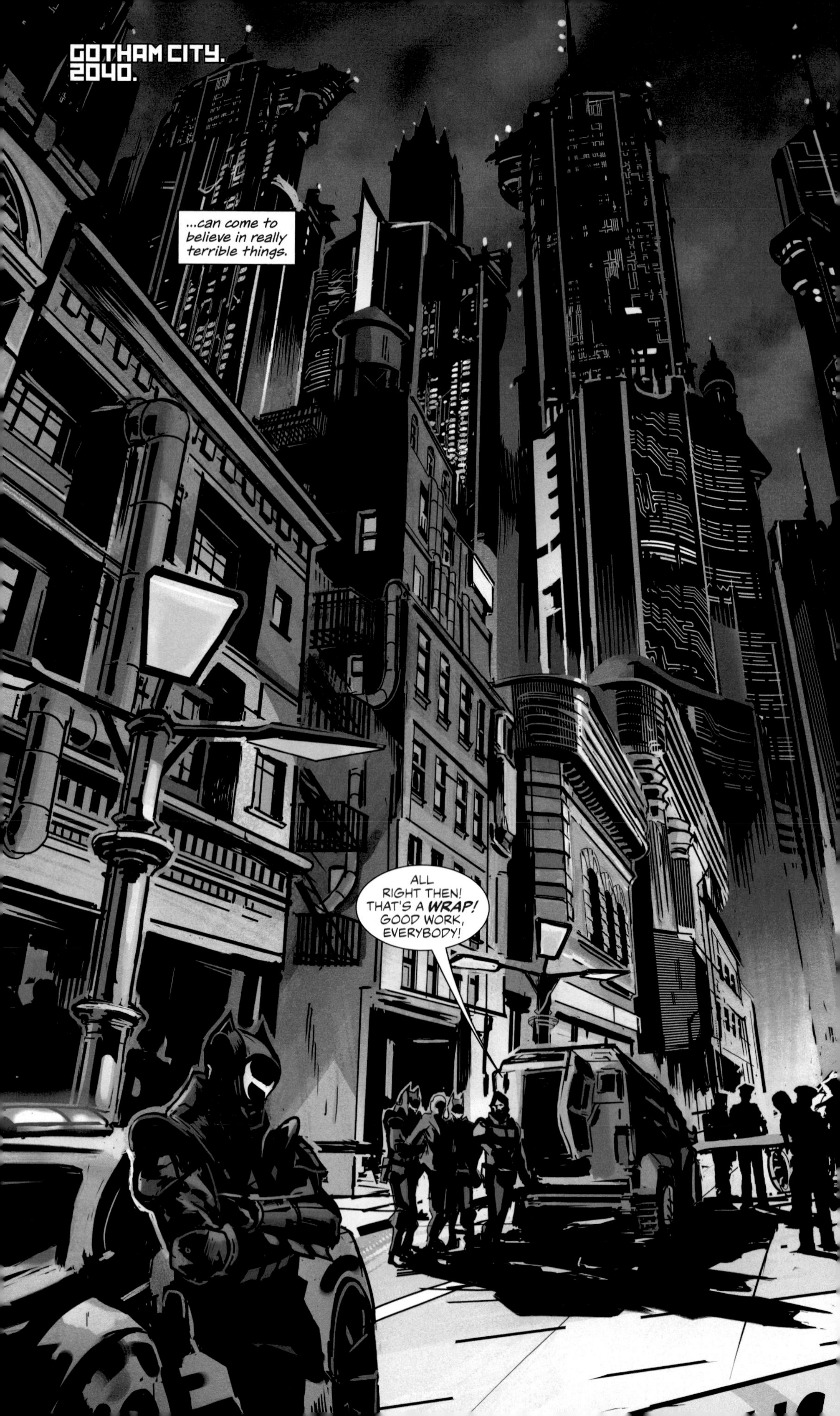
GOTHAM CITY. 2040.
...can come to believe in really terrible things.
ALL RIGHT THEN! THAT'S A WRAP! GOOD WORK, EVERYBODY!

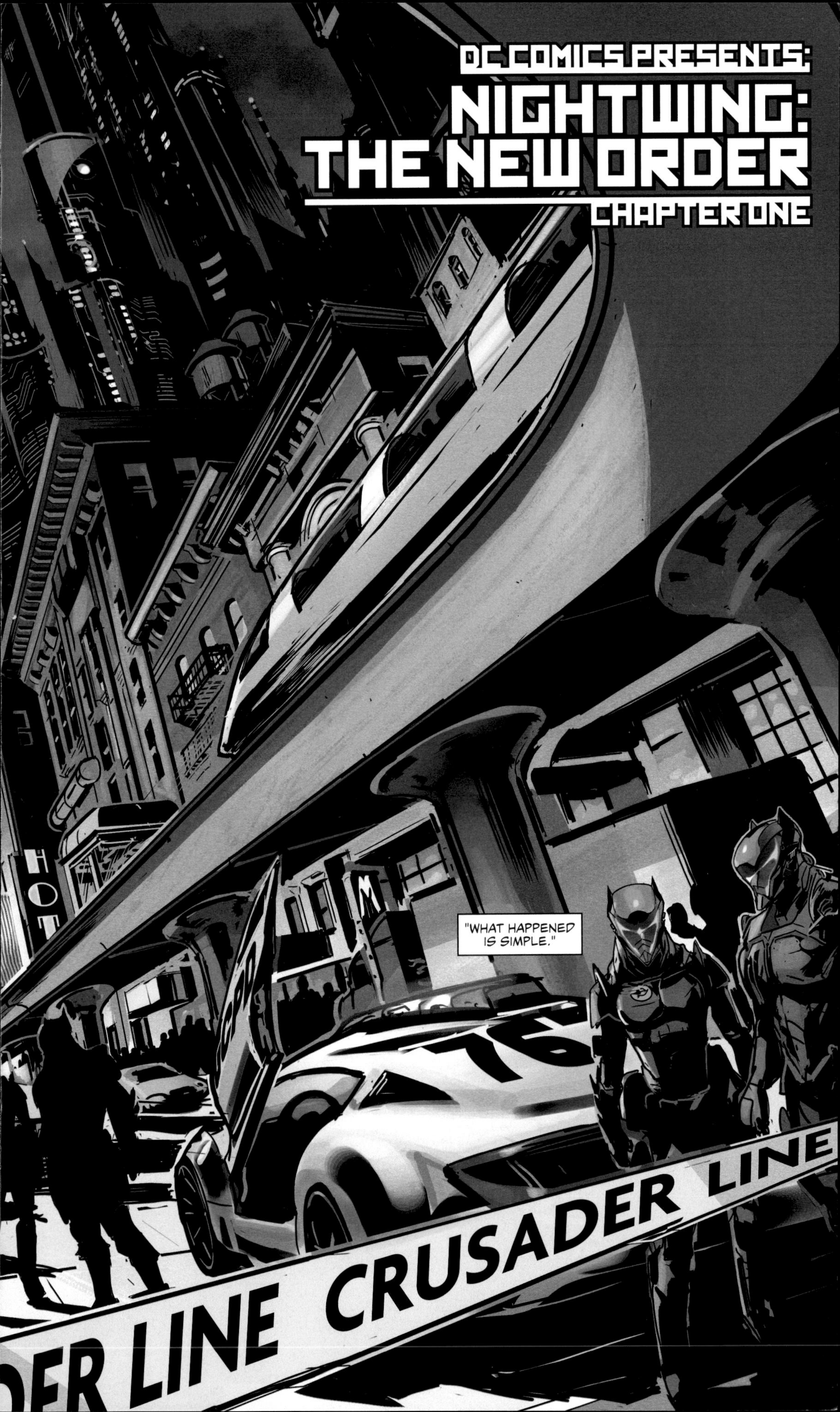
DC COMICS PRESENTS:
NIGHTWING:
THE NEW ORDER
CHAPTER ONE
"WHAT HAPPENED IS SIMPLE."
HOT
76
DER LINE CRUSADER LINE

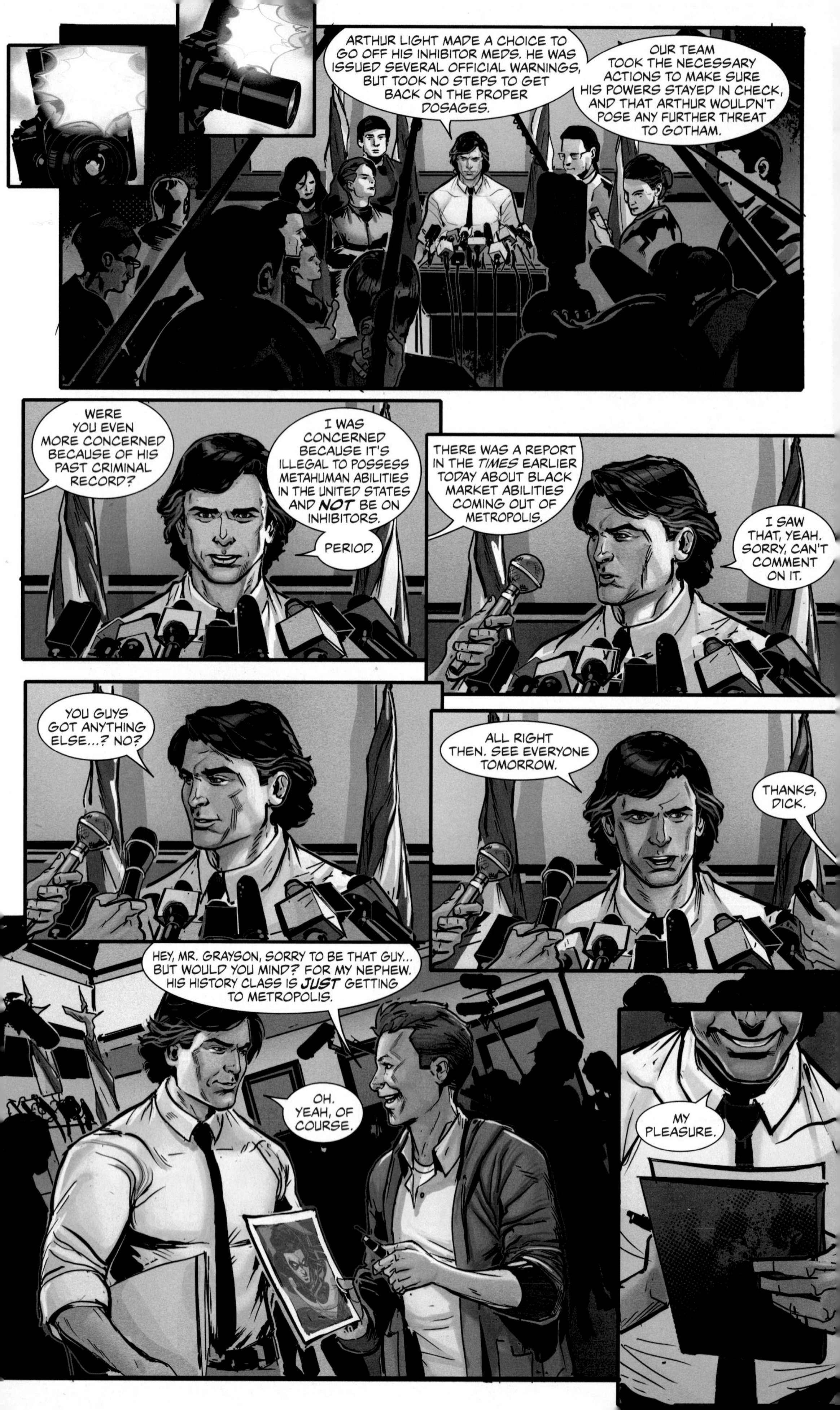

ARTHUR LIGHT MADE A CHOICE TO GO OFF HIS INHIBITOR MEDS. HE WAS ISSUED SEVERAL OFFICIAL WARNINGS, BUT TOOK NO STEPS TO GET BACK ON THE PROPER DOSAGES.
OUR TEAM TOOK THE NECESSARY ACTIONS TO MAKE SURE HIS POWERS STAYED IN CHECK, AND THAT ARTHUR WOULDN'T POSE ANY FURTHER THREAT TO GOTHAM.
WERE YOU EVEN MORE CONCERNED BECAUSE OF HIS PAST CRIMINAL RECORD?
I WAS CONCERNED BECAUSE IT'S ILLEGAL TO POSSESS METAHUMAN ABILITIES IN THE UNITED STATES AND ***NOT*** BE ON INHIBITORS.
PERIOD.
THERE WAS A REPORT IN THE *TIMES* EARLIER TODAY ABOUT BLACK MARKET ABILITIES COMING OUT OF METROPOLIS.
I SAW THAT, YEAH. SORRY, CAN'T COMMENT ON IT.
YOU GUYS GOT ANYTHING ELSE...? NO?
ALL RIGHT THEN. SEE EVERYONE TOMORROW.
THANKS, DICK.
HEY, MR. GRAYSON, SORRY TO BE THAT GUY... BUT WOULD YOU MIND? FOR MY NEPHEW. HIS HISTORY CLASS IS ***JUST*** GETTING TO METROPOLIS.
OH. YEAH, OF COURSE.
MY PLEASURE.

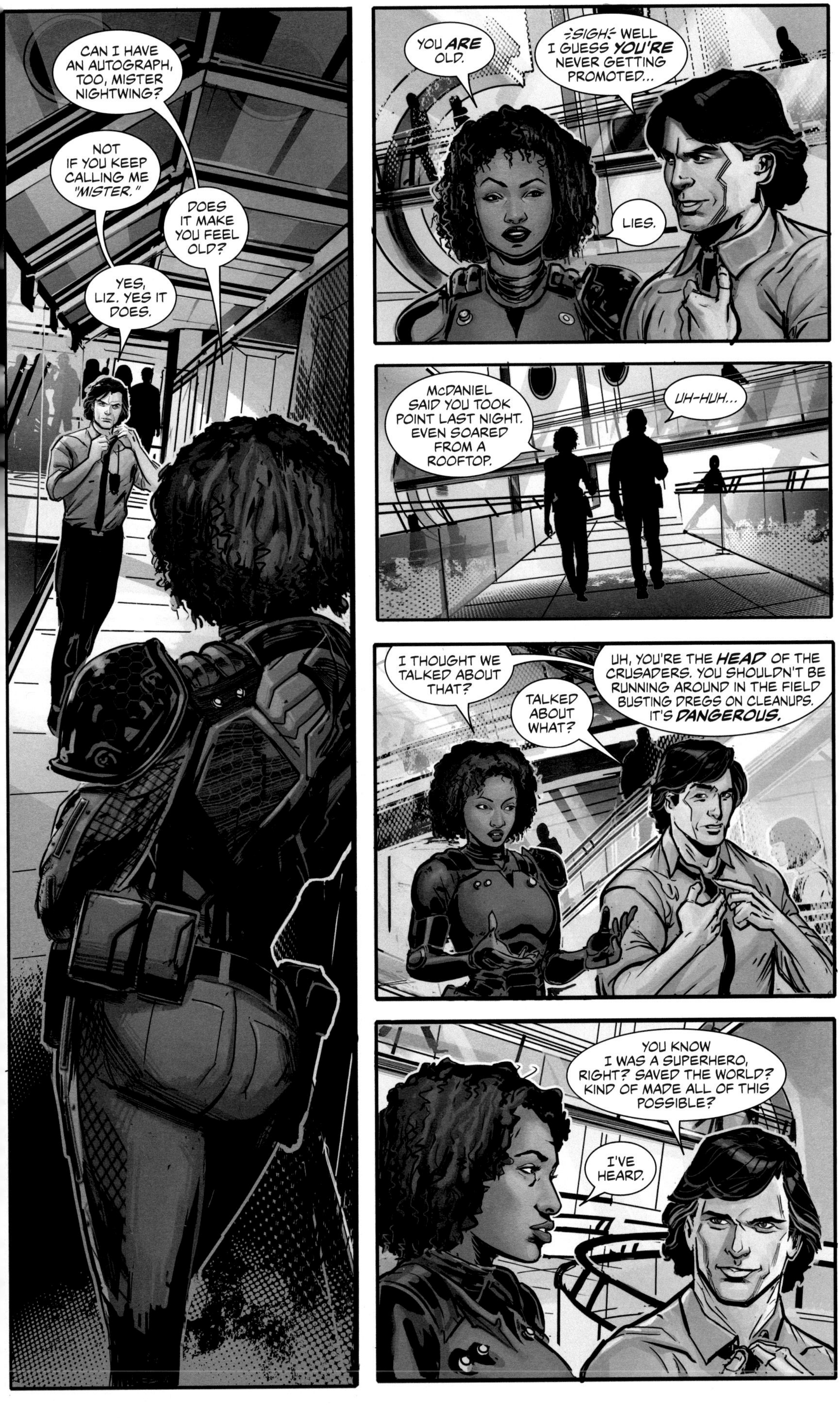
CAN I HAVE AN AUTOGRAPH, TOO, MISTER NIGHTWING?
NOT IF YOU KEEP CALLING ME "MISTER."
DOES IT MAKE YOU FEEL OLD?
YES, LIZ. YES IT DOES.
YOU ARE OLD.
-SIGH- WELL I GUESS YOU'RE NEVER GETTING PROMOTED...
LIES.
McDANIEL SAID YOU TOOK POINT LAST NIGHT. EVEN SOARED FROM A ROOFTOP.
UH-HUH...
I THOUGHT WE TALKED ABOUT THAT?
TALKED ABOUT WHAT?
UH, YOU'RE THE HEAD OF THE CRUSADERS. YOU SHOULDN'T BE RUNNING AROUND IN THE FIELD BUSTING DREGS ON CLEANUPS. IT'S DANGEROUS.
YOU KNOW I WAS A SUPERHERO, RIGHT? SAVED THE WORLD? KIND OF MADE ALL OF THIS POSSIBLE?
I'VE HEARD.

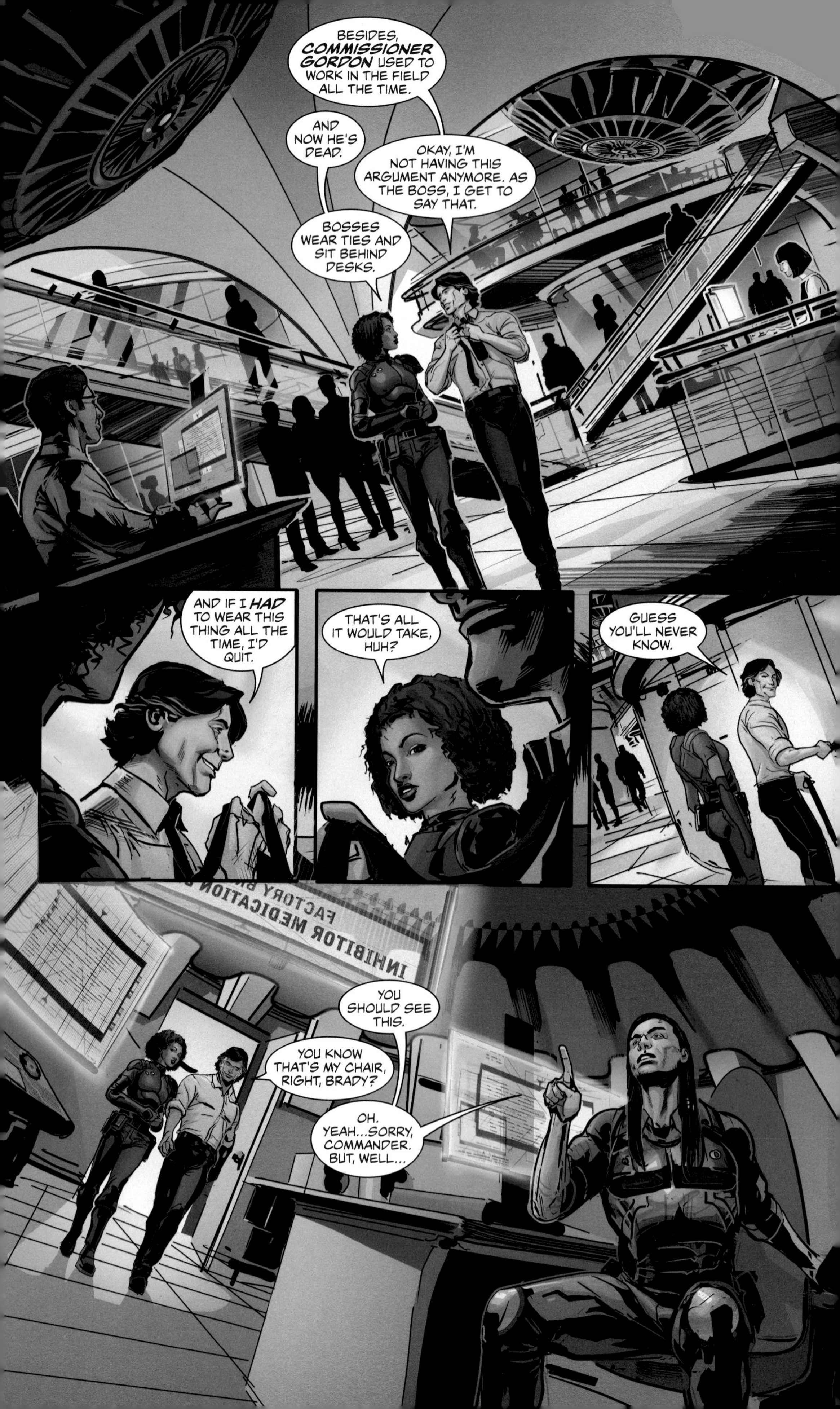

BESIDES, COMMISSIONER GORDON USED TO WORK IN THE FIELD ALL THE TIME.
AND NOW HE'S DEAD.
OKAY, I'M NOT HAVING THIS ARGUMENT ANYMORE. AS THE BOSS, I GET TO SAY THAT.
BOSSES WEAR TIES AND SIT BEHIND DESKS.
AND IF I HAD TO WEAR THIS THING ALL THE TIME, I'D QUIT.
THAT'S ALL IT WOULD TAKE, HUH?
GUESS YOU'LL NEVER KNOW.
INHIBITOR MEDICATION FACTORY
YOU SHOULD SEE THIS.
YOU KNOW THAT'S MY CHAIR, RIGHT, BRADY?
OH. YEAH...SORRY, COMMANDER. BUT, WELL...

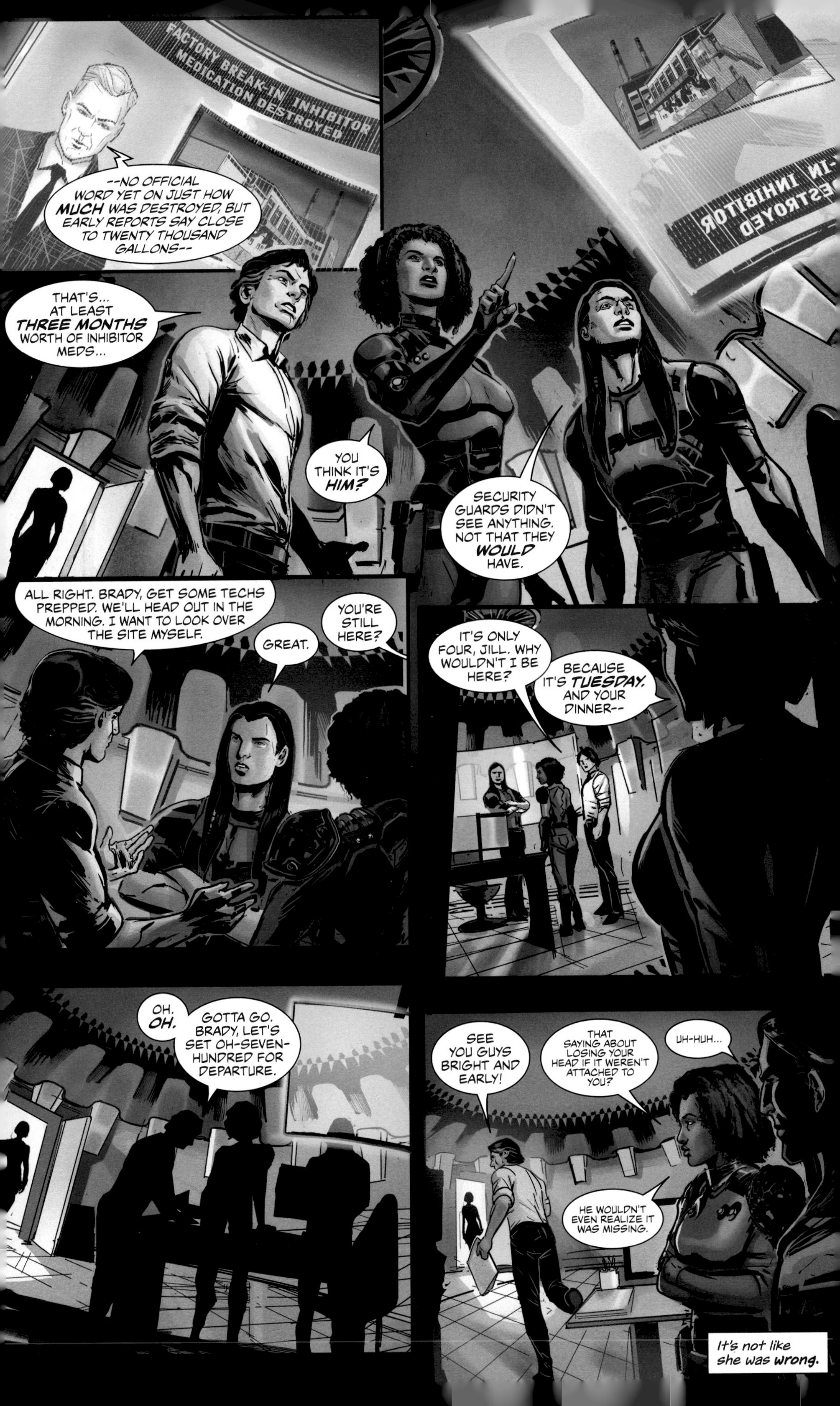
FACTORY BREAK-IN INHIBITOR MEDICATION DESTROYED
--NO OFFICIAL WORD YET ON JUST HOW MUCH WAS DESTROYED, BUT EARLY REPORTS SAY CLOSE TO TWENTY THOUSAND GALLONS--
THAT'S... AT LEAST THREE MONTHS WORTH OF INHIBITOR MEDS...
YOU THINK IT'S HIM?
SECURITY GUARDS DIDN'T SEE ANYTHING. NOT THAT THEY WOULD HAVE.
ALL RIGHT. BRADY, GET SOME TECHS PREPPED. WE'LL HEAD OUT IN THE MORNING. I WANT TO LOOK OVER THE SITE MYSELF.
GREAT.
YOU'RE STILL HERE?
IT'S ONLY FOUR, JILL. WHY WOULDN'T I BE HERE?
BECAUSE IT'S TUESDAY. AND YOUR DINNER--
OH. OH.
GOTTA GO. BRADY, LET'S SET OH-SEVEN-HUNDRED FOR DEPARTURE.
SEE YOU GUYS BRIGHT AND EARLY!
THAT SAYING ABOUT LOSING YOUR HEAD IF IT WEREN'T ATTACHED TO YOU?
UH-HUH...
HE WOULDN'T EVEN REALIZE IT WAS MISSING.
It's not like she was wrong.

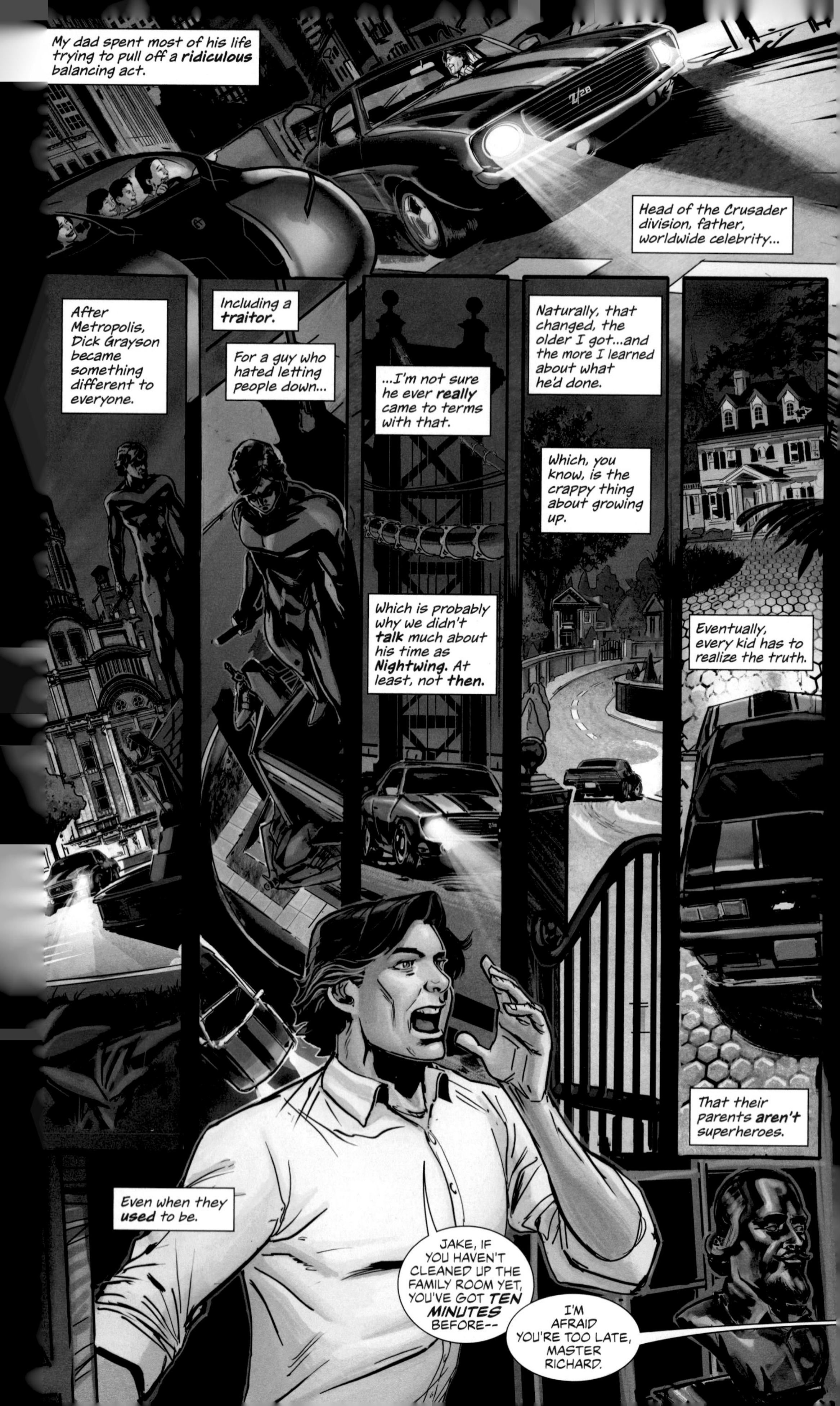
My dad spent most of his life trying to pull off a **ridiculous** balancing act.
Z/28
Head of the Crusader division, father, worldwide celebrity...
After Metropolis, Dick Grayson became something different to everyone.
Including a **traitor**.
For a guy who hated letting people down...
...I'm not sure he ever **really** came to terms with that.
Which is probably why we didn't **talk** much about his time as **Nightwing**. At least, not **then**.
Naturally, that changed, the older I got...and the more I learned about what he'd done.
Which, you know, is the crappy thing about growing up.
Eventually, every kid has to realize the truth.
That their parents **aren't** superheroes.
Even when they **used** to be.
JAKE, IF YOU HAVEN'T CLEANED UP THE FAMILY ROOM YET, YOU'VE GOT ***TEN MINUTES*** BEFORE--
I'M AFRAID YOU'RE TOO LATE, MASTER RICHARD.

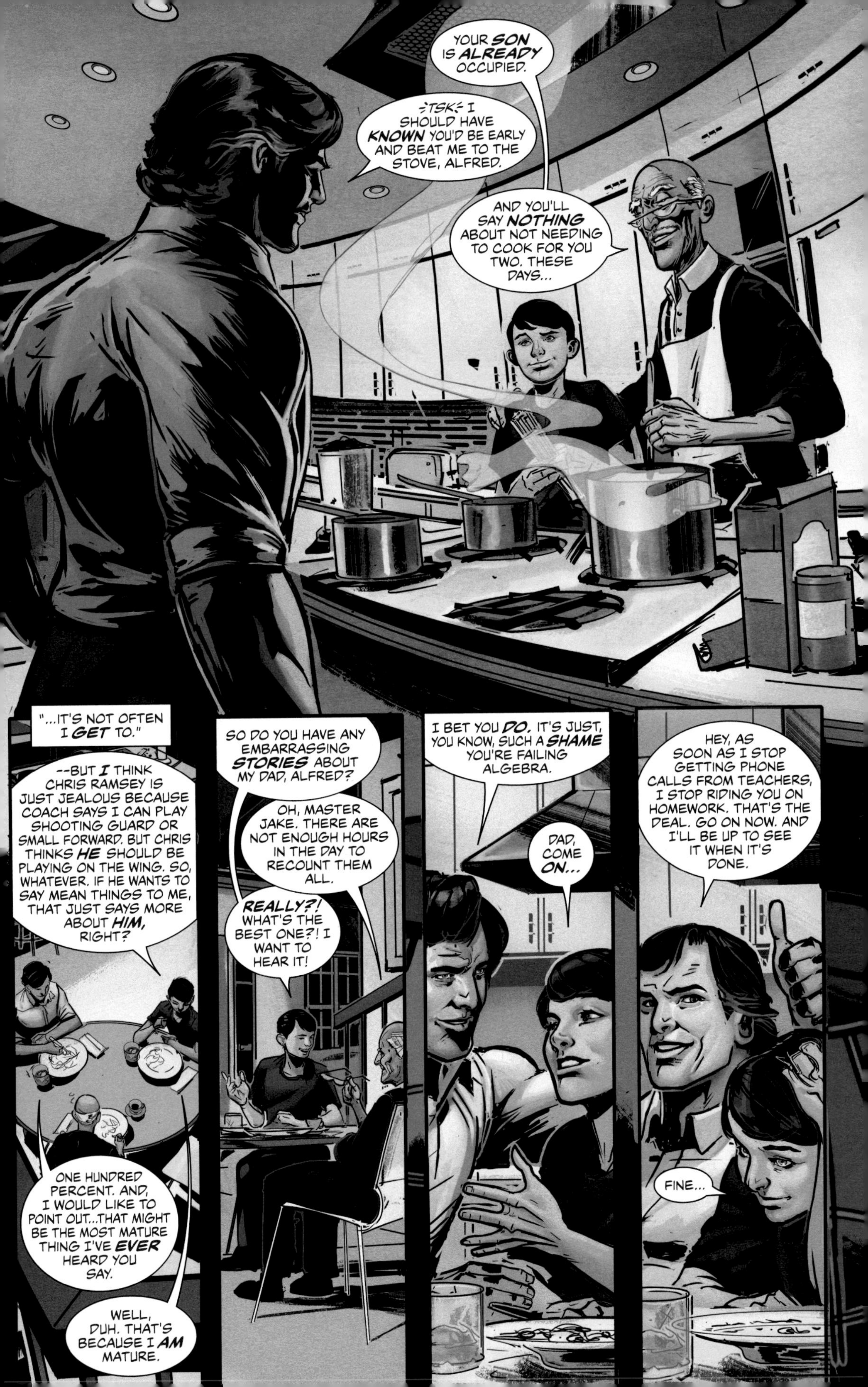
=TSK= I SHOULD HAVE KNOWN YOU'D BE EARLY AND BEAT ME TO THE STOVE, ALFRED.
YOUR SON IS ALREADY OCCUPIED.
AND YOU'LL SAY NOTHING ABOUT NOT NEEDING TO COOK FOR YOU TWO. THESE DAYS...
"...IT'S NOT OFTEN I GET TO."
--BUT I THINK CHRIS RAMSEY IS JUST JEALOUS BECAUSE COACH SAYS I CAN PLAY SHOOTING GUARD OR SMALL FORWARD. BUT CHRIS THINKS HE SHOULD BE PLAYING ON THE WING. SO, WHATEVER. IF HE WANTS TO SAY MEAN THINGS TO ME, THAT JUST SAYS MORE ABOUT HIM, RIGHT?
ONE HUNDRED PERCENT. AND, I WOULD LIKE TO POINT OUT...THAT MIGHT BE THE MOST MATURE THING I'VE EVER HEARD YOU SAY.
WELL, DUH. THAT'S BECAUSE I AM MATURE.
SO DO YOU HAVE ANY EMBARRASSING STORIES ABOUT MY DAD, ALFRED?
OH, MASTER JAKE. THERE ARE NOT ENOUGH HOURS IN THE DAY TO RECOUNT THEM ALL.
REALLY?! WHAT'S THE BEST ONE?! I WANT TO HEAR IT!
I BET YOU DO. IT'S JUST, YOU KNOW, SUCH A SHAME YOU'RE FAILING ALGEBRA.
DAD, COME ON...
HEY, AS SOON AS I STOP GETTING PHONE CALLS FROM TEACHERS, I STOP RIDING YOU ON HOMEWORK. THAT'S THE DEAL. GO ON NOW. AND I'LL BE UP TO SEE IT WHEN IT'S DONE.
FINE...

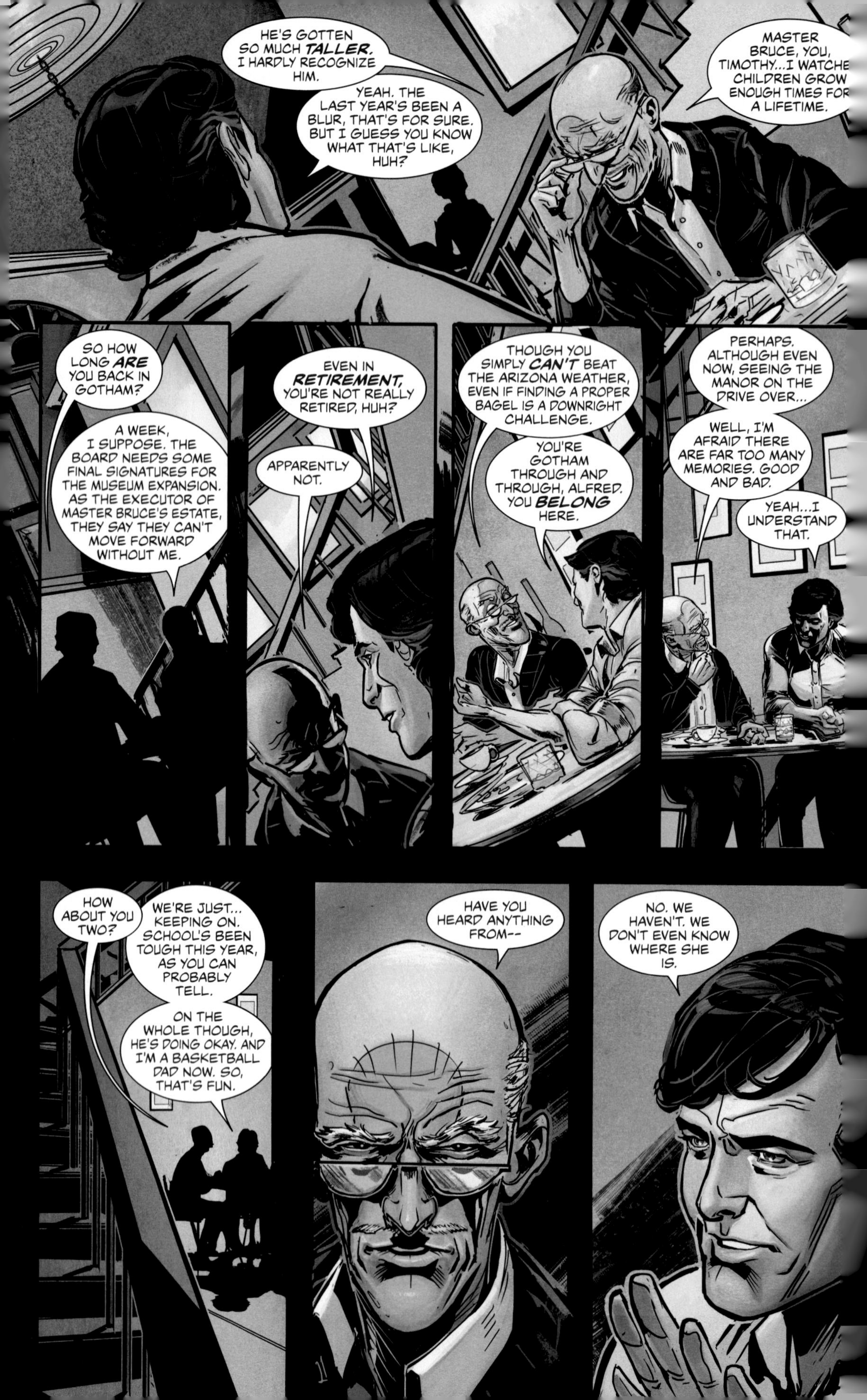
HE'S GOTTEN SO MUCH TALLER. I HARDLY RECOGNIZE HIM.
YEAH. THE LAST YEAR'S BEEN A BLUR, THAT'S FOR SURE. BUT I GUESS YOU KNOW WHAT THAT'S LIKE, HUH?
MASTER BRUCE, YOU, TIMOTHY...I WATCHED CHILDREN GROW ENOUGH TIMES FOR A LIFETIME.
SO HOW LONG ARE YOU BACK IN GOTHAM?
A WEEK, I SUPPOSE. THE BOARD NEEDS SOME FINAL SIGNATURES FOR THE MUSEUM EXPANSION. AS THE EXECUTOR OF MASTER BRUCE'S ESTATE, THEY SAY THEY CAN'T MOVE FORWARD WITHOUT ME.
EVEN IN RETIREMENT, YOU'RE NOT REALLY RETIRED, HUH?
APPARENTLY NOT.
THOUGH YOU SIMPLY CAN'T BEAT THE ARIZONA WEATHER, EVEN IF FINDING A PROPER BAGEL IS A DOWNRIGHT CHALLENGE.
YOU'RE GOTHAM THROUGH AND THROUGH, ALFRED. YOU BELONG HERE.
PERHAPS. ALTHOUGH EVEN NOW, SEEING THE MANOR ON THE DRIVE OVER...
WELL, I'M AFRAID THERE ARE FAR TOO MANY MEMORIES. GOOD AND BAD.
YEAH...I UNDERSTAND THAT.
HOW ABOUT YOU TWO?
WE'RE JUST... KEEPING ON. SCHOOL'S BEEN TOUGH THIS YEAR, AS YOU CAN PROBABLY TELL.
ON THE WHOLE THOUGH, HE'S DOING OKAY. AND I'M A BASKETBALL DAD NOW. SO, THAT'S FUN.
HAVE YOU HEARD ANYTHING FROM--
NO. WE HAVEN'T. WE DON'T EVEN KNOW WHERE SHE IS.

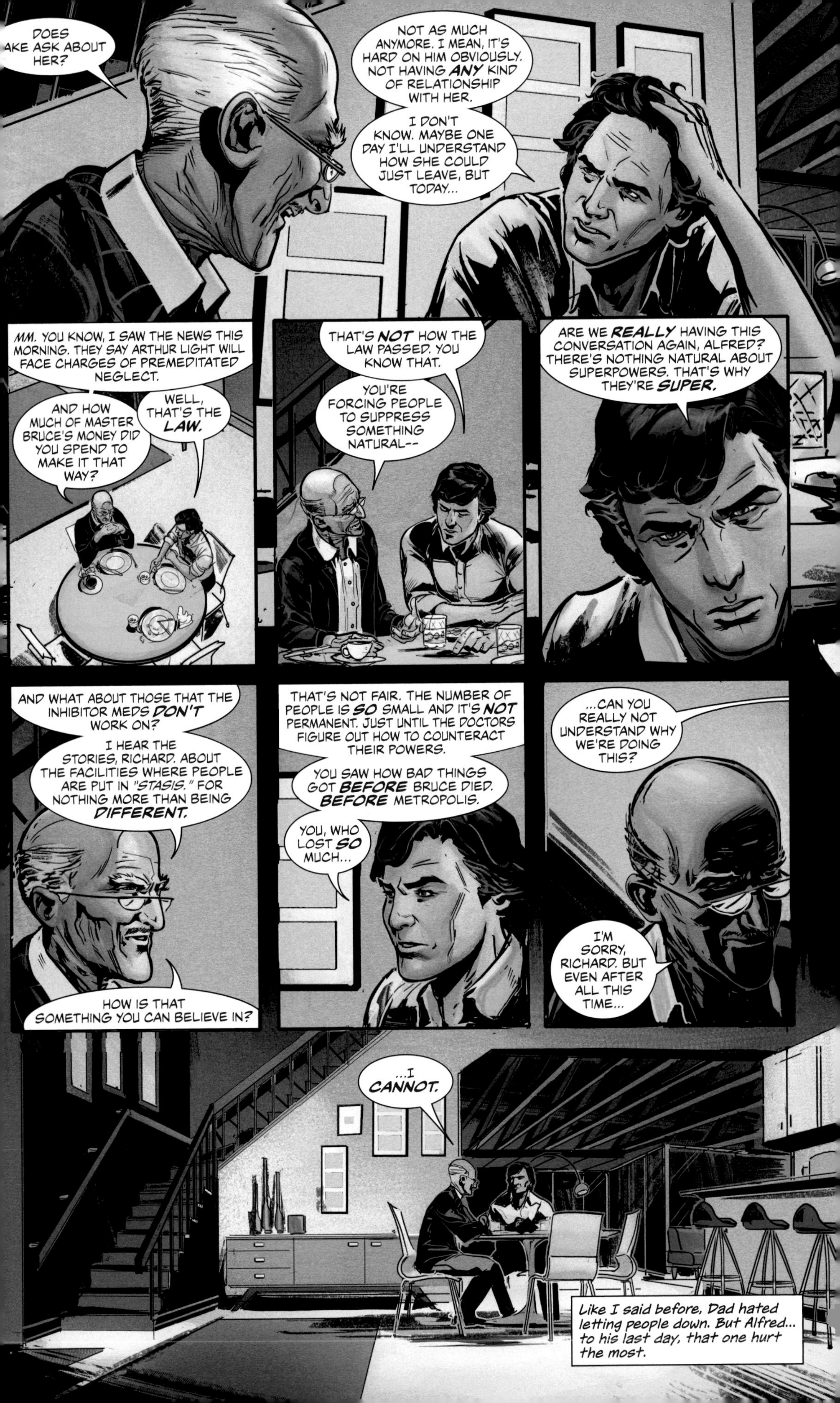
DOES
AKE ASK ABOUT
HER?
NOT AS MUCH ANYMORE. I MEAN, IT'S HARD ON HIM OBVIOUSLY. NOT HAVING ANY KIND OF RELATIONSHIP WITH HER.
I DON'T KNOW. MAYBE ONE DAY I'LL UNDERSTAND HOW SHE COULD JUST LEAVE, BUT TODAY...
MM. YOU KNOW, I SAW THE NEWS THIS MORNING. THEY SAY ARTHUR LIGHT WILL FACE CHARGES OF PREMEDITATED NEGLECT.
WELL, THAT'S THE LAW.
AND HOW MUCH OF MASTER BRUCE'S MONEY DID YOU SPEND TO MAKE IT THAT WAY?
THAT'S NOT HOW THE LAW PASSED. YOU KNOW THAT.
YOU'RE FORCING PEOPLE TO SUPPRESS SOMETHING NATURAL--
ARE WE REALLY HAVING THIS CONVERSATION AGAIN, ALFRED? THERE'S NOTHING NATURAL ABOUT SUPERPOWERS. THAT'S WHY THEY'RE SUPER.
AND WHAT ABOUT THOSE THAT THE INHIBITOR MEDS DON'T WORK ON?
I HEAR THE STORIES, RICHARD. ABOUT THE FACILITIES WHERE PEOPLE ARE PUT IN "STASIS." FOR NOTHING MORE THAN BEING DIFFERENT.
HOW IS THAT SOMETHING YOU CAN BELIEVE IN?
THAT'S NOT FAIR. THE NUMBER OF PEOPLE IS SO SMALL AND IT'S NOT PERMANENT. JUST UNTIL THE DOCTORS FIGURE OUT HOW TO COUNTERACT THEIR POWERS.
YOU SAW HOW BAD THINGS GOT BEFORE BRUCE DIED. BEFORE METROPOLIS.
YOU, WHO LOST SO MUCH...
...CAN YOU REALLY NOT UNDERSTAND WHY WE'RE DOING THIS?
I'M SORRY, RICHARD. BUT EVEN AFTER ALL THIS TIME...
...I CANNOT.
Like I said before, Dad hated letting people down. But Alfred... to his last day, that one hurt the most.

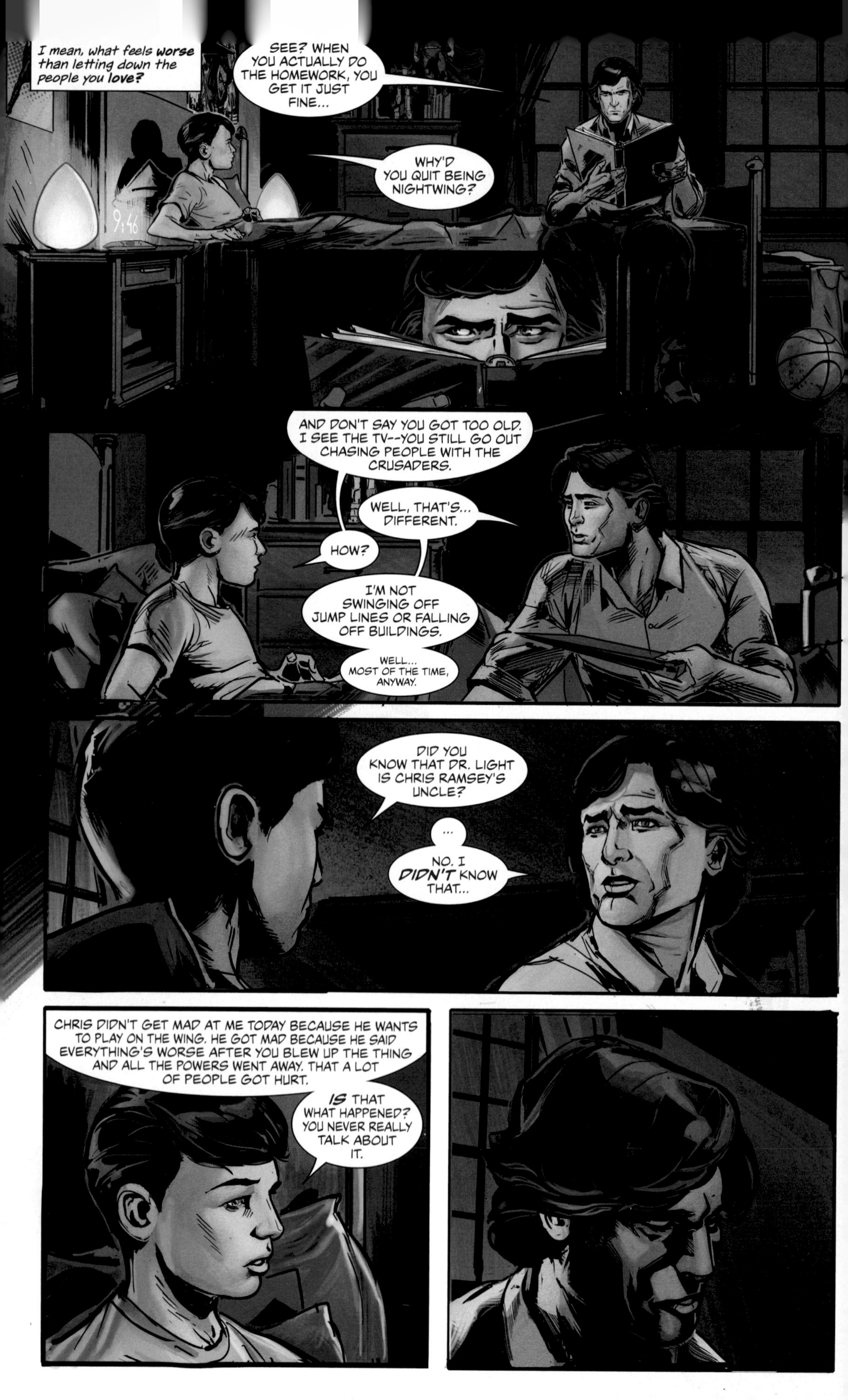

I mean, what feels **worse** than letting down the people you **love?**
SEE? WHEN YOU ACTUALLY DO THE HOMEWORK, YOU GET IT JUST FINE...
WHY'D YOU QUIT BEING NIGHTWING?
AND DON'T SAY YOU GOT TOO OLD. I SEE THE TV--YOU STILL GO OUT CHASING PEOPLE WITH THE CRUSADERS.
WELL, THAT'S... DIFFERENT.
HOW?
I'M NOT SWINGING OFF JUMP LINES OR FALLING OFF BUILDINGS.
WELL... MOST OF THE TIME, ANYWAY.
DID YOU KNOW THAT DR. LIGHT IS CHRIS RAMSEY'S UNCLE?
...
NO. I *DIDN'T* KNOW THAT...
CHRIS DIDN'T GET MAD AT ME TODAY BECAUSE HE WANTS TO PLAY ON THE WING. HE GOT MAD BECAUSE HE SAID EVERYTHING'S WORSE AFTER YOU BLEW UP THE THING AND ALL THE POWERS WENT AWAY. THAT A LOT OF PEOPLE GOT HURT.
IS THAT WHAT HAPPENED? YOU NEVER REALLY TALK ABOUT IT.
9:46

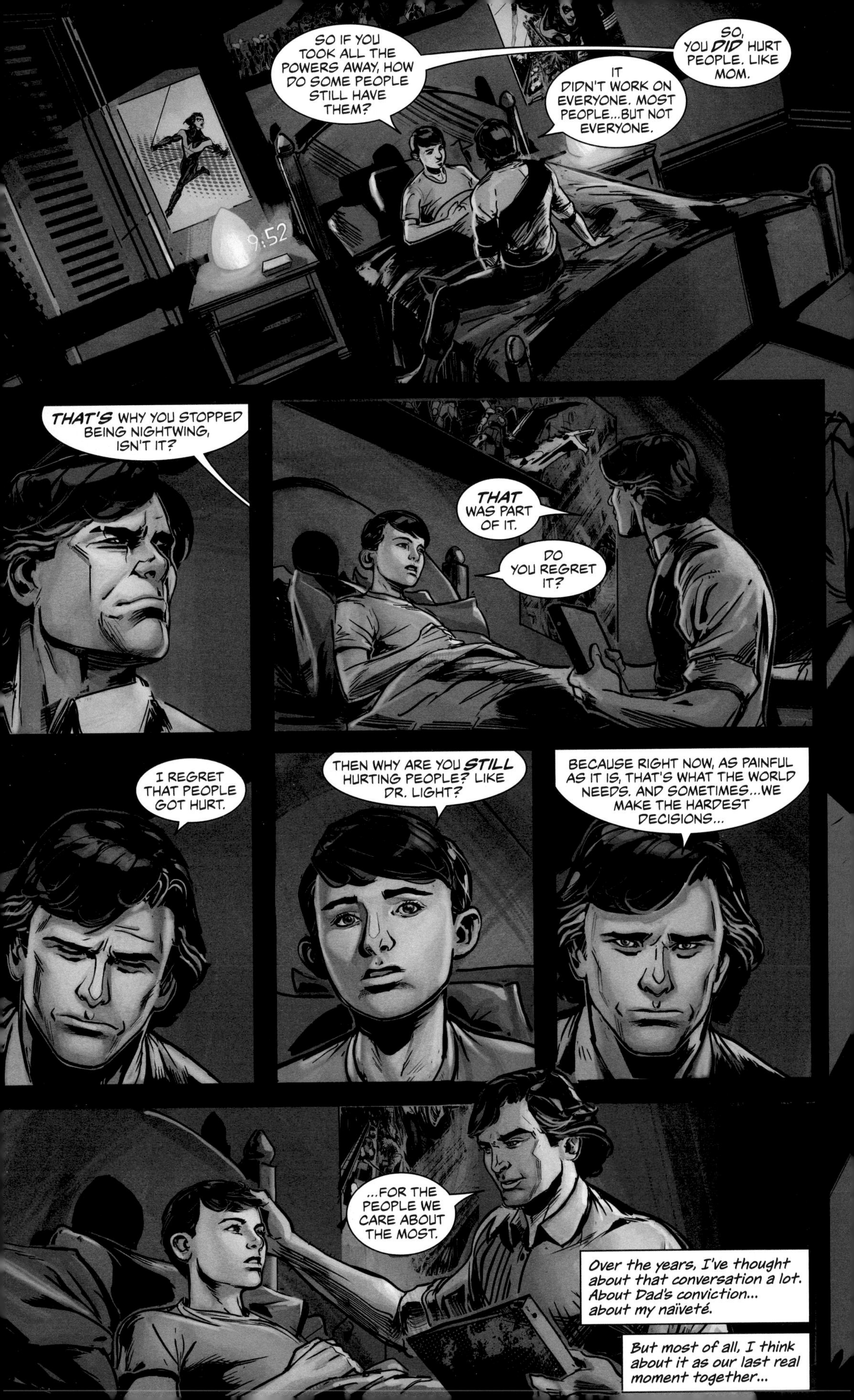
SO IF YOU TOOK ALL THE POWERS AWAY, HOW DO SOME PEOPLE STILL HAVE THEM?
IT DIDN'T WORK ON EVERYONE. MOST PEOPLE...BUT NOT EVERYONE.
SO, YOU DID HURT PEOPLE. LIKE MOM.
9:52
THAT'S WHY YOU STOPPED BEING NIGHTWING, ISN'T IT?
THAT WAS PART OF IT.
DO YOU REGRET IT?
I REGRET THAT PEOPLE GOT HURT.
THEN WHY ARE YOU STILL HURTING PEOPLE? LIKE DR. LIGHT?
BECAUSE RIGHT NOW, AS PAINFUL AS IT IS, THAT'S WHAT THE WORLD NEEDS. AND SOMETIMES...WE MAKE THE HARDEST DECISIONS...
...FOR THE PEOPLE WE CARE ABOUT THE MOST.
Over the years, I've thought about that conversation a lot. About Dad's conviction... about my naïveté.
But most of all, I think about it as our last real moment together...

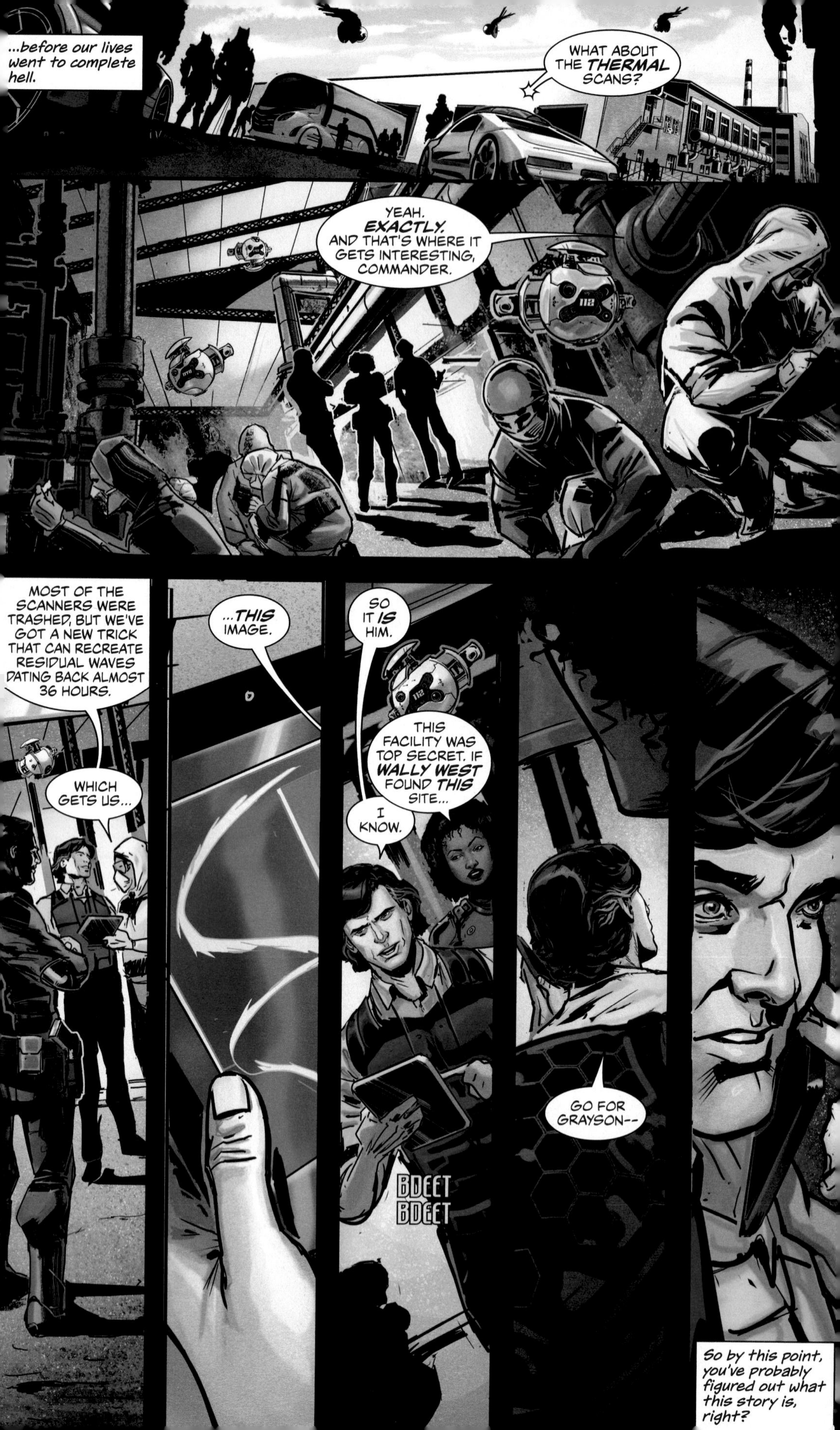
...before our lives went to complete hell.
WHAT ABOUT THE THERMAL SCANS?
YEAH. EXACTLY. AND THAT'S WHERE IT GETS INTERESTING, COMMANDER.
MOST OF THE SCANNERS WERE TRASHED, BUT WE'VE GOT A NEW TRICK THAT CAN RECREATE RESIDUAL WAVES DATING BACK ALMOST 36 HOURS.
WHICH GETS US...
...THIS IMAGE.
SO IT IS HIM.
THIS FACILITY WAS TOP SECRET. IF WALLY WEST FOUND THIS SITE...
I KNOW.
BDEET BDEET
GO FOR GRAYSON--
So by this point, you've probably figured out what this story is, right?

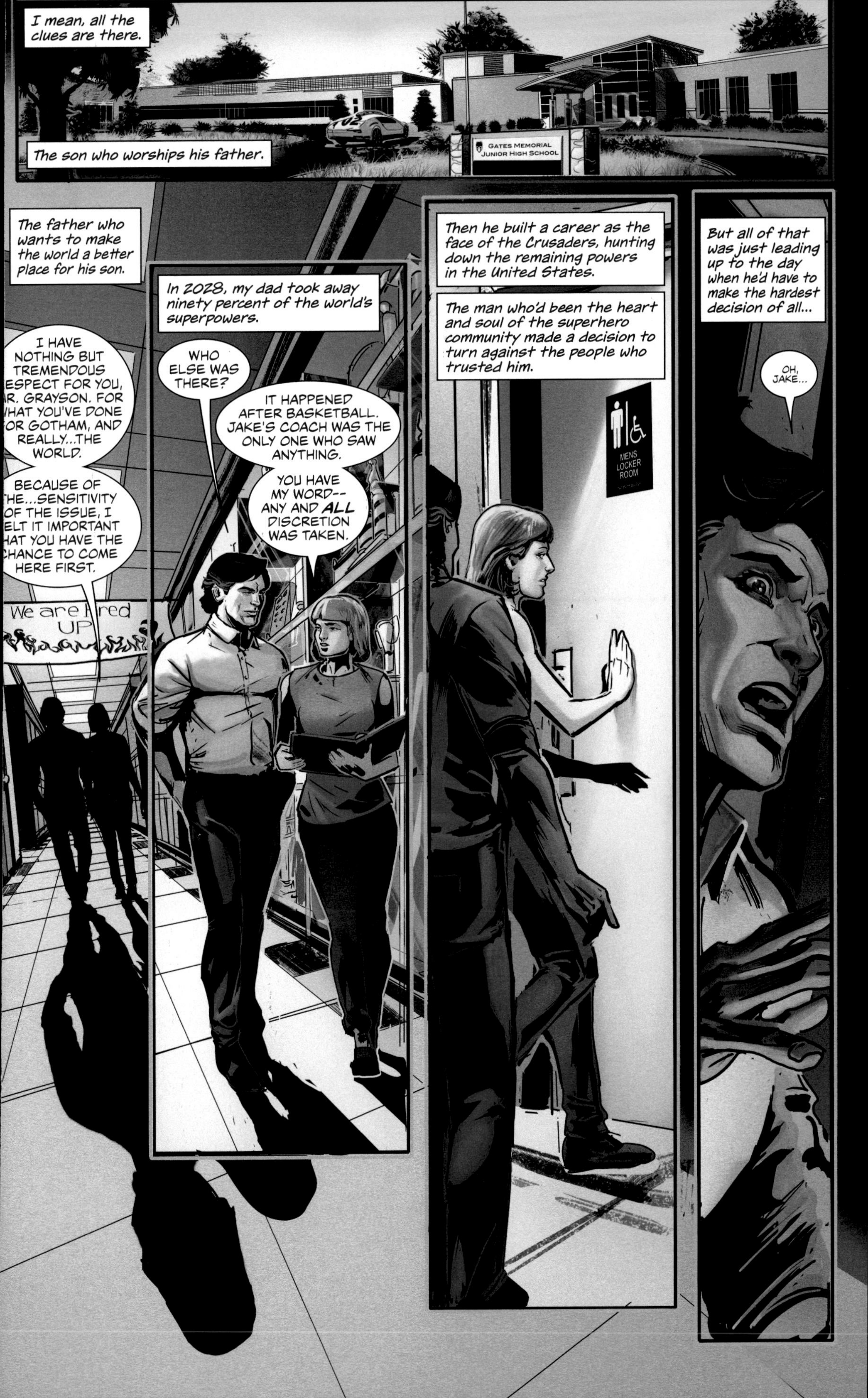
I mean, all the clues are there.
Gates Memorial Junior High School
The son who worships his father.
The father who wants to make the world a better place for his son.
I HAVE NOTHING BUT TREMENDOUS RESPECT FOR YOU, MR. GRAYSON. FOR WHAT YOU'VE DONE FOR GOTHAM, AND REALLY...THE WORLD.
BECAUSE OF THE...SENSITIVITY OF THE ISSUE, I FELT IT IMPORTANT THAT YOU HAVE THE CHANCE TO COME HERE FIRST.
We are Fired UP
In 2028, my dad took away ninety percent of the world's superpowers.
WHO ELSE WAS THERE?
IT HAPPENED AFTER BASKETBALL. JAKE'S COACH WAS THE ONLY ONE WHO SAW ANYTHING.
YOU HAVE MY WORD-- ANY AND ALL DISCRETION WAS TAKEN.
Then he built a career as the face of the Crusaders, hunting down the remaining powers in the United States.
The man who'd been the heart and soul of the superhero community made a decision to turn against the people who trusted him.
MENS LOCKER ROOM
But all of that was just leading up to the day when he'd have to make the hardest decision of all...
OH, JAKE...

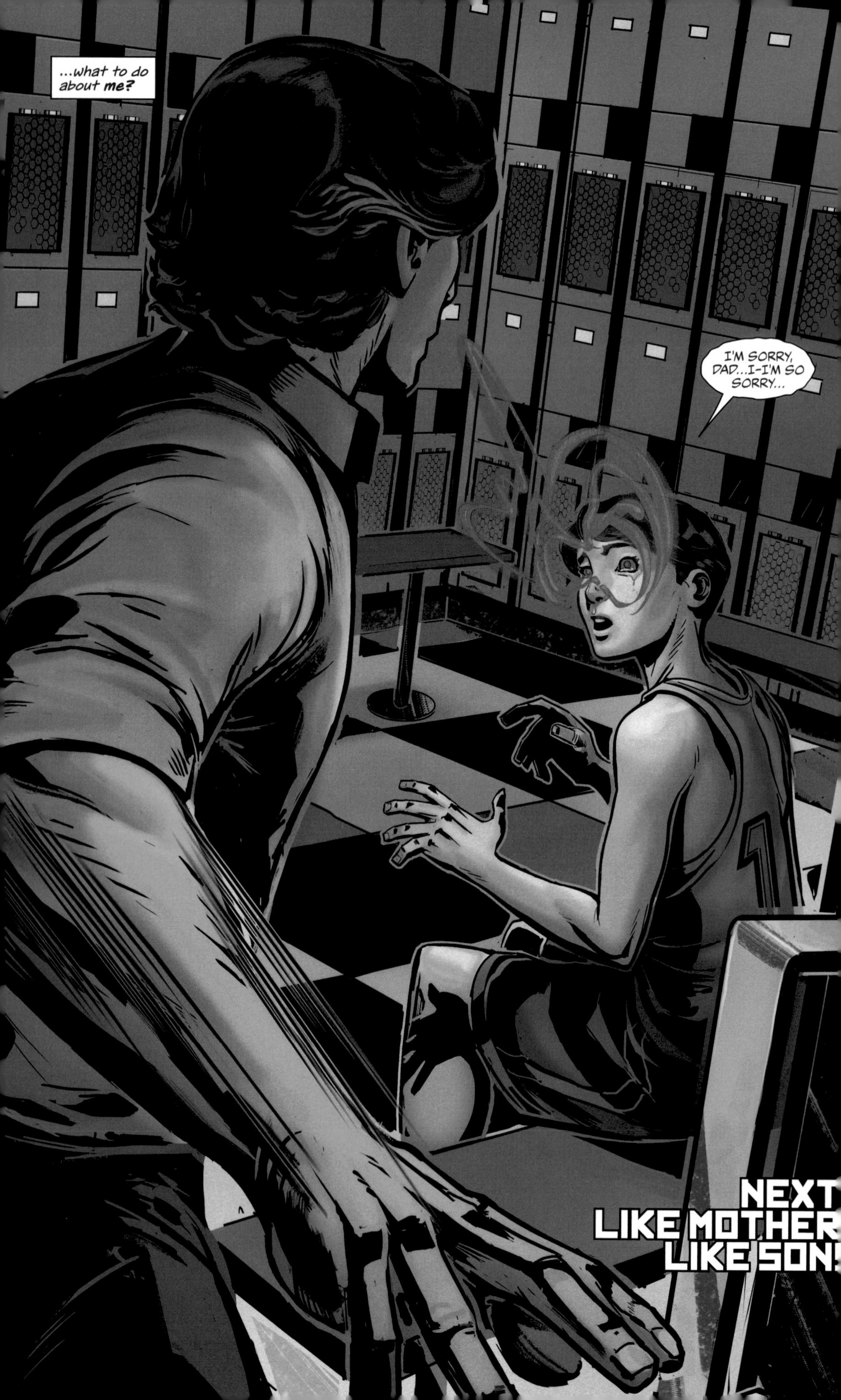
...what to do about **me?**
I'M SORRY, DAD...I-I'M SO SORRY...
NEXT
LIKE MOTHER LIKE SON!

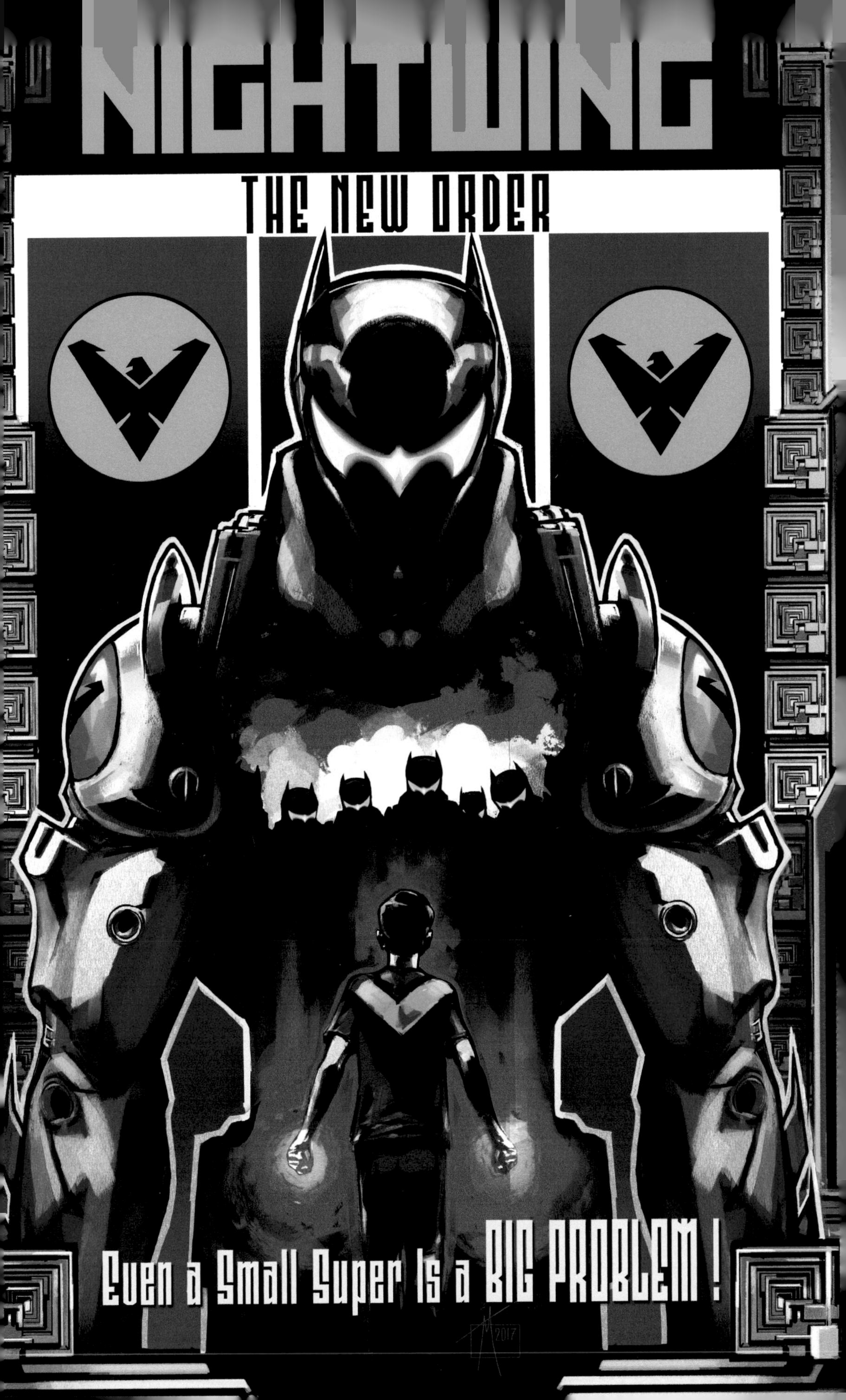
NIGHTWING
THE NEW ORDER
Even a Small Super Is a BIG PROBLEM !
2017

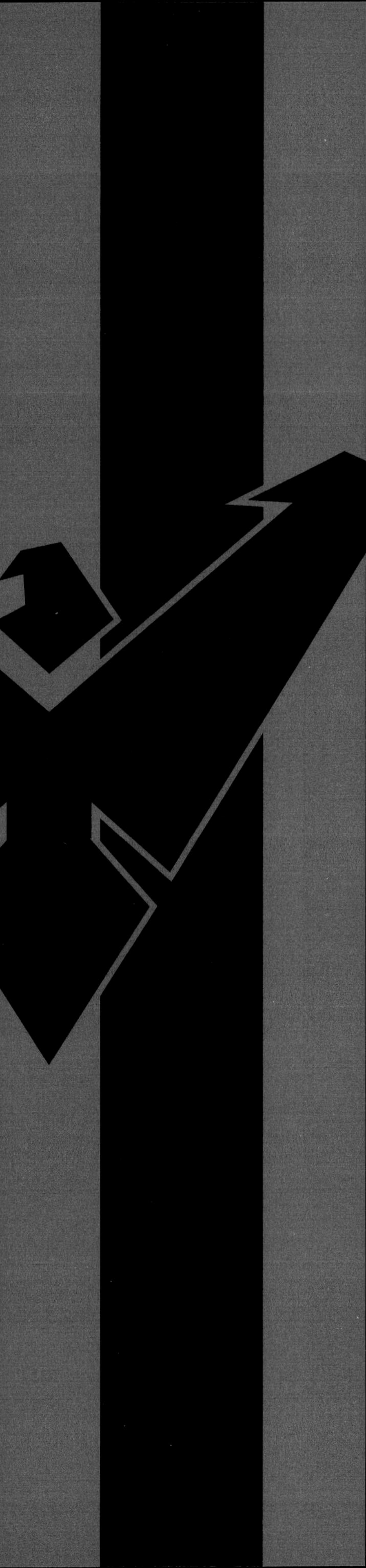

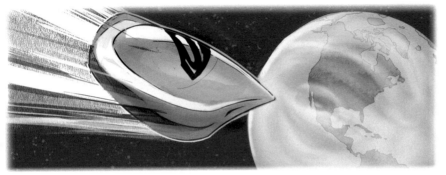

With rare exception, the world almost never changes overnight.

Shifts are usually slow and layered.

It takes **years** before anyone even realizes they're **happening**.

Or how they're going to **affect** us.

And then one day you wake up...

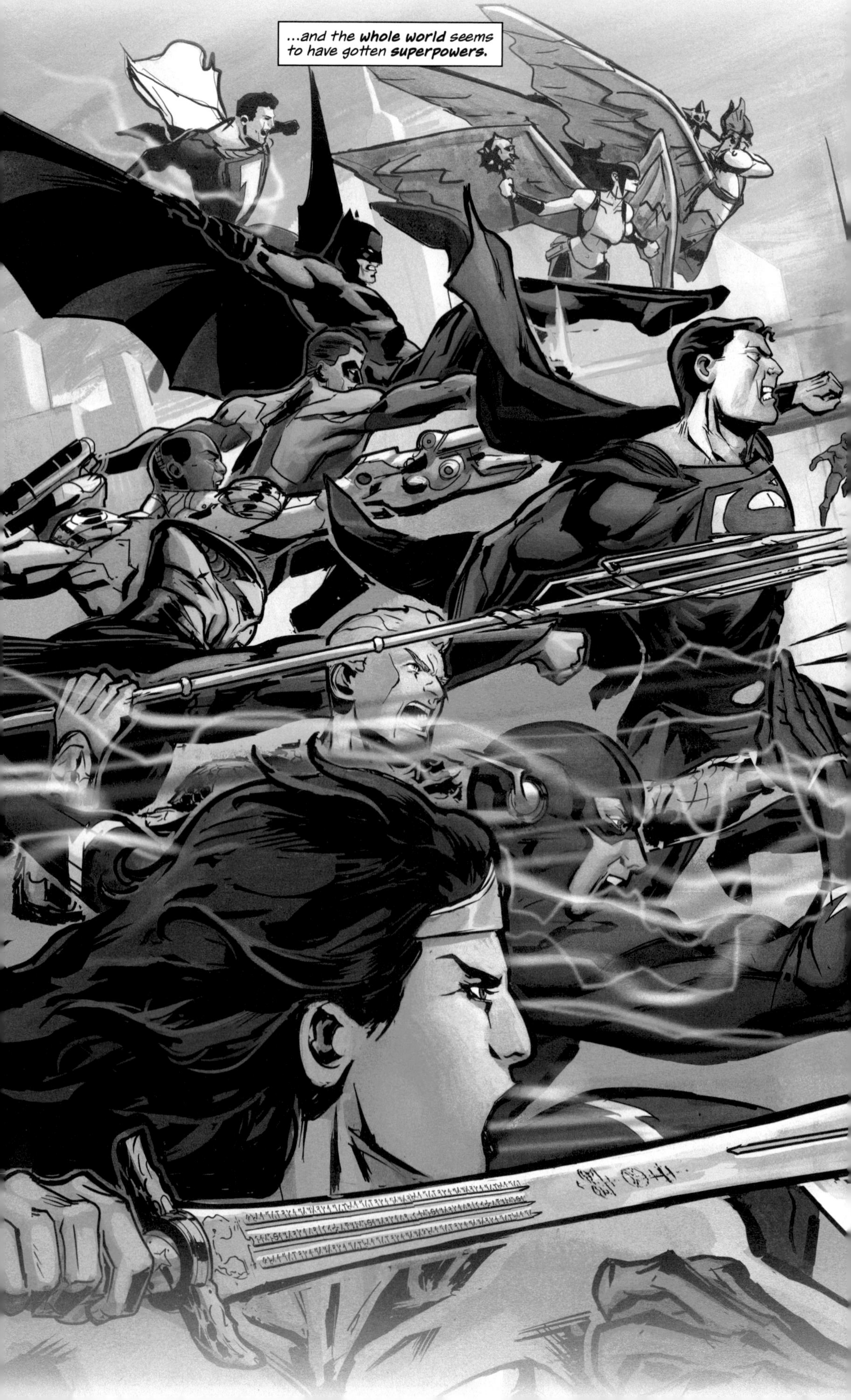
...and the **whole world** seems to have gotten **superpowers.**

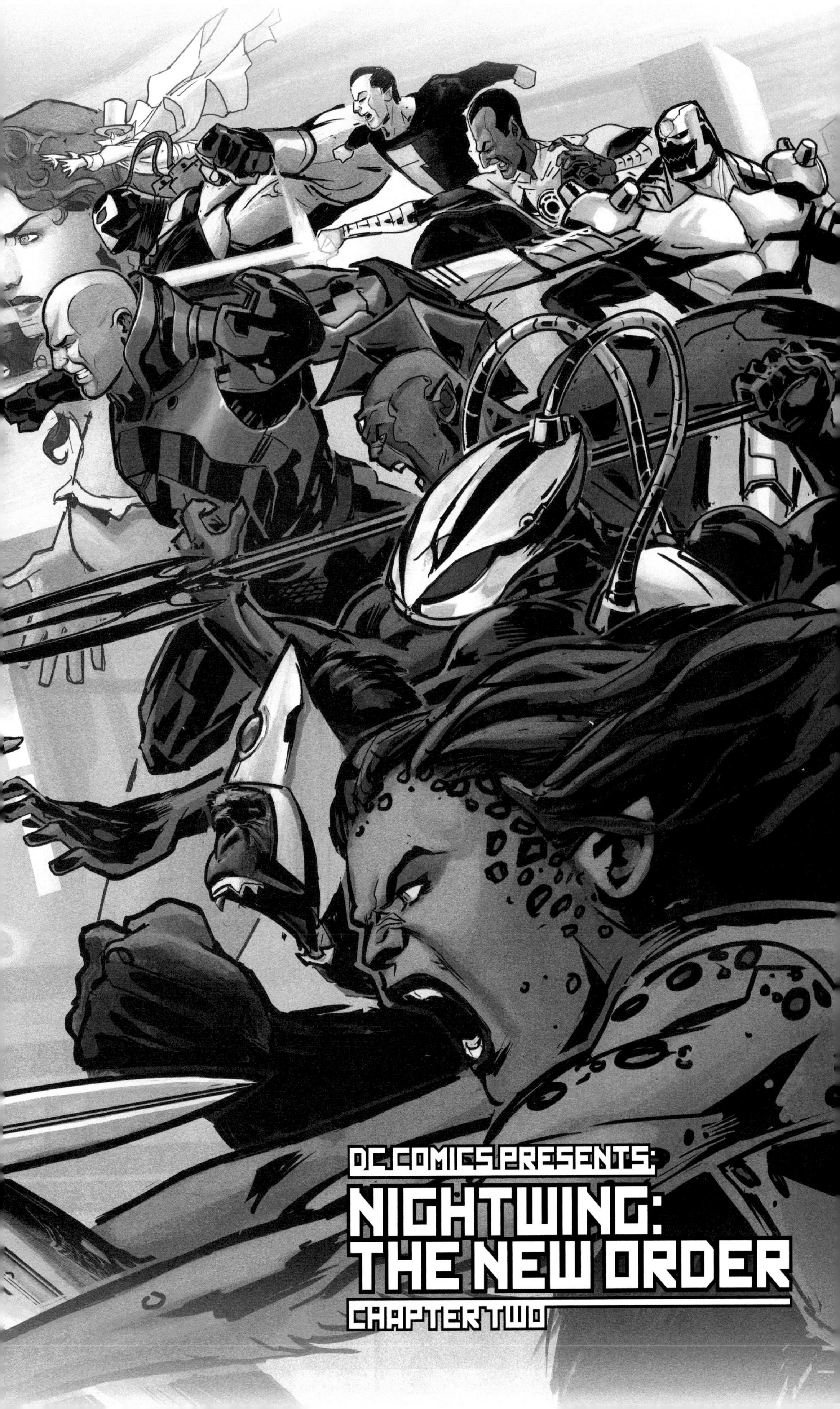
DC COMICS PRESENTS:
NIGHTWING: THE NEW ORDER
CHAPTER TWO

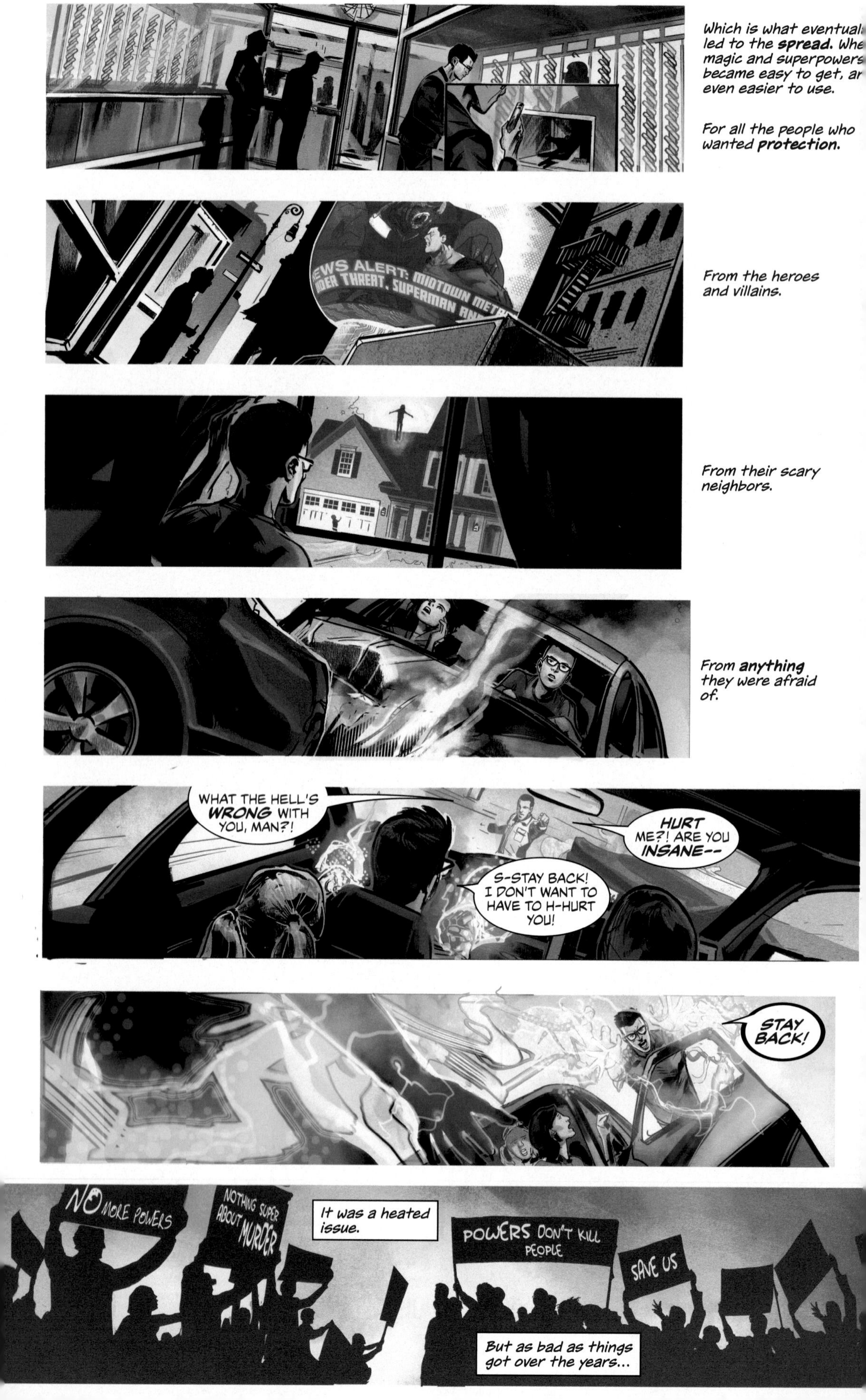
Which is what eventual
led to the **spread.** Whe
magic and superpowers
became easy to get, ar
even easier to use.
For all the people who wanted **protection.**
EWS ALERT: MIDTOWN METR
DER THREAT. SUPERMAN AN
From the heroes and villains.
From their scary neighbors.
From **anything** they were afraid of.
WHAT THE HELL'S **WRONG** WITH YOU, MAN?!
HURT ME?! ARE YOU **INSANE--**
S-STAY BACK! I DON'T WANT TO HAVE TO H-HURT YOU!
STAY BACK!
NO MORE POWERS
NOTHING SUPER ABOUT MURDER
It was a heated issue.
POWERS DON'T KILL PEOPLE
SAVE US
But as bad as things got over the years...

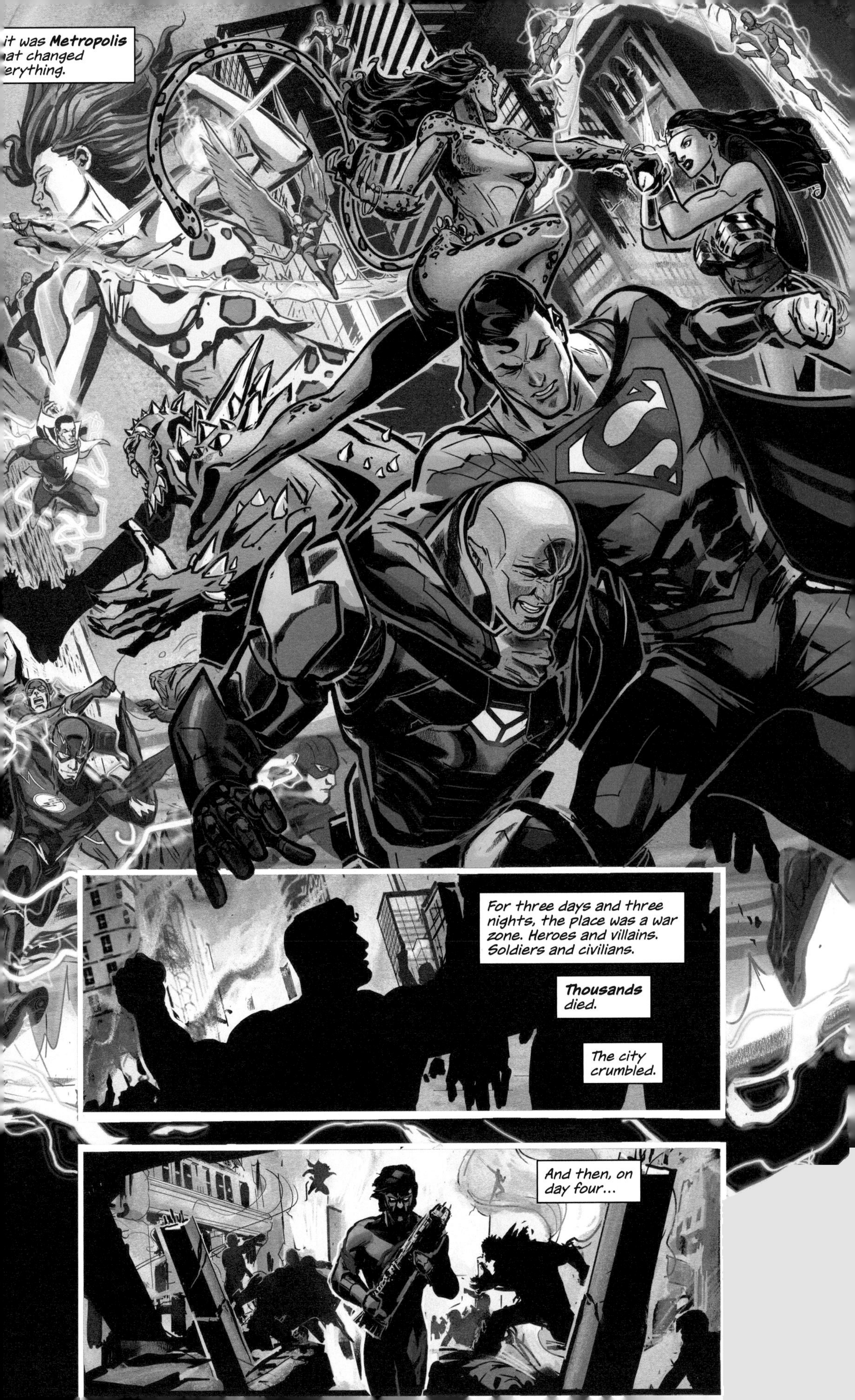

it was **Metropolis**
at changed
erything.
For three days and three nights, the place was a war zone. Heroes and villains. Soldiers and civilians.
Thousands died.
The city crumbled.
And then, on day four...

...my dad put an end to it.

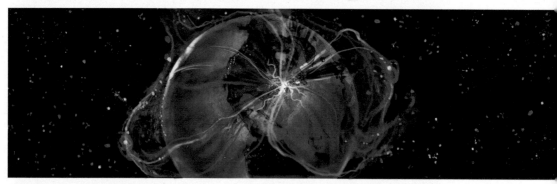

In total, the device wiped out ninety percent of Earth's powers.

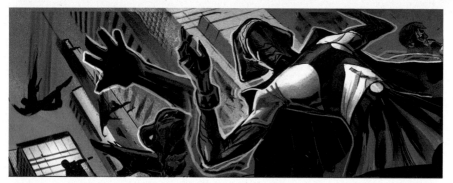

And yeah, that included my mom's.

I wasn't born yet when Metropolis happened. So I don't remember-- firsthand-- the years right after.

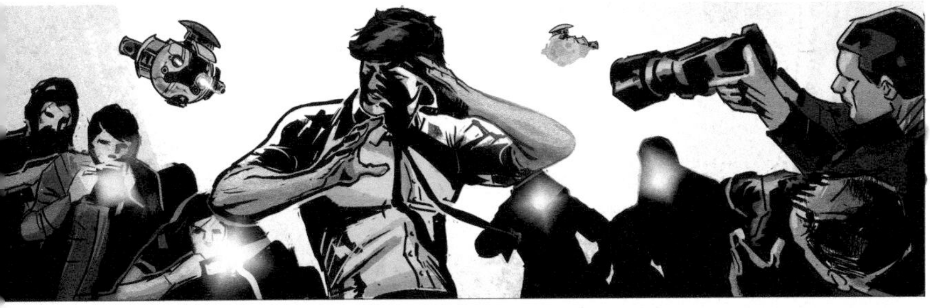

When Dad's secret identity was ***exposed.***

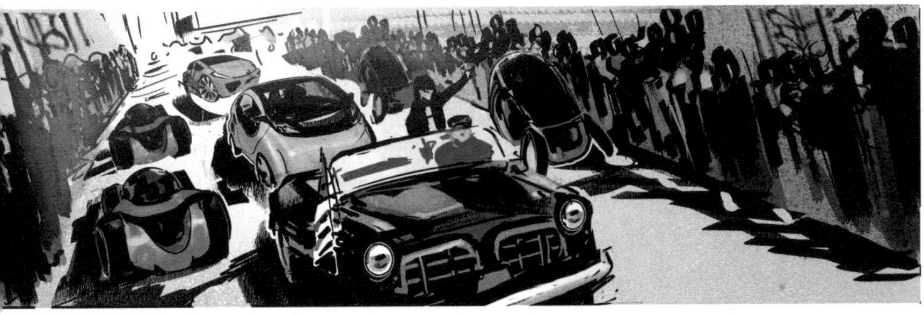

When the president threw him a ***parade.***

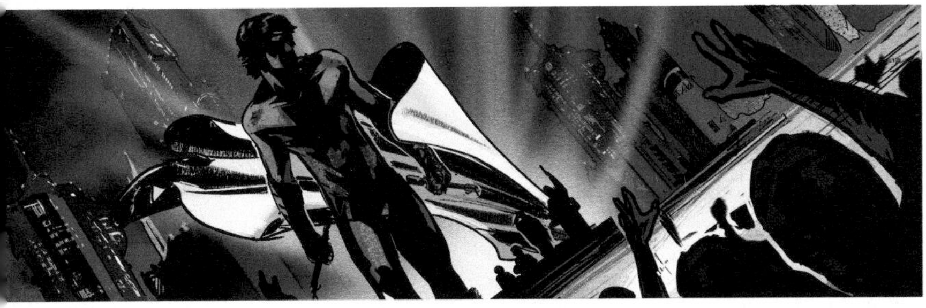

When Gotham built him a ***statue.***

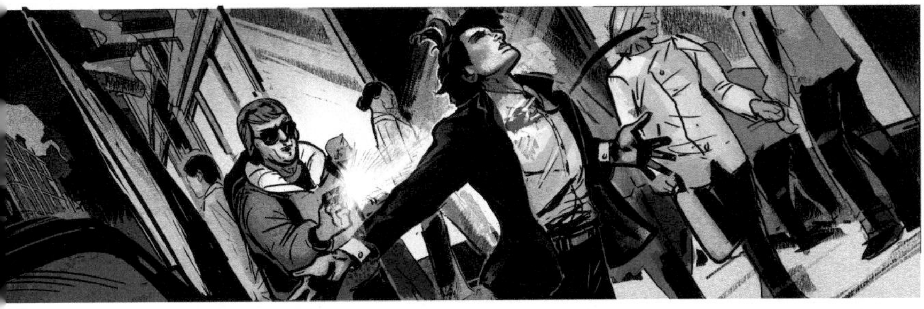

When he survived the ***assassination*** *attempt.*

Like I said before-- it was all pretty complicated.

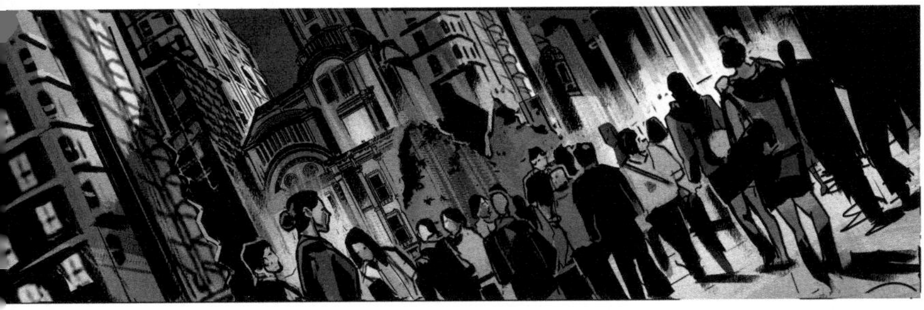

But no matter what side of the fence you were on, it was hard to argue that the world ***hadn't*** *become safer.*

Eventually, that led to laws that made the remaining superpowers-- and any new ones-- ***illegal.***

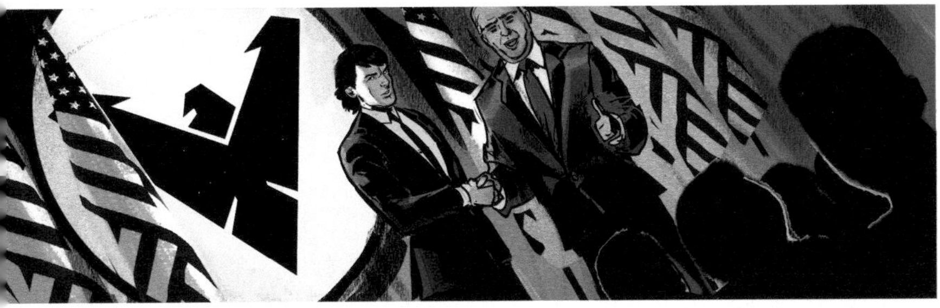

With Dad becoming the face of it.

And while it ***didn't*** *happen overnight, the one thing I* ***can*** *attest to from that time, is that he genuinely believed we'd turned a corner.*

That our country was ***better off*** *without superpowers. Which is why...*

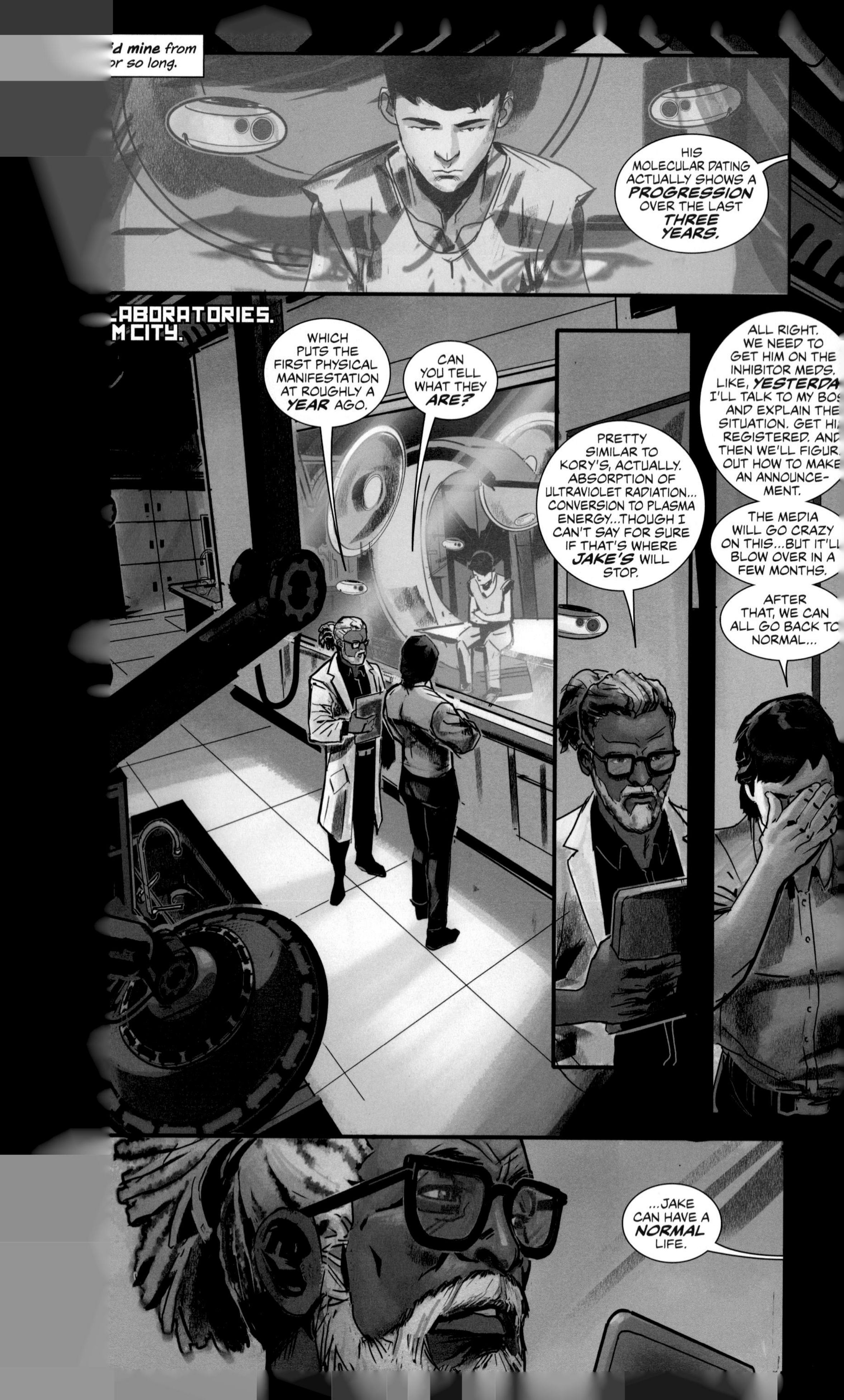

...d mine from
...or so long.
HIS MOLECULAR DATING ACTUALLY SHOWS A PROGRESSION OVER THE LAST THREE YEARS.
...LABORATORIES.
...M CITY.
WHICH PUTS THE FIRST PHYSICAL MANIFESTATION AT ROUGHLY A YEAR AGO.
CAN YOU TELL WHAT THEY ARE?
PRETTY SIMILAR TO KORY'S, ACTUALLY. ABSORPTION OF ULTRAVIOLET RADIATION... CONVERSION TO PLASMA ENERGY...THOUGH I CAN'T SAY FOR SURE IF THAT'S WHERE JAKE'S WILL STOP.
ALL RIGHT. WE NEED TO GET HIM ON THE INHIBITOR MEDS. LIKE, YESTERDA... I'LL TALK TO MY BOS... AND EXPLAIN THE SITUATION. GET HI... REGISTERED. AND THEN WE'LL FIGUR... OUT HOW TO MAKE AN ANNOUNCE-MENT.
THE MEDIA WILL GO CRAZY ON THIS...BUT IT'L... BLOW OVER IN A FEW MONTHS.
AFTER THAT, WE CAN ALL GO BACK TO NORMAL...
...JAKE CAN HAVE A NORMAL LIFE.

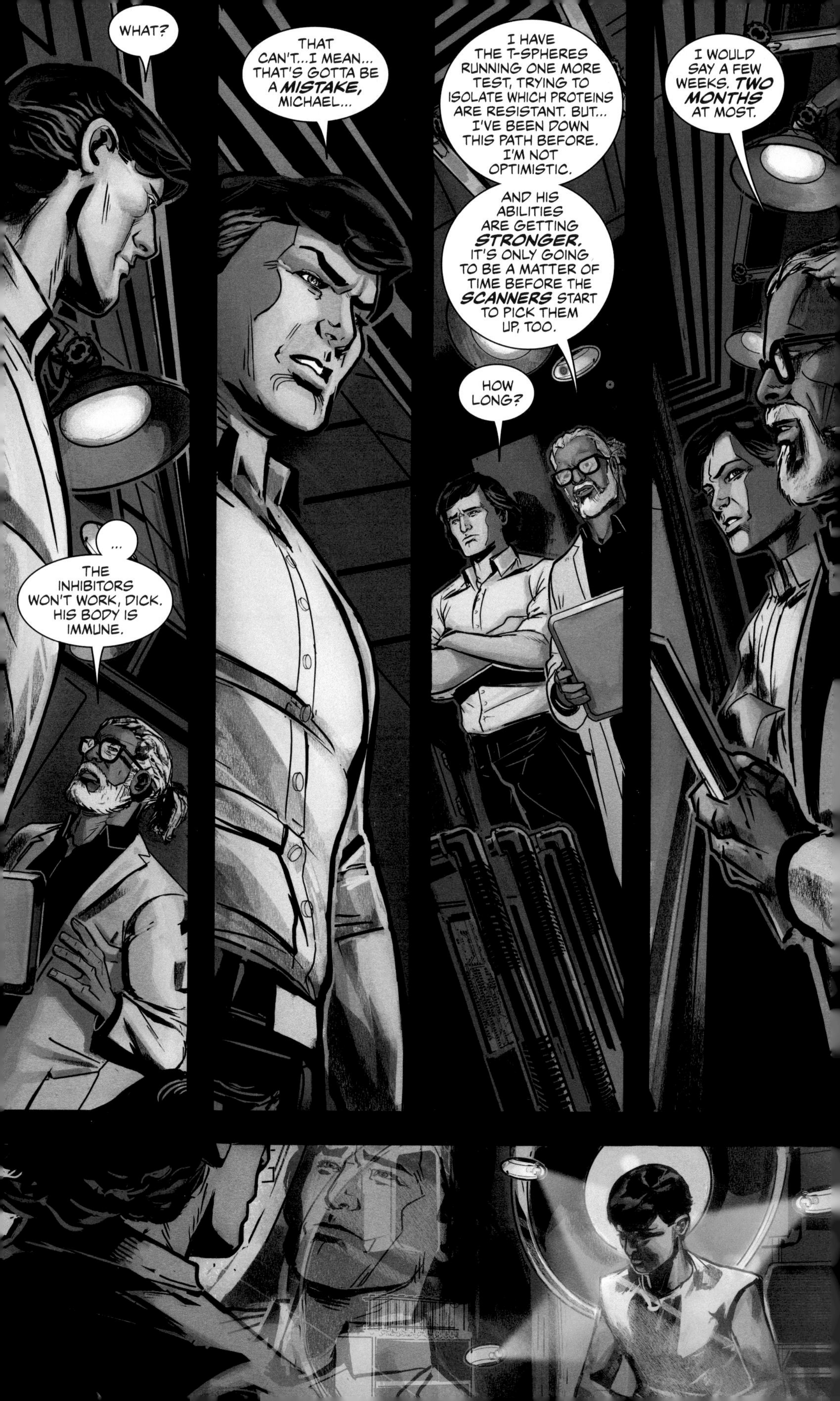
WHAT?
...
THE INHIBITORS WON'T WORK, DICK. HIS BODY IS IMMUNE.
THAT CAN'T...I MEAN... THAT'S GOTTA BE A MISTAKE, MICHAEL...
I HAVE THE T-SPHERES RUNNING ONE MORE TEST, TRYING TO ISOLATE WHICH PROTEINS ARE RESISTANT. BUT... I'VE BEEN DOWN THIS PATH BEFORE. I'M NOT OPTIMISTIC.
AND HIS ABILITIES ARE GETTING STRONGER. IT'S ONLY GOING TO BE A MATTER OF TIME BEFORE THE SCANNERS START TO PICK THEM UP, TOO.
HOW LONG?
I WOULD SAY A FEW WEEKS. TWO MONTHS AT MOST.

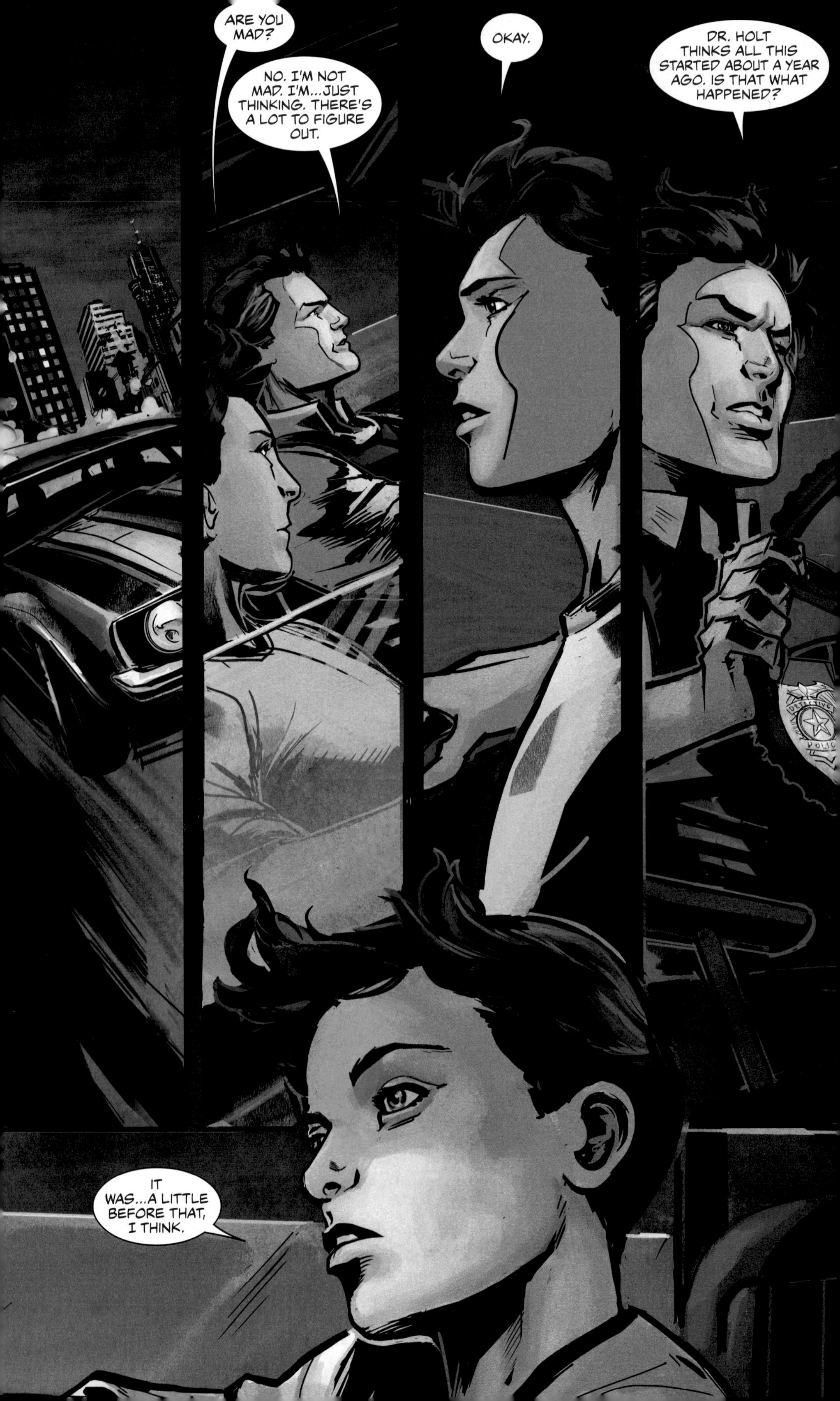
ARE YOU MAD?
NO. I'M NOT MAD. I'M...JUST THINKING. THERE'S A LOT TO FIGURE OUT.
OKAY.
DR. HOLT THINKS ALL THIS STARTED ABOUT A YEAR AGO. IS THAT WHAT HAPPENED?
IT WAS...A LITTLE BEFORE THAT, I THINK.

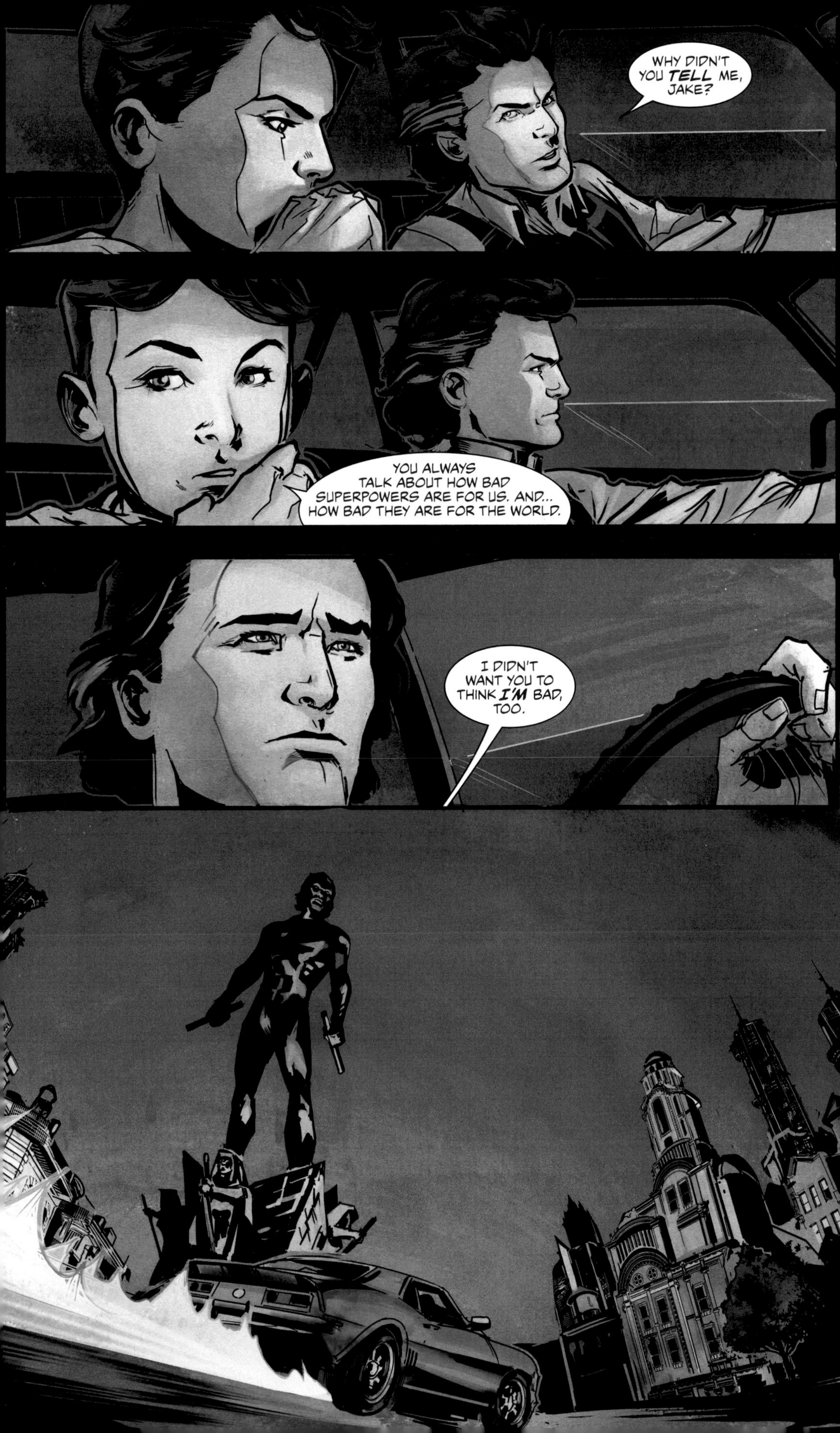
WHY DIDN'T YOU TELL ME, JAKE?
YOU ALWAYS TALK ABOUT HOW BAD SUPERPOWERS ARE FOR US. AND... HOW BAD THEY ARE FOR THE WORLD.
I DIDN'T WANT YOU TO THINK I'M BAD, TOO.

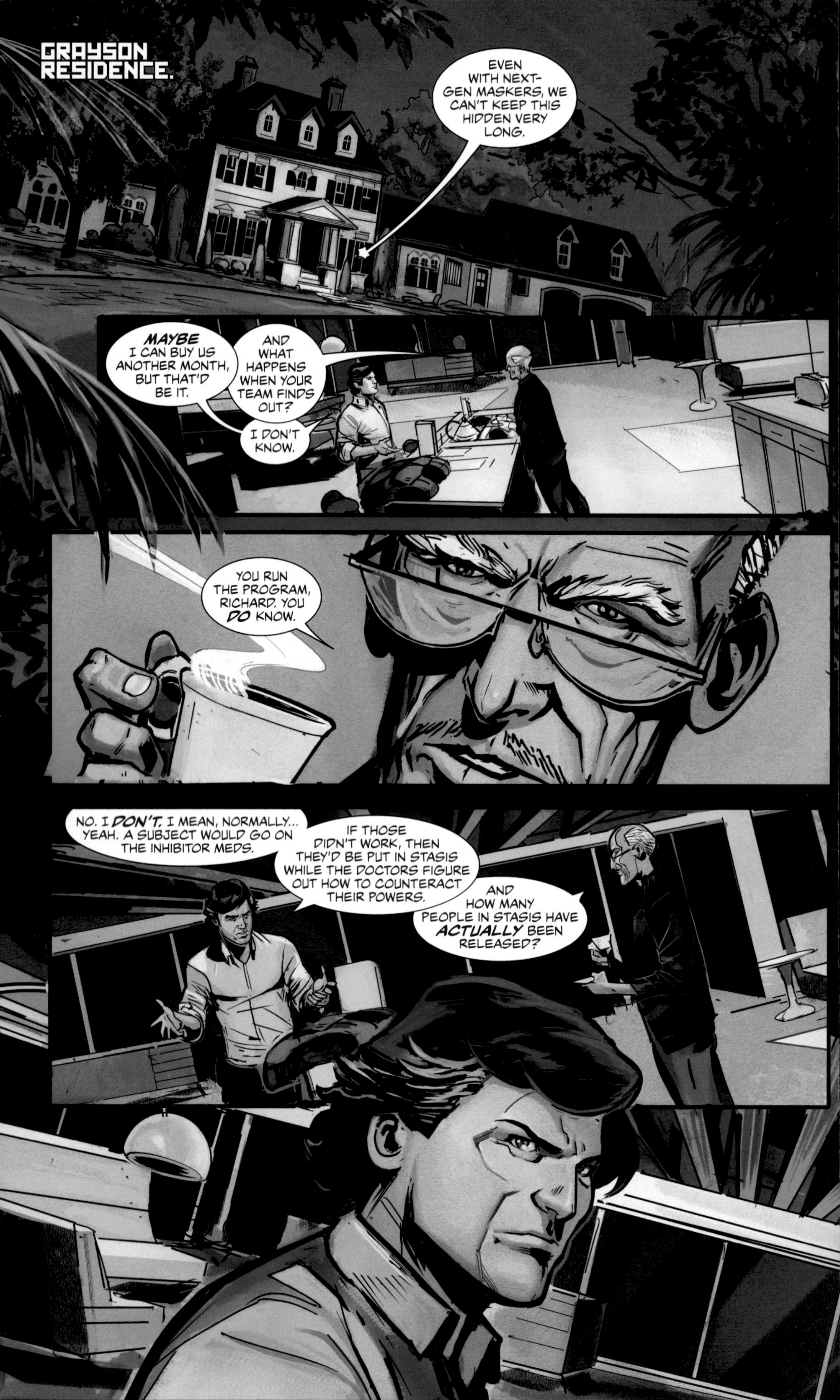
GRAYSON RESIDENCE.
EVEN WITH NEXT-GEN MASKERS, WE CAN'T KEEP THIS HIDDEN VERY LONG.
MAYBE I CAN BUY US ANOTHER MONTH, BUT THAT'D BE IT.
AND WHAT HAPPENS WHEN YOUR TEAM FINDS OUT?
I DON'T KNOW.
YOU RUN THE PROGRAM, RICHARD. YOU DO KNOW.
NO. I DON'T. I MEAN, NORMALLY... YEAH. A SUBJECT WOULD GO ON THE INHIBITOR MEDS.
IF THOSE DIDN'T WORK, THEN THEY'D BE PUT IN STASIS WHILE THE DOCTORS FIGURE OUT HOW TO COUNTERACT THEIR POWERS.
AND HOW MANY PEOPLE IN STASIS HAVE ACTUALLY BEEN RELEASED?

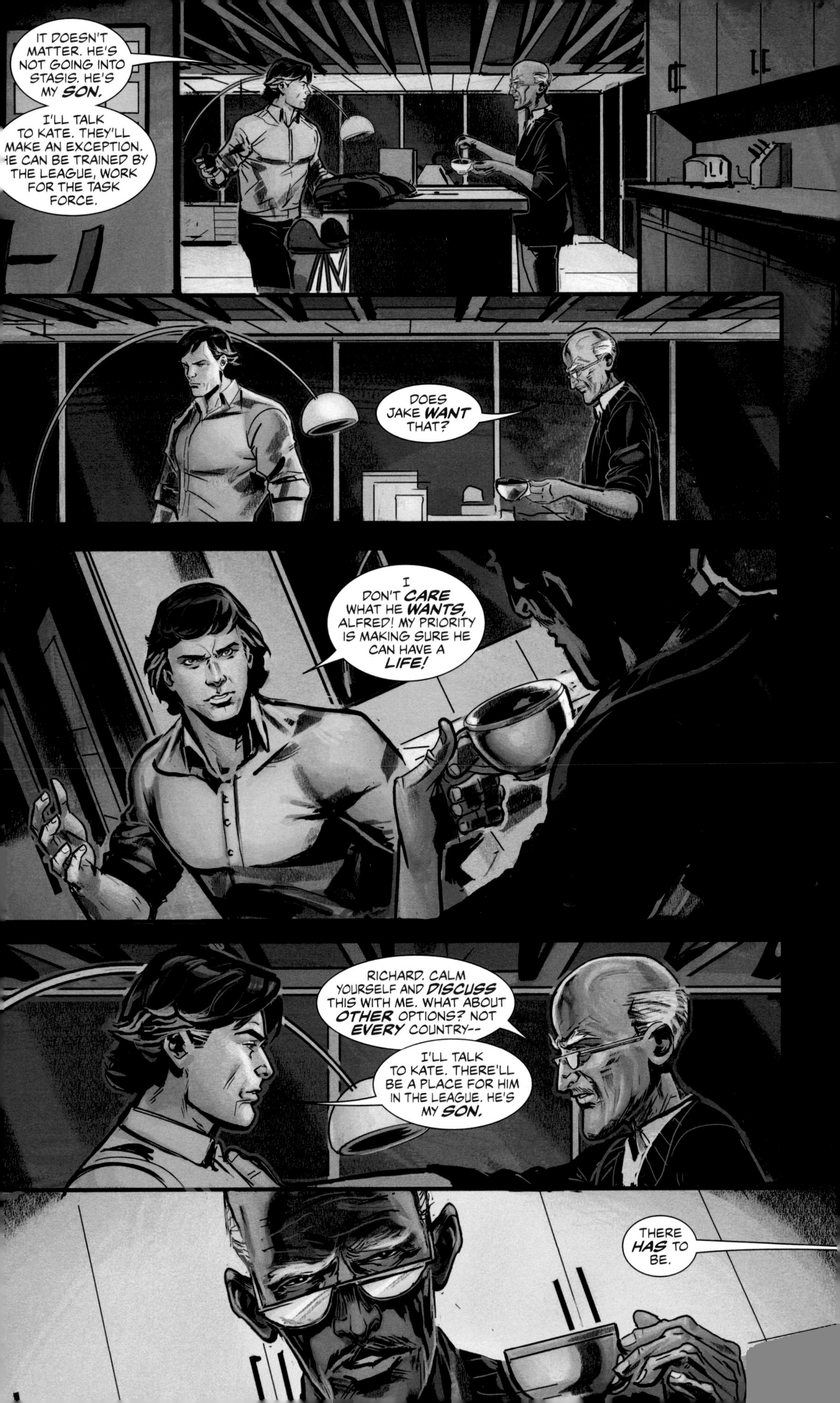
IT DOESN'T MATTER. HE'S NOT GOING INTO STASIS. HE'S MY SON.
I'LL TALK TO KATE. THEY'LL MAKE AN EXCEPTION. HE CAN BE TRAINED BY THE LEAGUE, WORK FOR THE TASK FORCE.
DOES JAKE WANT THAT?
I DON'T CARE WHAT HE WANTS, ALFRED! MY PRIORITY IS MAKING SURE HE CAN HAVE A LIFE!
RICHARD. CALM YOURSELF AND DISCUSS THIS WITH ME. WHAT ABOUT OTHER OPTIONS? NOT EVERY COUNTRY--
I'LL TALK TO KATE. THERE'LL BE A PLACE FOR HIM IN THE LEAGUE. HE'S MY SON.
THERE HAS TO BE.

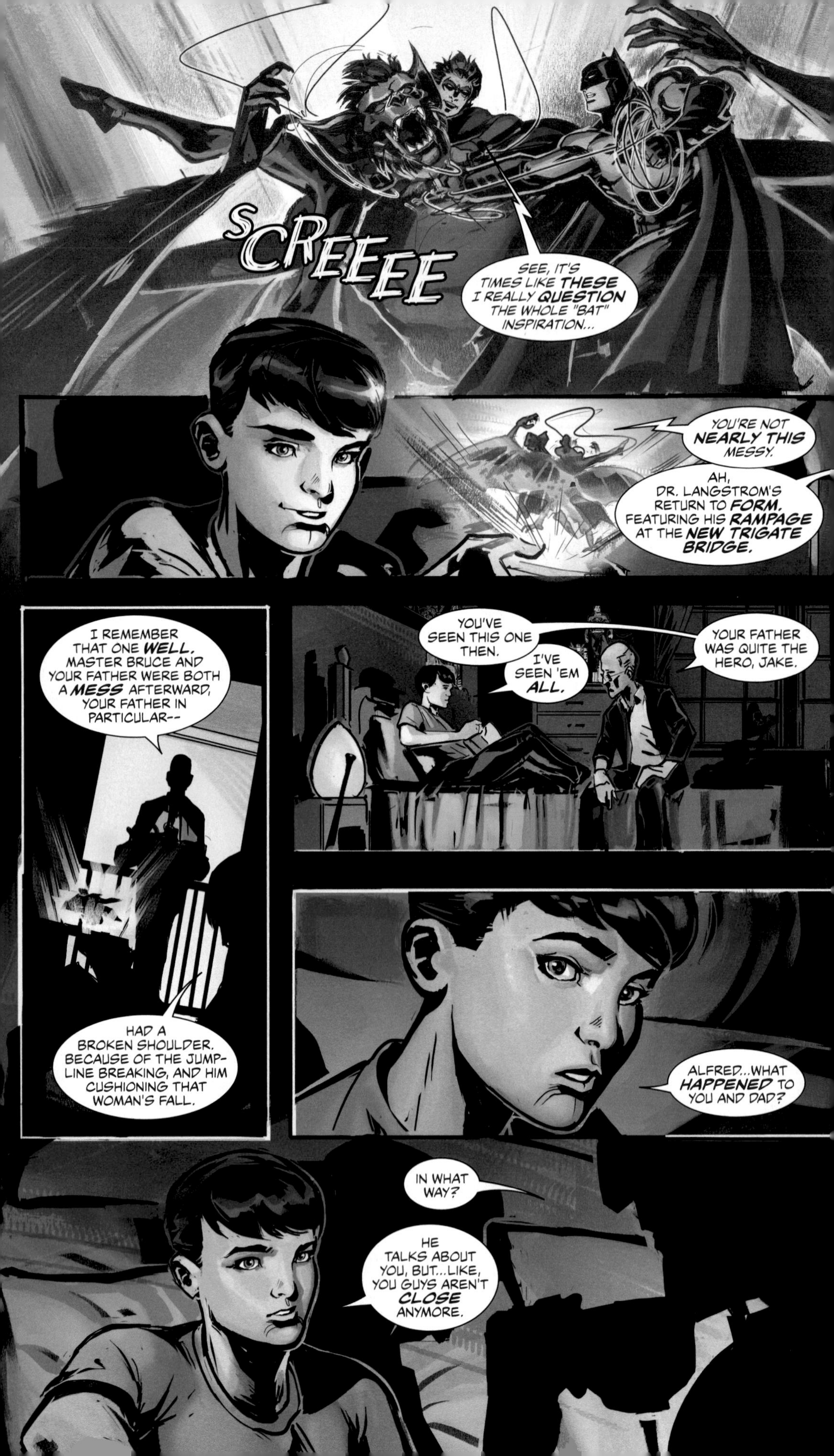
SCREEEE
SEE, IT'S TIMES LIKE THESE I REALLY QUESTION THE WHOLE "BAT" INSPIRATION...
YOU'RE NOT NEARLY THIS MESSY.
AH, DR. LANGSTROM'S RETURN TO FORM. FEATURING HIS RAMPAGE AT THE NEW TRIGATE BRIDGE.
I REMEMBER THAT ONE WELL. MASTER BRUCE AND YOUR FATHER WERE BOTH A MESS AFTERWARD, YOUR FATHER IN PARTICULAR--
HAD A BROKEN SHOULDER. BECAUSE OF THE JUMP-LINE BREAKING, AND HIM CUSHIONING THAT WOMAN'S FALL.
YOU'VE SEEN THIS ONE THEN.
I'VE SEEN 'EM ALL.
YOUR FATHER WAS QUITE THE HERO, JAKE.
ALFRED...WHAT HAPPENED TO YOU AND DAD?
IN WHAT WAY?
HE TALKS ABOUT YOU, BUT...LIKE, YOU GUYS AREN'T CLOSE ANYMORE.

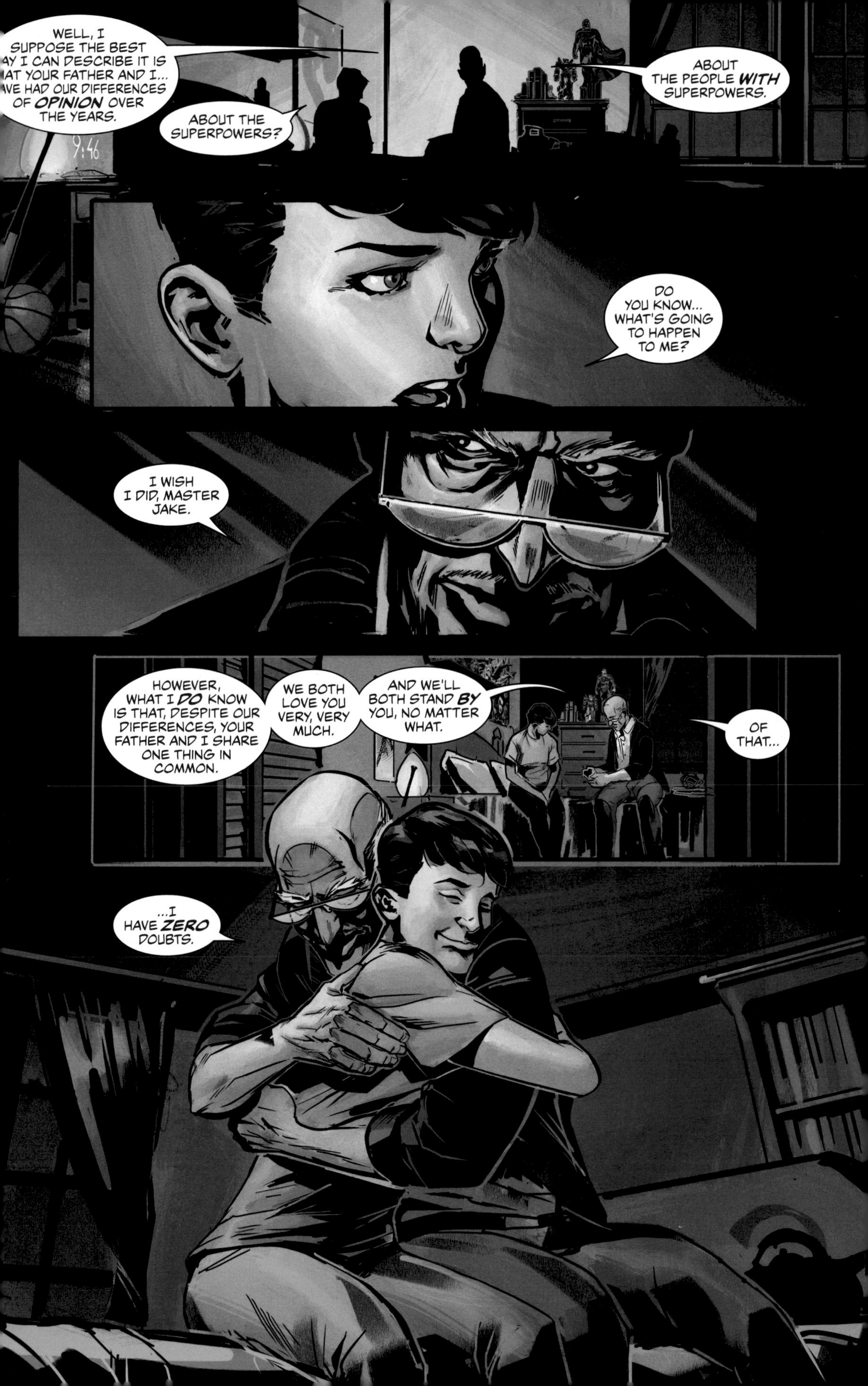
WELL, I SUPPOSE THE BEST AY I CAN DESCRIBE IT IS AT YOUR FATHER AND I... VE HAD OUR DIFFERENCES OF OPINION OVER THE YEARS.
ABOUT THE SUPERPOWERS?
ABOUT THE PEOPLE WITH SUPERPOWERS.
9:46
DO YOU KNOW... WHAT'S GOING TO HAPPEN TO ME?
I WISH I DID, MASTER JAKE.
HOWEVER, WHAT I DO KNOW IS THAT, DESPITE OUR DIFFERENCES, YOUR FATHER AND I SHARE ONE THING IN COMMON.
WE BOTH LOVE YOU VERY, VERY MUCH.
AND WE'LL BOTH STAND BY YOU, NO MATTER WHAT.
OF THAT...
...I HAVE ZERO DOUBTS.

VRRRR
VRRRR
VRRRRRRRRRR
JAKE! GET AWAY FROM THE WINDOWS--

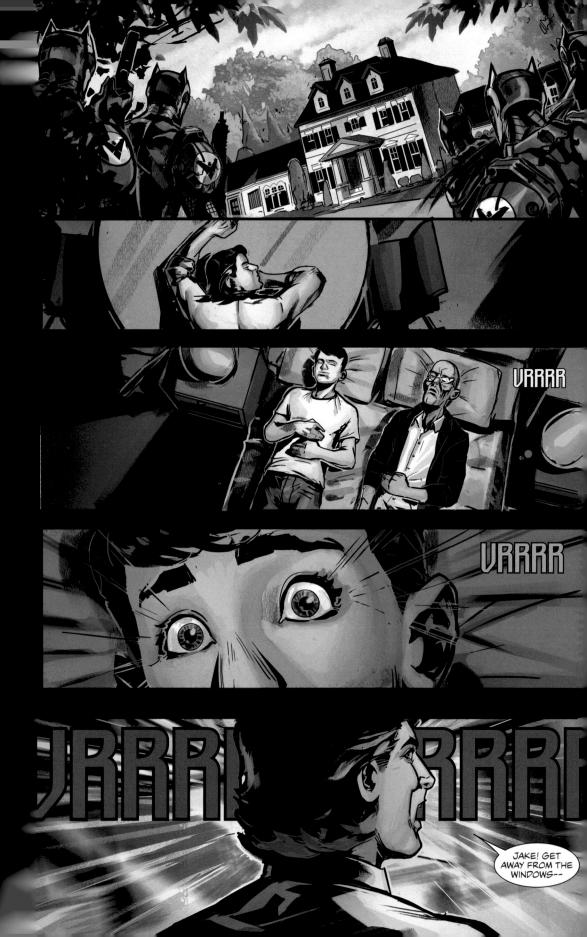

AHHH!

MASTER JAKE, *HURRY!*

I'M SORRY, DICK--THIS WASN'T OUR CALL!

W-WHAT... WHO...

NICE AND EASY, COMMANDER-- I'VE GOT YOU.
M-MY HEAD...
YOU'VE GOT A CONCUSSION. JUST TRY TO RELAX AND--
YOU'RE MAKING THE SITUATION WORSE!
DAD!
JAKE!
GHNN!
OH, I WHOLEHEARTEDLY DISAGREE, YOUNG MAN...
ACKK!
...YOU HAVE ENTERED A PRIVATE RESIDENCE IN THE MOST INCENDIARY WAY POSSIBLE--
--AND UNNECESSARILY PUT OUR LIVES AT RISK!
I'M NOT GONNA TELL YOU AGAIN!
BRADY! WHAT ARE YOU DOING?!

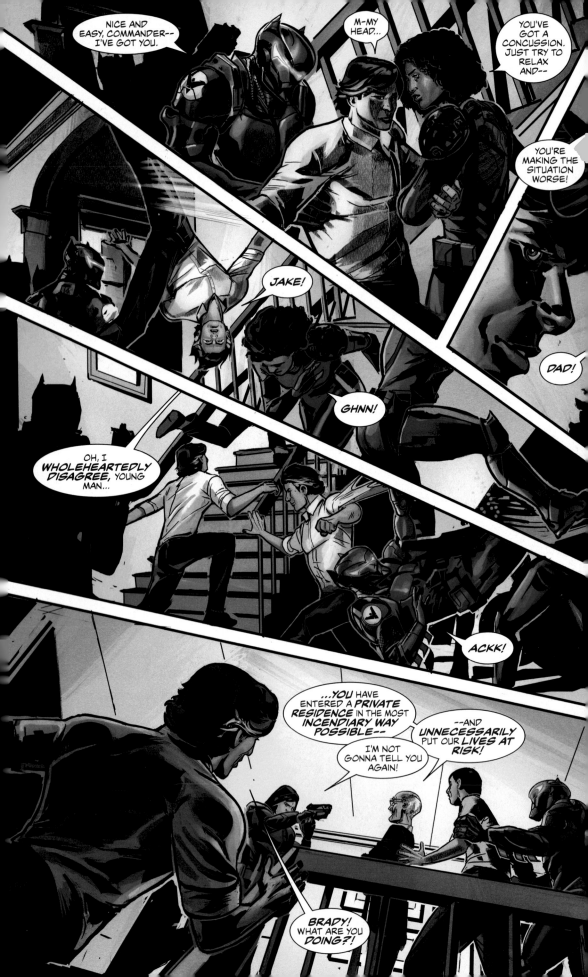

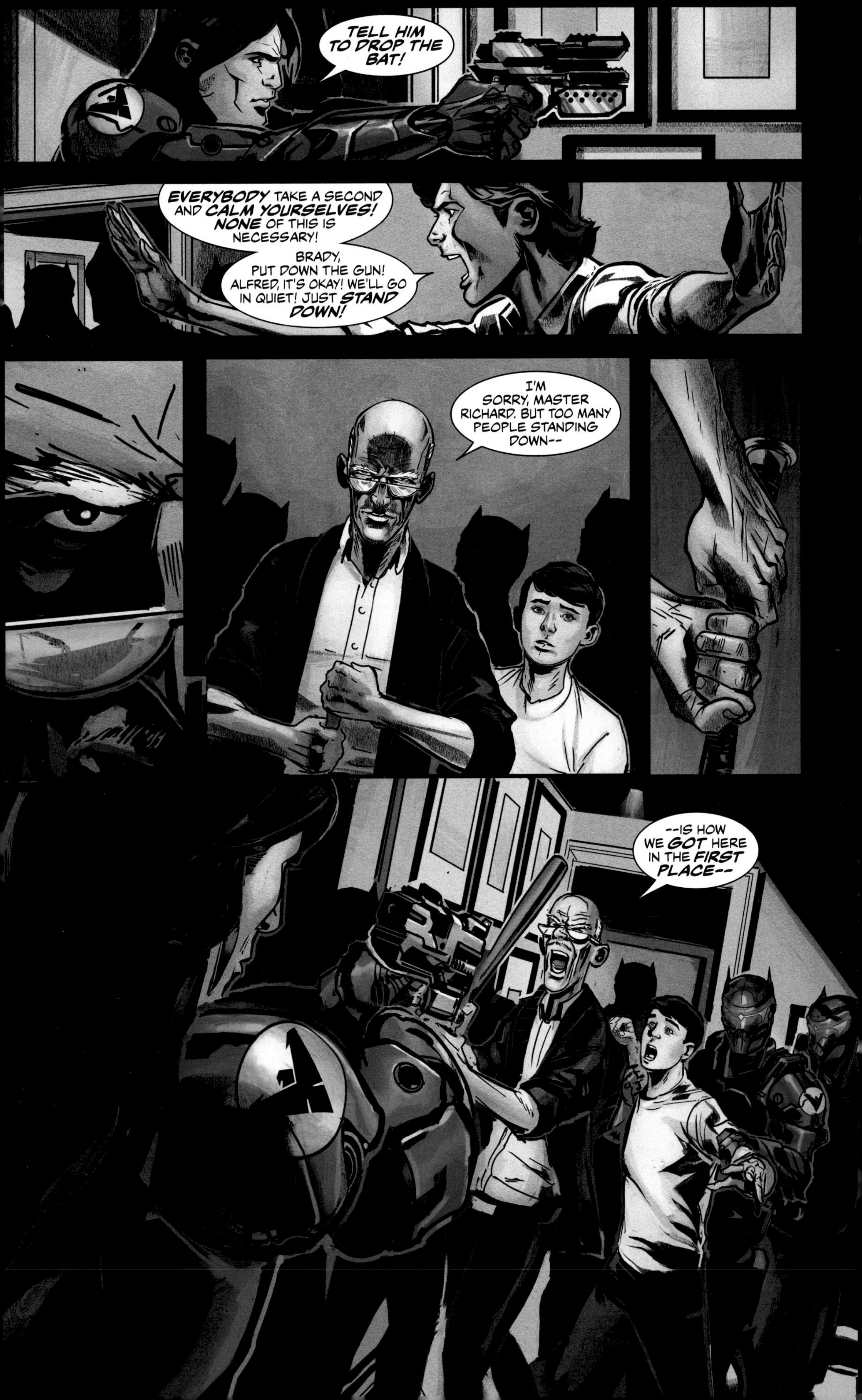
TELL HIM TO DROP THE BAT!
EVERYBODY TAKE A SECOND AND CALM YOURSELVES! NONE OF THIS IS NECESSARY!
BRADY, PUT DOWN THE GUN! ALFRED, IT'S OKAY! WE'LL GO IN QUIET! JUST STAND DOWN!
I'M SORRY, MASTER RICHARD. BUT TOO MANY PEOPLE STANDING DOWN--
--IS HOW WE GOT HERE IN THE FIRST PLACE--

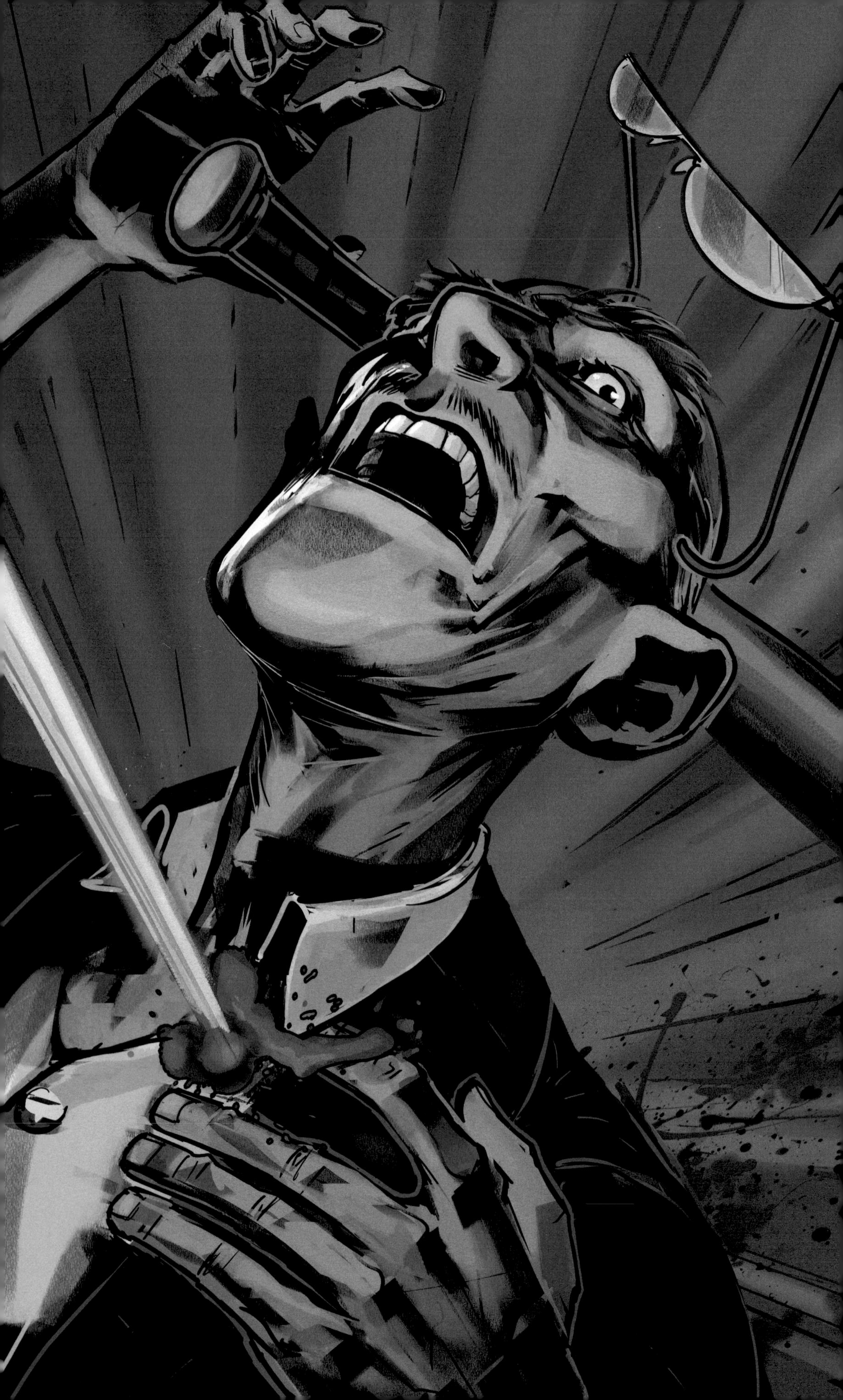

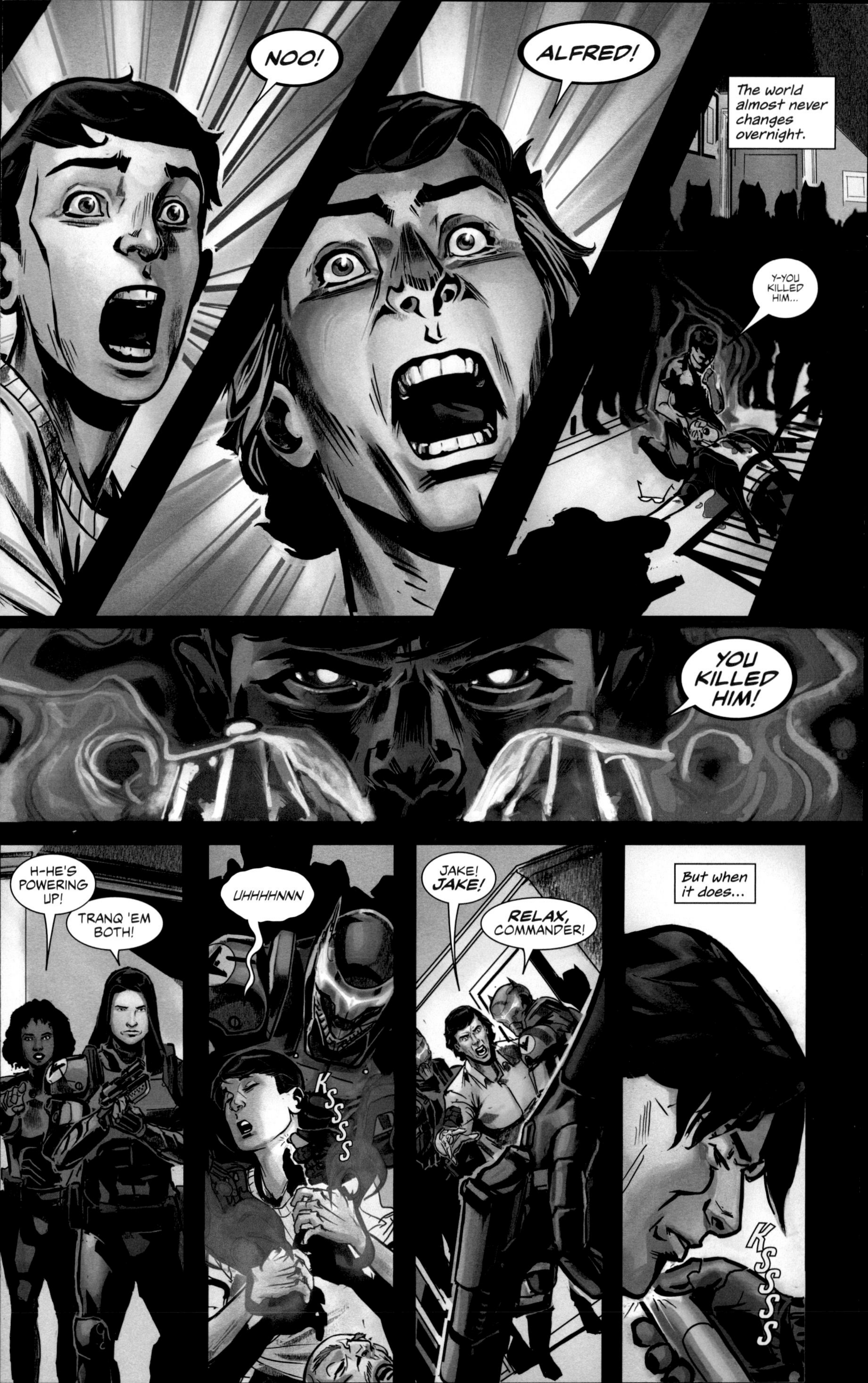
NOO!
ALFRED!
The world almost never changes overnight.
Y-YOU KILLED HIM...
YOU KILLED HIM!
H-HE'S POWERING UP!
TRANQ 'EM BOTH!
UHHHHNNN
KSSSS
JAKE! JAKE!
RELAX, COMMANDER!
But when it does...
KSSSS

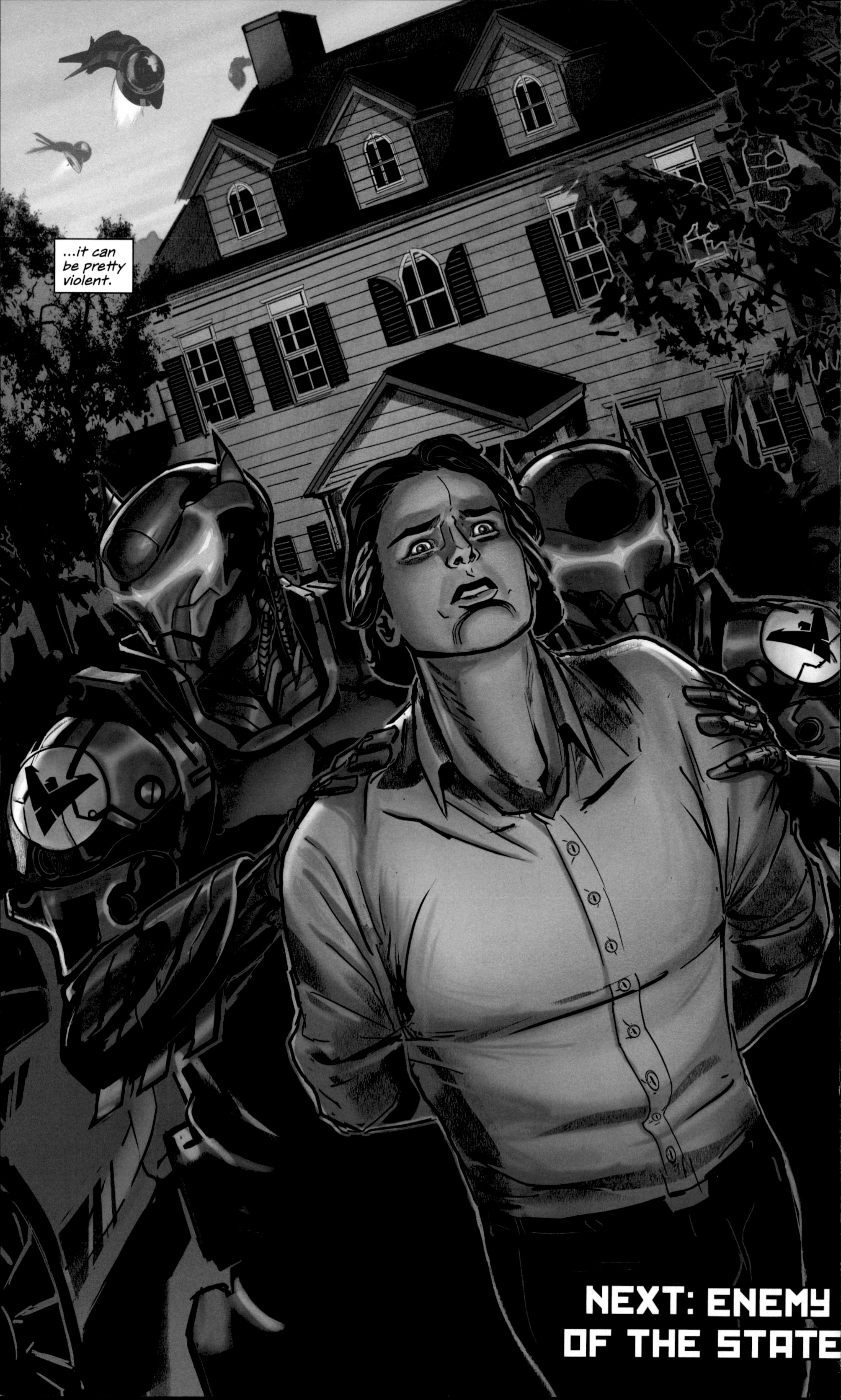

...it can be pretty violent.
NEXT: ENEMY OF THE STATE

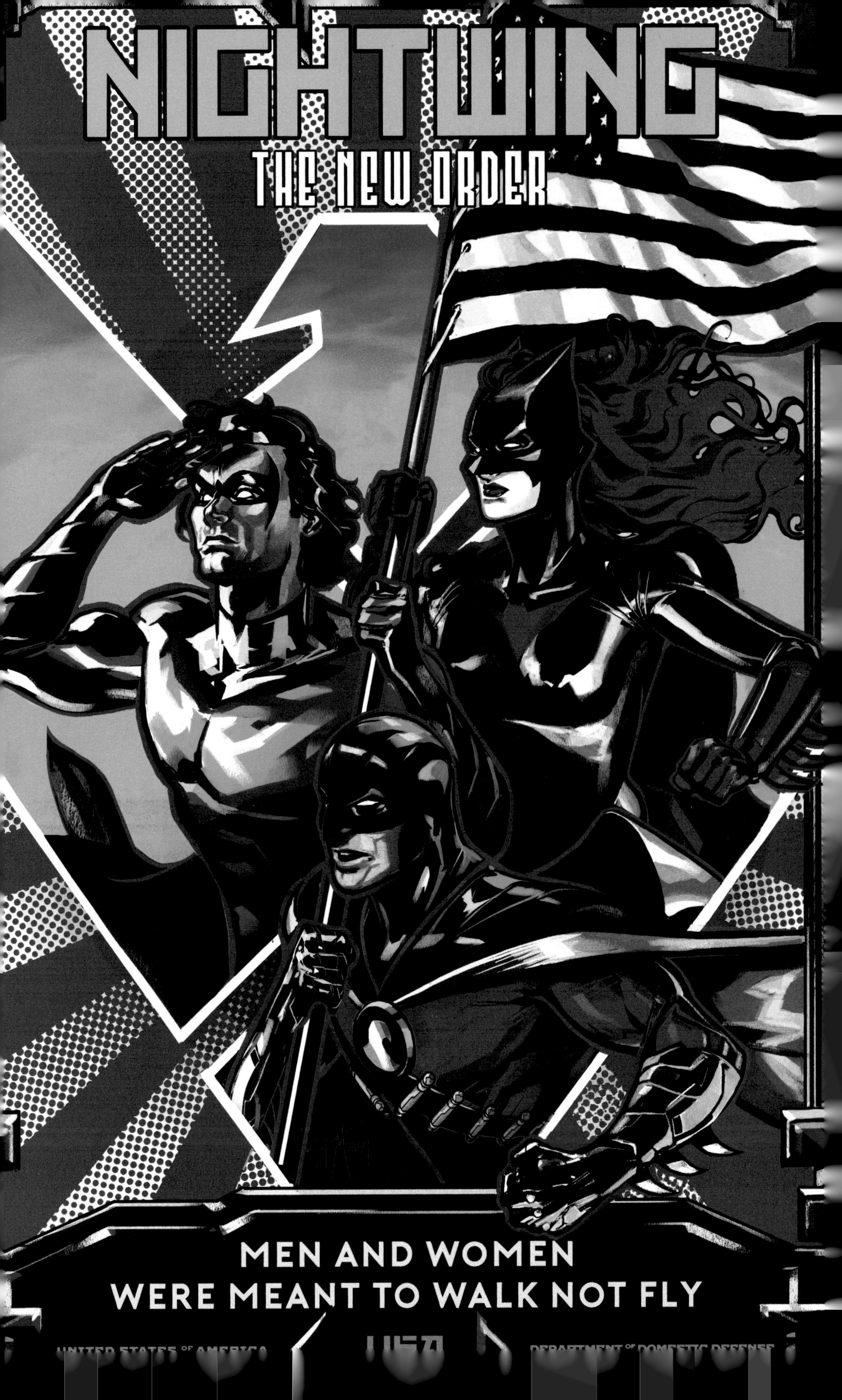
NIGHTWING
THE NEW ORDER
MEN AND WOMEN
WERE MEANT TO WALK NOT FLY

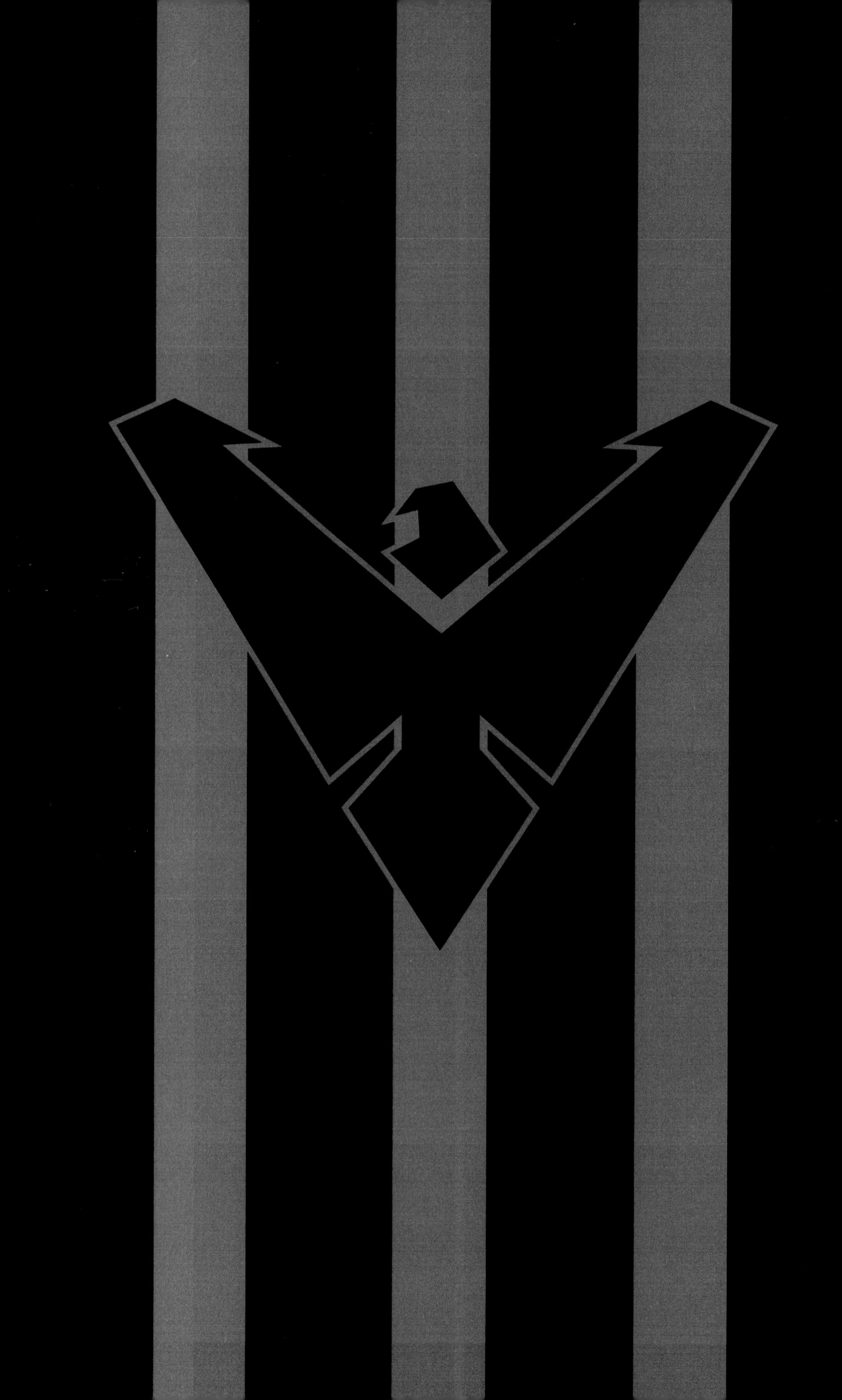

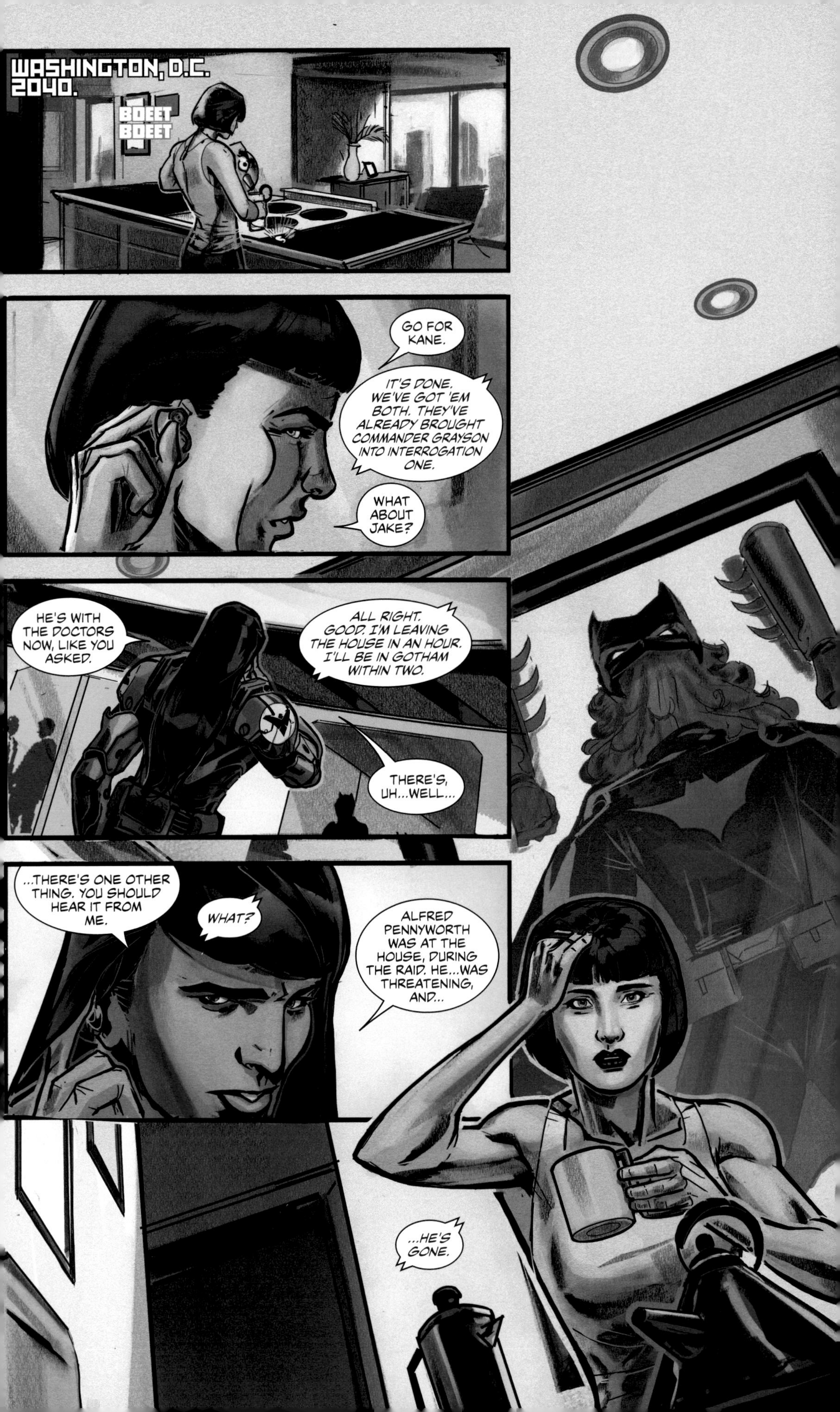
WASHINGTON, D.C. 2040.
BDEET BDEET
GO FOR KANE.
IT'S DONE. WE'VE GOT 'EM BOTH. THEY'VE ALREADY BROUGHT COMMANDER GRAYSON INTO INTERROGATION ONE.
WHAT ABOUT JAKE?
HE'S WITH THE DOCTORS NOW, LIKE YOU ASKED.
ALL RIGHT. GOOD. I'M LEAVING THE HOUSE IN AN HOUR. I'LL BE IN GOTHAM WITHIN TWO.
THERE'S, UH...WELL...
...THERE'S ONE OTHER THING. YOU SHOULD HEAR IT FROM ME.
WHAT?
ALFRED PENNYWORTH WAS AT THE HOUSE, DURING THE RAID. HE...WAS THREATENING, AND...
...HE'S GONE.

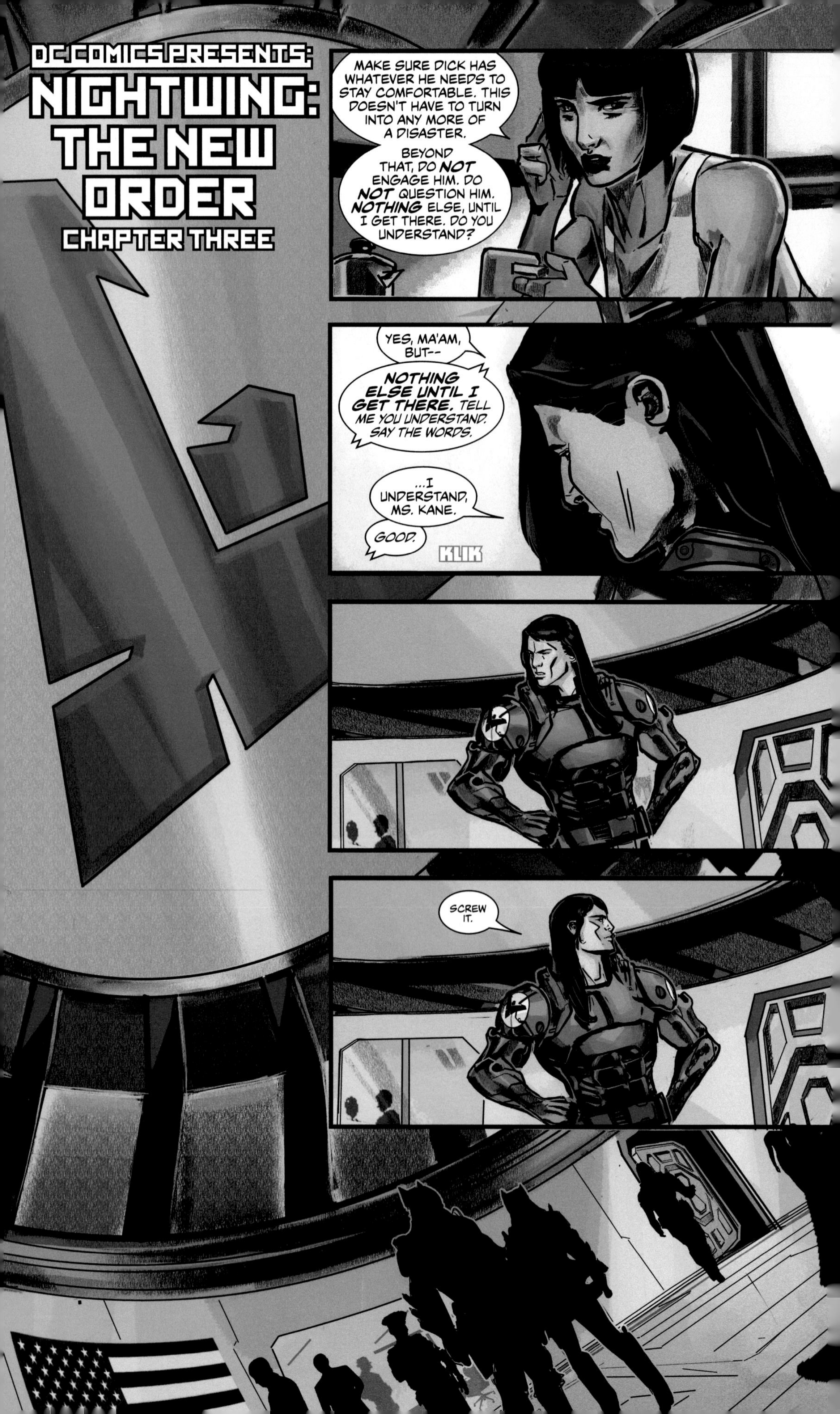
DC COMICS PRESENTS:
NIGHTWING: THE NEW ORDER
CHAPTER THREE
MAKE SURE DICK HAS WHATEVER HE NEEDS TO STAY COMFORTABLE. THIS DOESN'T HAVE TO TURN INTO ANY MORE OF A DISASTER.
BEYOND THAT, DO NOT ENGAGE HIM. DO NOT QUESTION HIM. NOTHING ELSE, UNTIL I GET THERE. DO YOU UNDERSTAND?
YES, MA'AM, BUT--
NOTHING ELSE UNTIL I GET THERE. TELL ME YOU UNDERSTAND. SAY THE WORDS.
...I UNDERSTAND, MS. KANE.
GOOD.
KLIK
SCREW IT.

I JUST GOT OFF THE PHONE WITH MS. KANE. SHE'LL BE HERE IN A FEW HOURS.

IS THERE ANYTHING YOU WANT? WATER? COFFEE? I'M SUPPOSED TO MAKE YOU... *COMFORTABLE.*

IF YOU'RE WONDERING...MICHAEL HOLT DIDN'T RAT YOU OUT. DATA TECH JUST STARTED MONITORING HIS STREAMS. I GUESS YOU MISSED THAT MEETING, HUH? THAT'S ALL RIGHT. YOU'VE GOT *BIGGER* PROBLEMS NOW.

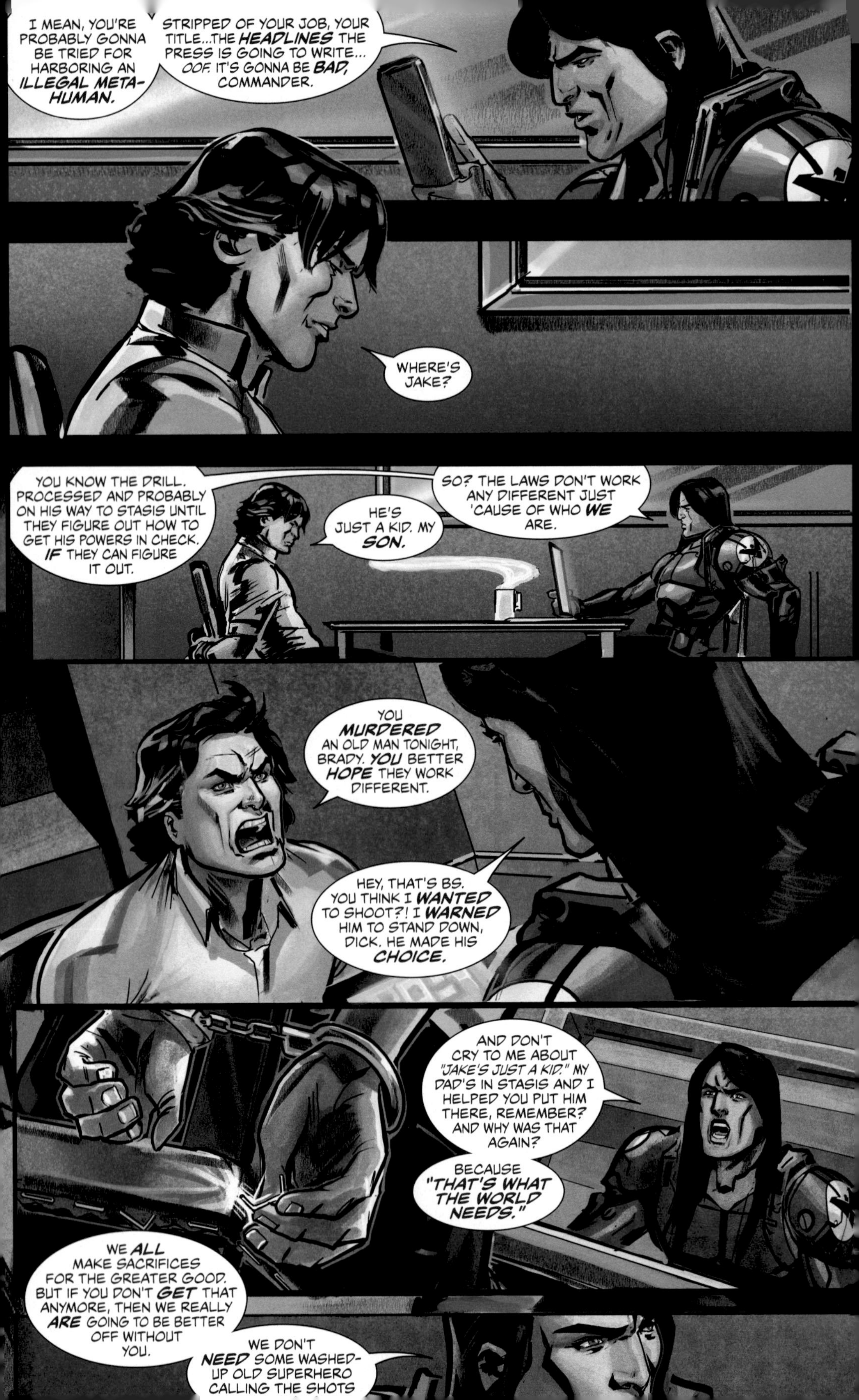
I MEAN, YOU'RE PROBABLY GONNA BE TRIED FOR HARBORING AN ILLEGAL META-HUMAN.
STRIPPED OF YOUR JOB, YOUR TITLE...THE HEADLINES THE PRESS IS GOING TO WRITE... OOF. IT'S GONNA BE BAD, COMMANDER.
WHERE'S JAKE?
YOU KNOW THE DRILL. PROCESSED AND PROBABLY ON HIS WAY TO STASIS UNTIL THEY FIGURE OUT HOW TO GET HIS POWERS IN CHECK. IF THEY CAN FIGURE IT OUT.
HE'S JUST A KID. MY SON.
SO? THE LAWS DON'T WORK ANY DIFFERENT JUST 'CAUSE OF WHO WE ARE.
YOU MURDERED AN OLD MAN TONIGHT, BRADY. YOU BETTER HOPE THEY WORK DIFFERENT.
HEY, THAT'S BS. YOU THINK I WANTED TO SHOOT?! I WARNED HIM TO STAND DOWN, DICK. HE MADE HIS CHOICE.
AND DON'T CRY TO ME ABOUT "JAKE'S JUST A KID." MY DAD'S IN STASIS AND I HELPED YOU PUT HIM THERE, REMEMBER? AND WHY WAS THAT AGAIN?
BECAUSE "THAT'S WHAT THE WORLD NEEDS."
WE ALL MAKE SACRIFICES FOR THE GREATER GOOD. BUT IF YOU DON'T GET THAT ANYMORE, THEN WE REALLY ARE GOING TO BE BETTER OFF WITHOUT YOU.
WE DON'T NEED SOME WASHED-UP OLD SUPERHERO CALLING THE SHOTS

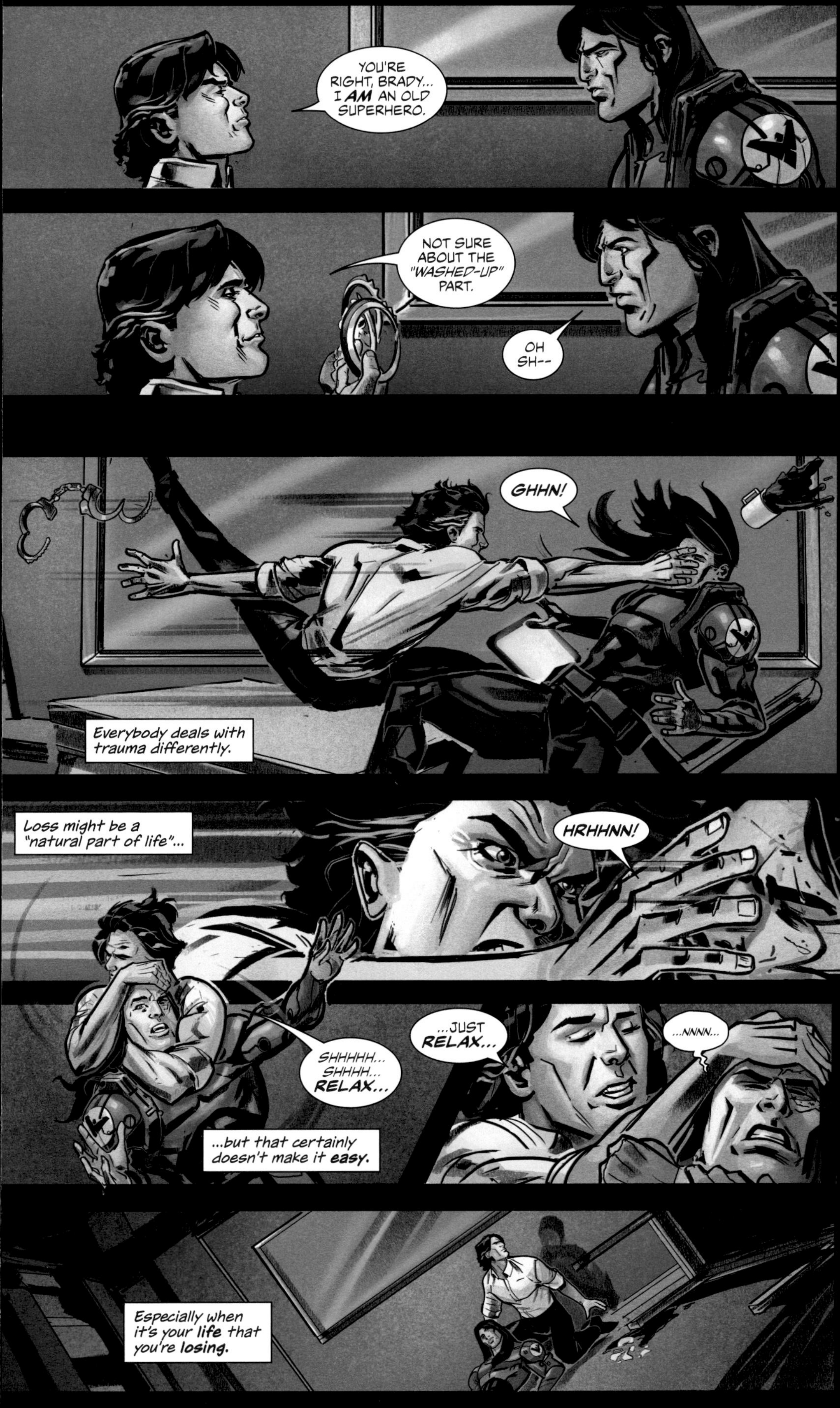
YOU'RE RIGHT, BRADY... I AM AN OLD SUPERHERO.
NOT SURE ABOUT THE "WASHED-UP" PART.
OH SH--
GHHN!
Everybody deals with trauma differently.
Loss might be a "natural part of life"...
HRHHNN!
SHHHHH... SHHHH... RELAX...
...JUST RELAX...
...NNNN...
...but that certainly doesn't make it easy.
Especially when it's your life that you're losing.

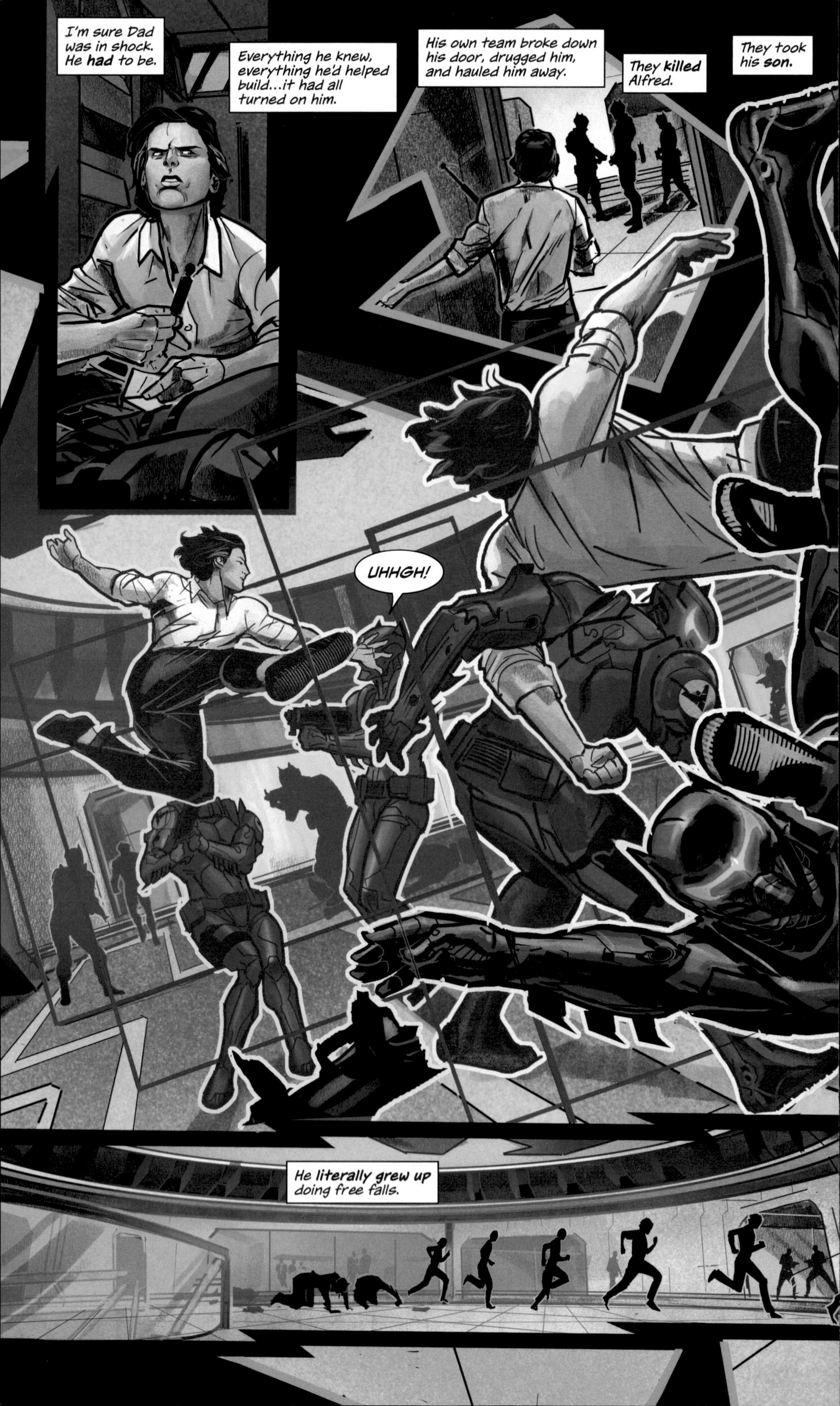
I'm sure Dad was in shock. He had to be.
Everything he knew, everything he'd helped build...it had all turned on him.
His own team broke down his door, drugged him, and hauled him away.
They killed Alfred.
They took his son.
UHHGH!
He literally grew up doing free falls.

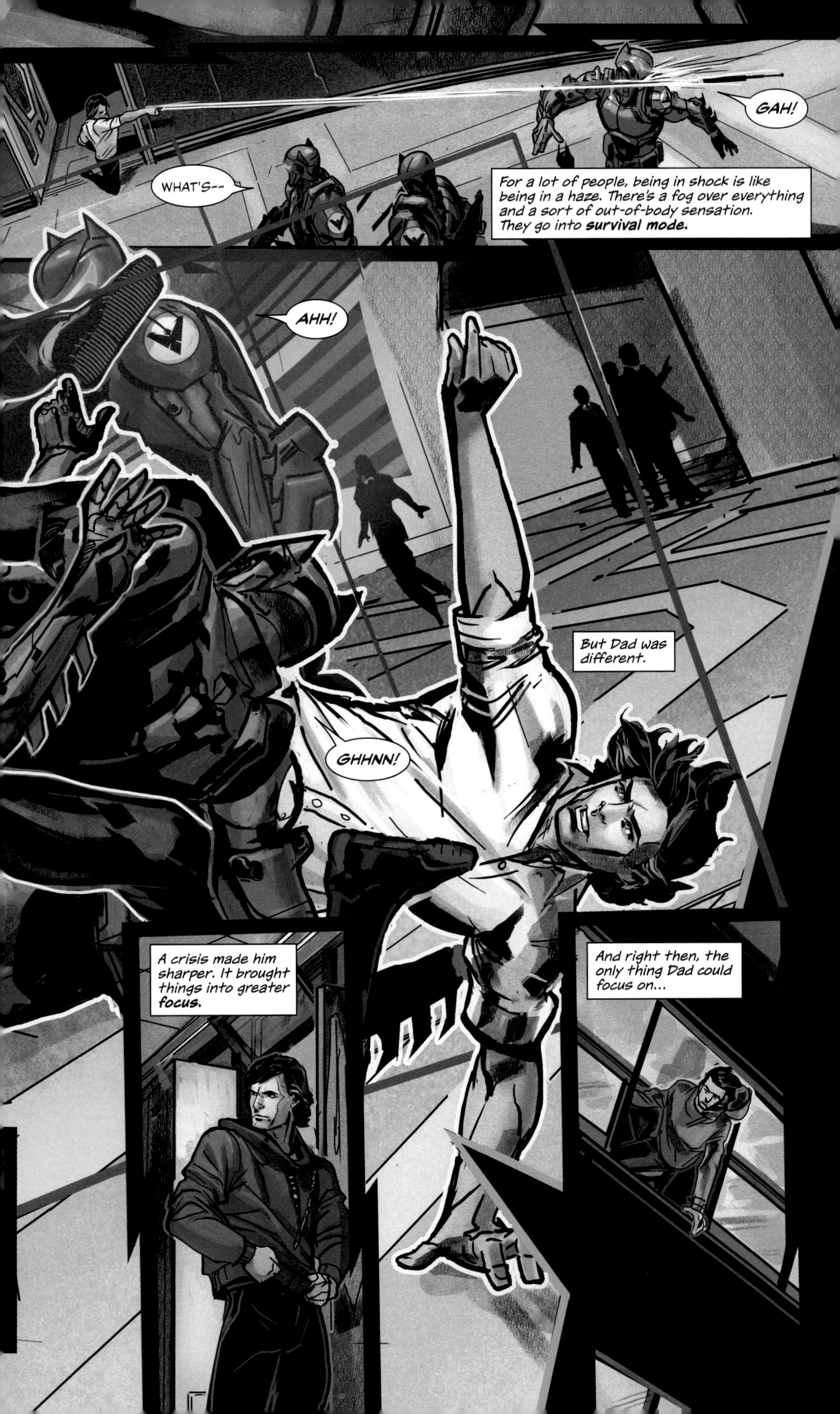
GAH!
WHAT'S--
For a lot of people, being in shock is like being in a haze. There's a fog over everything and a sort of out-of-body sensation. They go into **survival mode.**
AHH!
But Dad was different.
GHHNN!
A crisis made him sharper. It brought things into greater **focus.**
And right then, the only thing Dad could focus on...

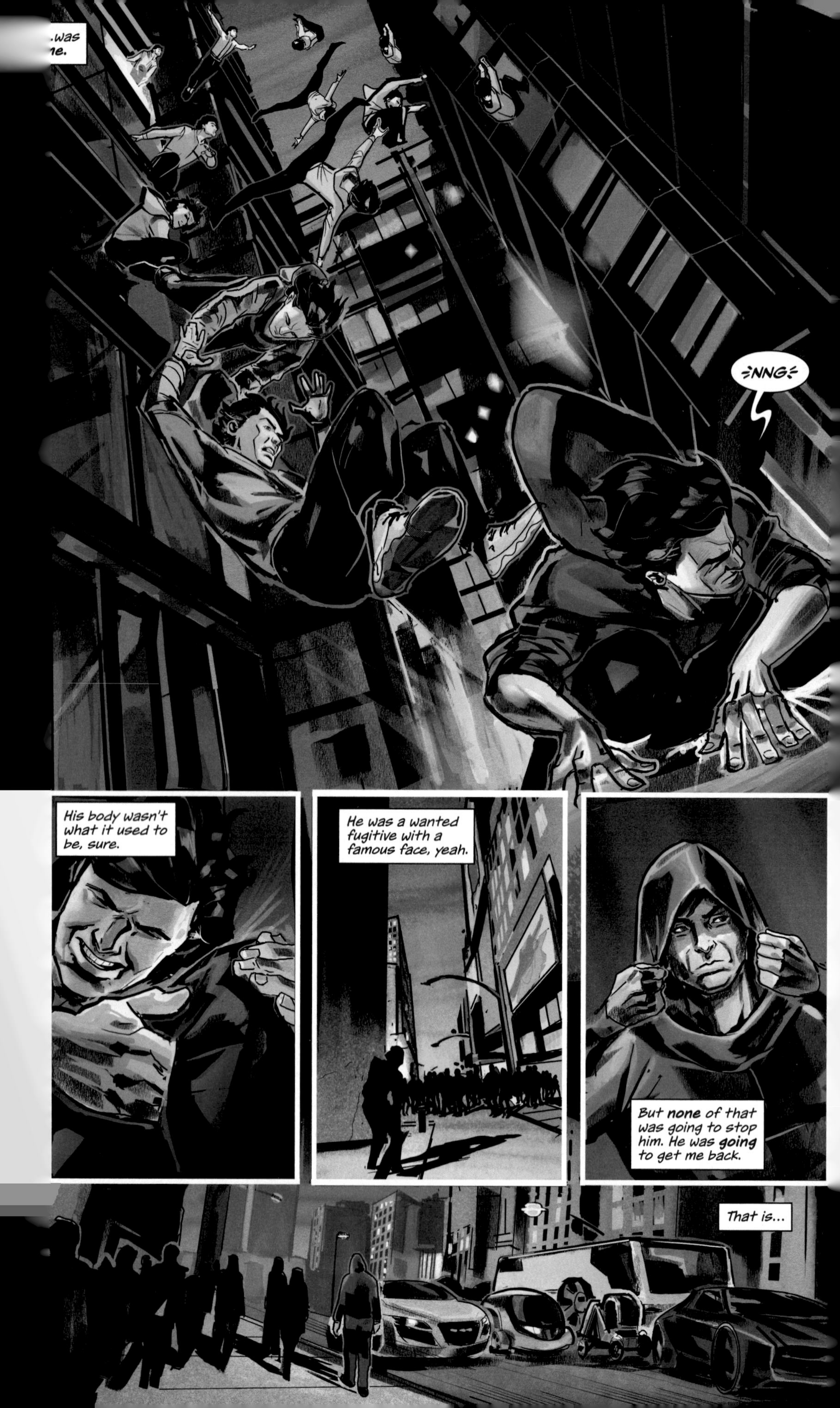
.was
ne.
NNG
His body wasn't what it used to be, sure.
He was a wanted fugitive with a famous face, yeah.
But none of that was going to stop him. He was going to get me back.
That is...

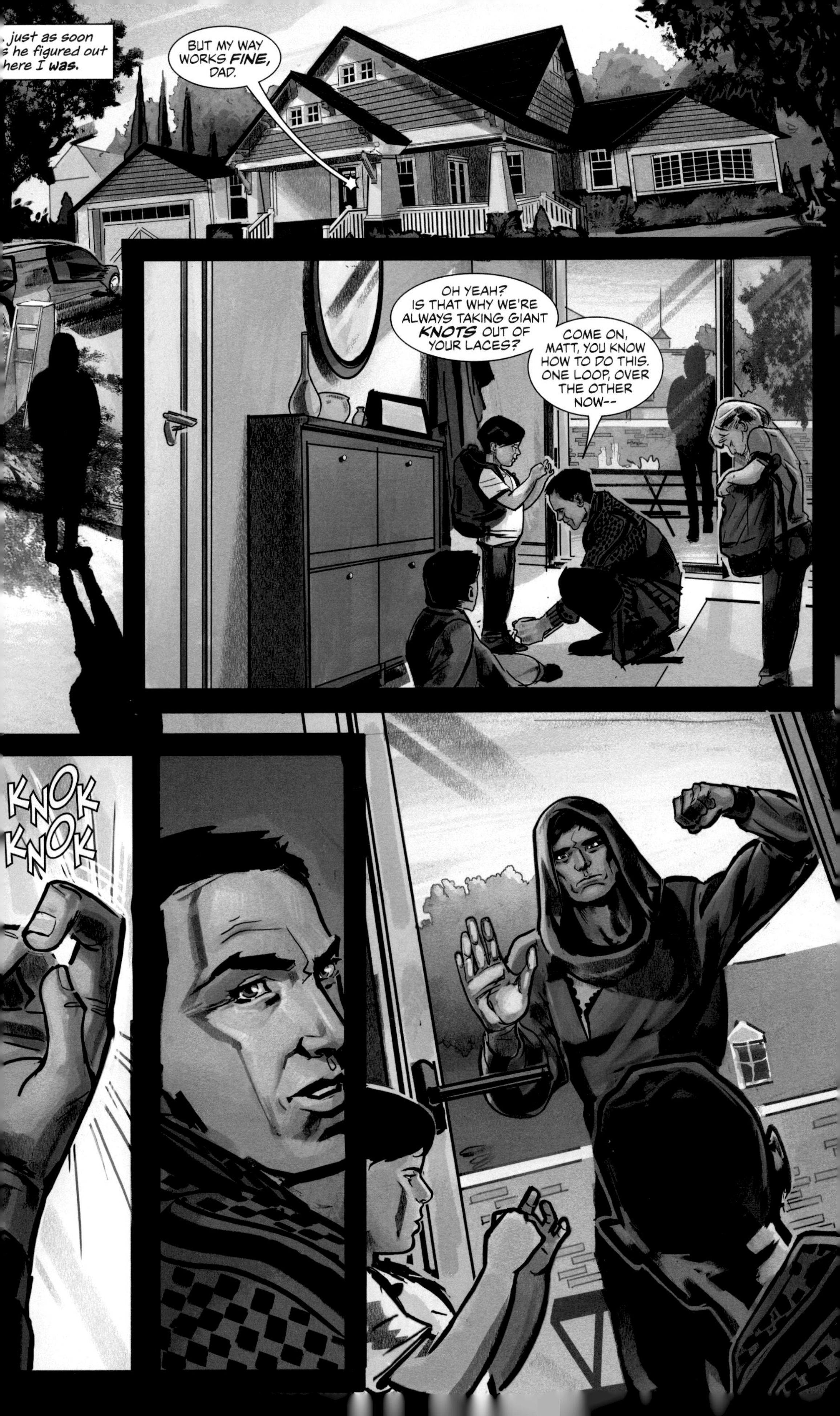

, just as soon
s he figured out
here I **was.**
BUT MY WAY WORKS **FINE,** DAD.
OH YEAH? IS THAT WHY WE'RE ALWAYS TAKING GIANT **KNOTS** OUT OF YOUR LACES?
COME ON, MATT, YOU KNOW HOW TO DO THIS. ONE LOOP, OVER THE OTHER NOW--
KNOK KNOK

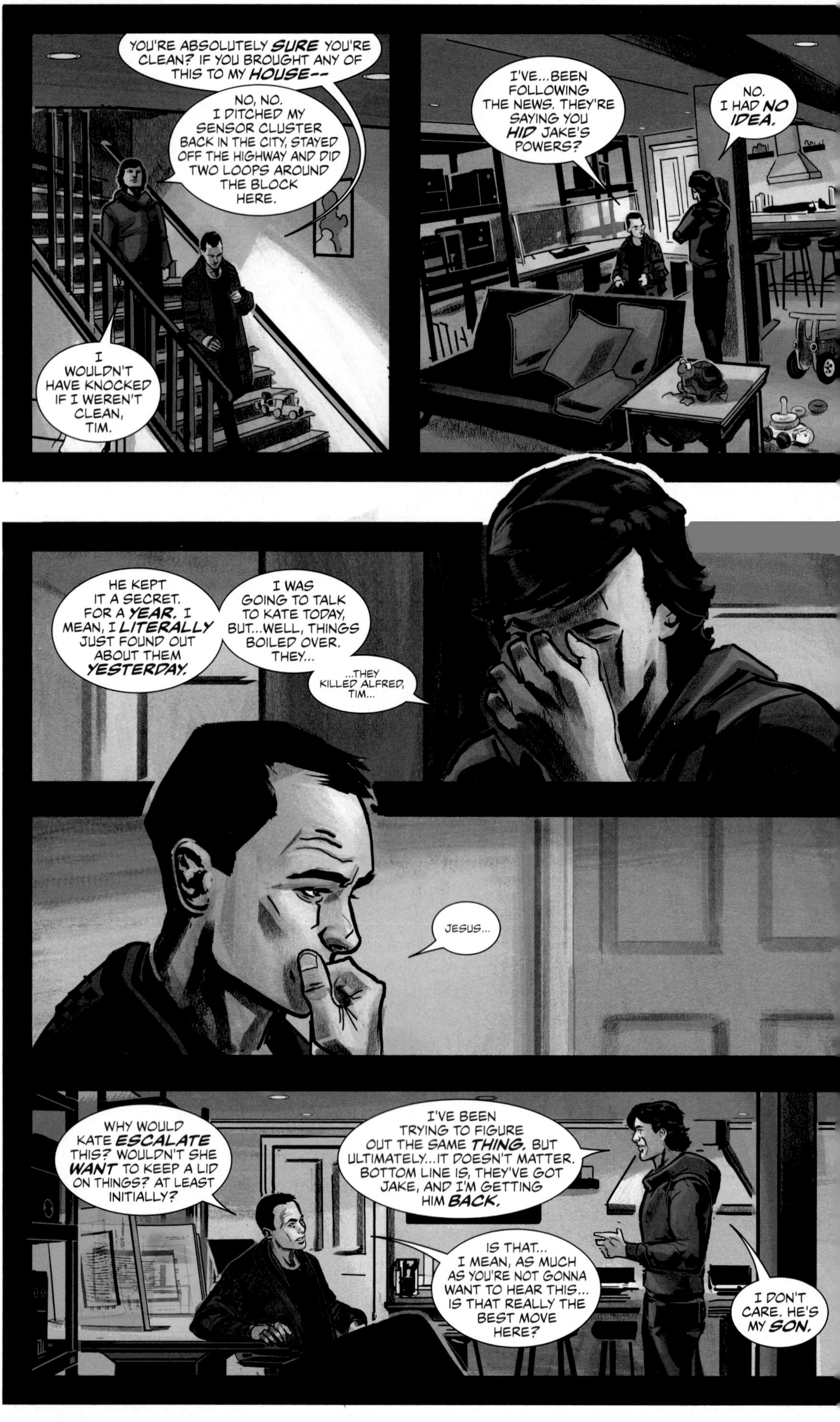
YOU'RE ABSOLUTELY SURE YOU'RE CLEAN? IF YOU BROUGHT ANY OF THIS TO MY HOUSE--
NO, NO. I DITCHED MY SENSOR CLUSTER BACK IN THE CITY, STAYED OFF THE HIGHWAY AND DID TWO LOOPS AROUND THE BLOCK HERE.
I WOULDN'T HAVE KNOCKED IF I WEREN'T CLEAN, TIM.
I'VE...BEEN FOLLOWING THE NEWS. THEY'RE SAYING YOU HID JAKE'S POWERS?
NO. I HAD NO IDEA.
HE KEPT IT A SECRET. FOR A YEAR. I MEAN, I LITERALLY JUST FOUND OUT ABOUT THEM YESTERDAY.
I WAS GOING TO TALK TO KATE TODAY, BUT...WELL, THINGS BOILED OVER. THEY...
...THEY KILLED ALFRED, TIM...
JESUS...
WHY WOULD KATE ESCALATE THIS? WOULDN'T SHE WANT TO KEEP A LID ON THINGS? AT LEAST INITIALLY?
I'VE BEEN TRYING TO FIGURE OUT THE SAME THING. BUT ULTIMATELY...IT DOESN'T MATTER. BOTTOM LINE IS, THEY'VE GOT JAKE, AND I'M GETTING HIM BACK.
IS THAT... I MEAN, AS MUCH AS YOU'RE NOT GONNA WANT TO HEAR THIS... IS THAT REALLY THE BEST MOVE HERE?
I DON'T CARE. HE'S MY SON.

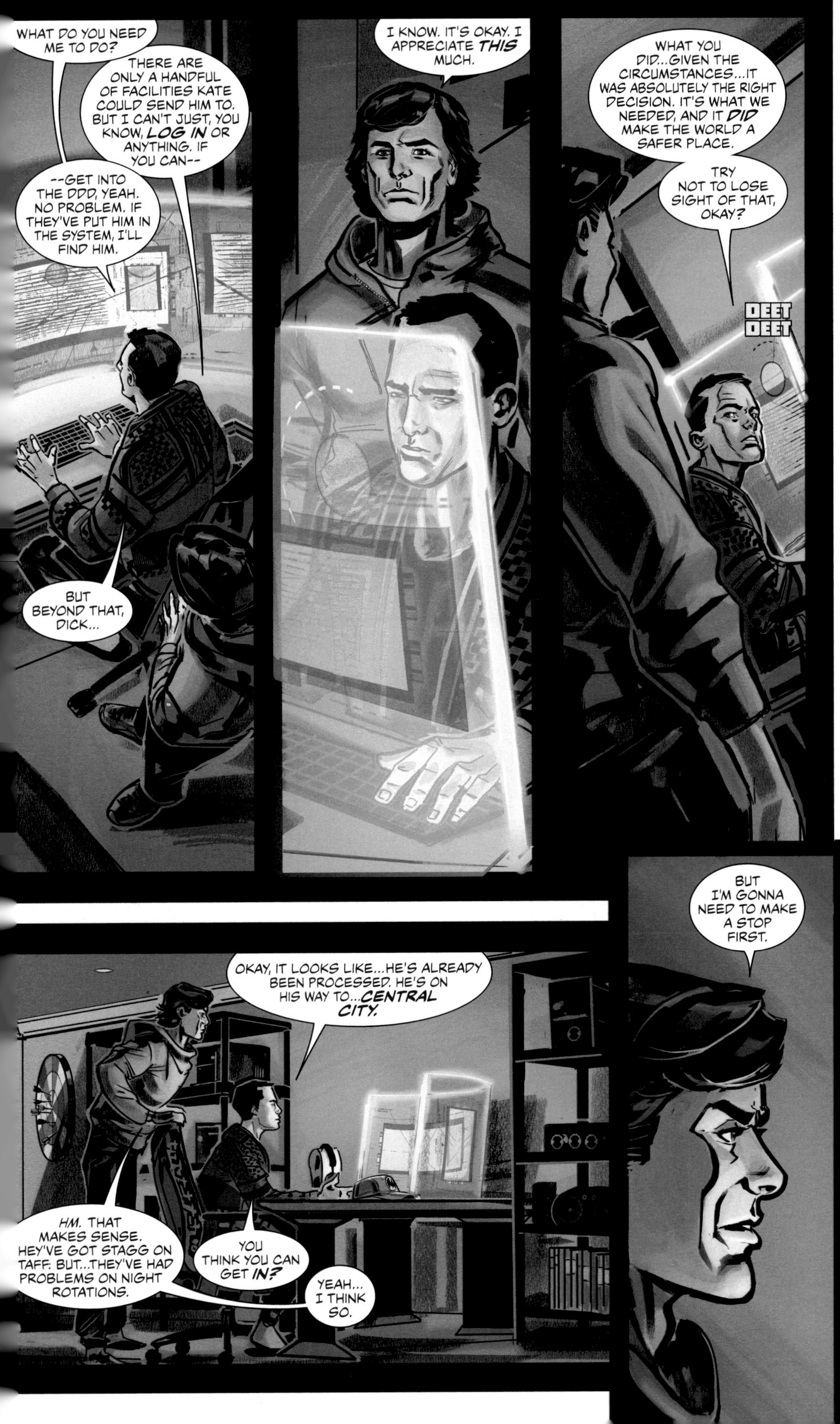
WHAT DO YOU NEED ME TO DO?
THERE ARE ONLY A HANDFUL OF FACILITIES KATE COULD SEND HIM TO. BUT I CAN'T JUST, YOU KNOW, LOG IN OR ANYTHING. IF YOU CAN--
--GET INTO THE DDD, YEAH. NO PROBLEM. IF THEY'VE PUT HIM IN THE SYSTEM, I'LL FIND HIM.
BUT BEYOND THAT, DICK...
I KNOW. IT'S OKAY. I APPRECIATE THIS MUCH.
WHAT YOU DID...GIVEN THE CIRCUMSTANCES...IT WAS ABSOLUTELY THE RIGHT DECISION. IT'S WHAT WE NEEDED, AND IT DID MAKE THE WORLD A SAFER PLACE.
TRY NOT TO LOSE SIGHT OF THAT, OKAY?
DEET DEET
OKAY, IT LOOKS LIKE...HE'S ALREADY BEEN PROCESSED. HE'S ON HIS WAY TO...CENTRAL CITY.
HM. THAT MAKES SENSE. HEY'VE GOT STAGG ON TAFF: BUT...THEY'VE HAD PROBLEMS ON NIGHT ROTATIONS.
YOU THINK YOU CAN GET IN?
YEAH... I THINK SO.
BUT I'M GONNA NEED TO MAKE A STOP FIRST.

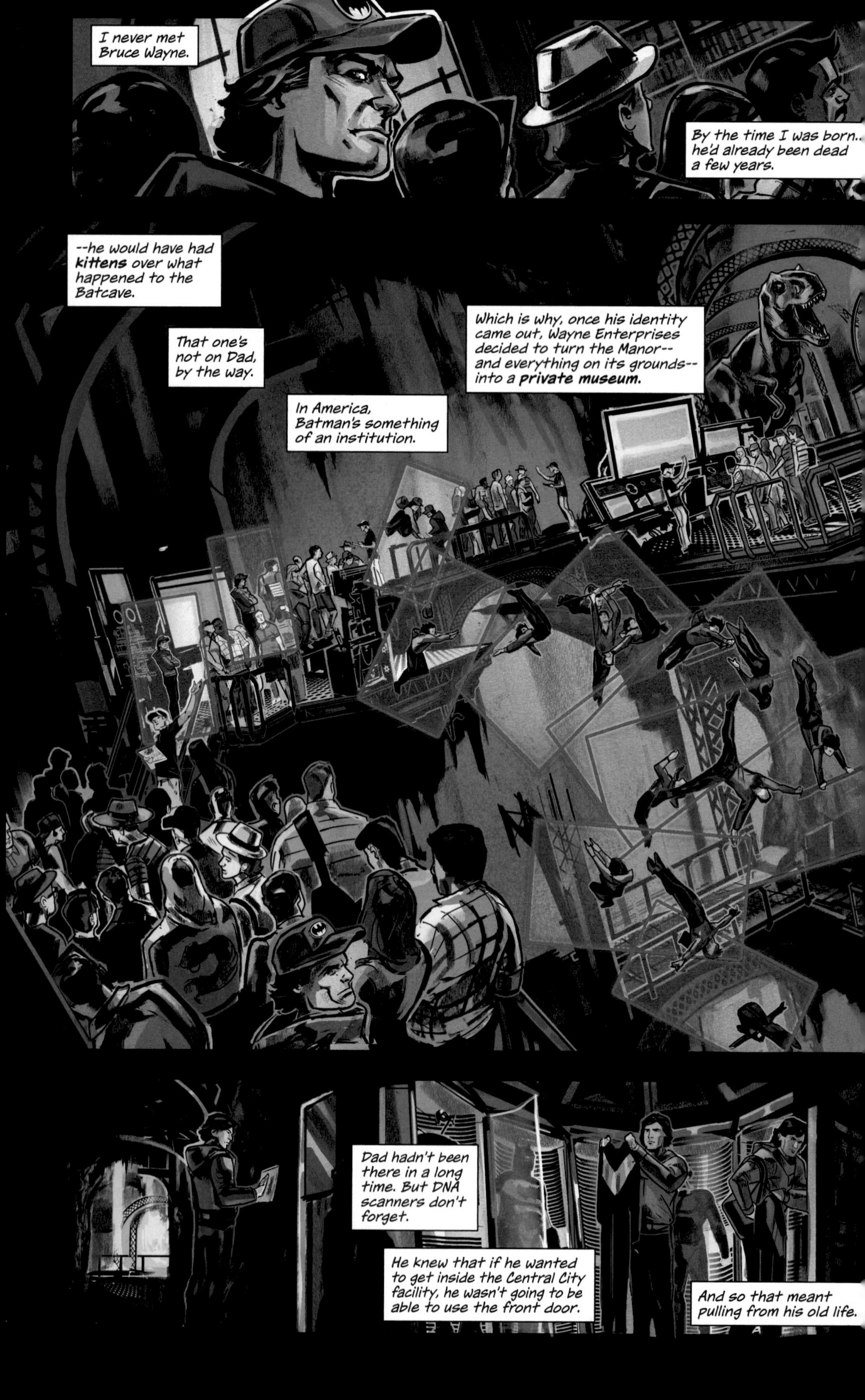
I never met Bruce Wayne.
By the time I was born... he'd already been dead a few years.
--he would have had **kittens** over what happened to the Batcave.
That one's not on Dad, by the way.
Which is why, once his identity came out, Wayne Enterprises decided to turn the Manor--and everything on its grounds--into a **private museum.**
In America, Batman's something of an institution.
Dad hadn't been there in a long time. But DNA scanners don't forget.
He knew that if he wanted to get inside the Central City facility, he wasn't going to be able to use the front door.
And so that meant pulling from his old life.

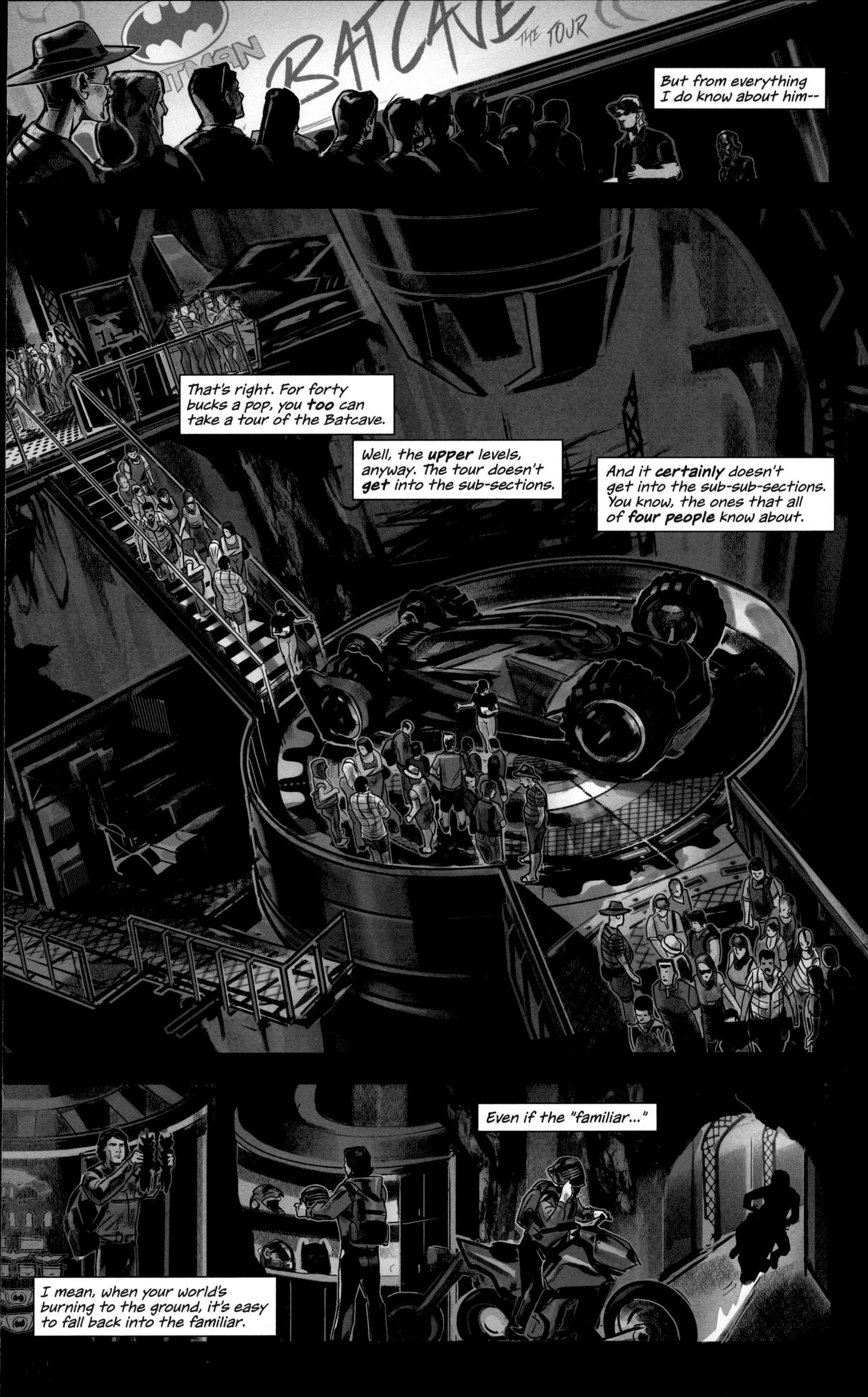
BATMAN
BATCAVE THE TOUR
But from everything I do know about him--
That's right. For forty bucks a pop, you **too** can take a tour of the Batcave.
Well, the **upper** levels, anyway. The tour doesn't **get** into the sub-sections.
And it **certainly** doesn't get into the sub-sub-sections. You know, the ones that all of **four people** know about.
I mean, when your world's burning to the ground, it's easy to fall back into the familiar.
Even if the "familiar..."

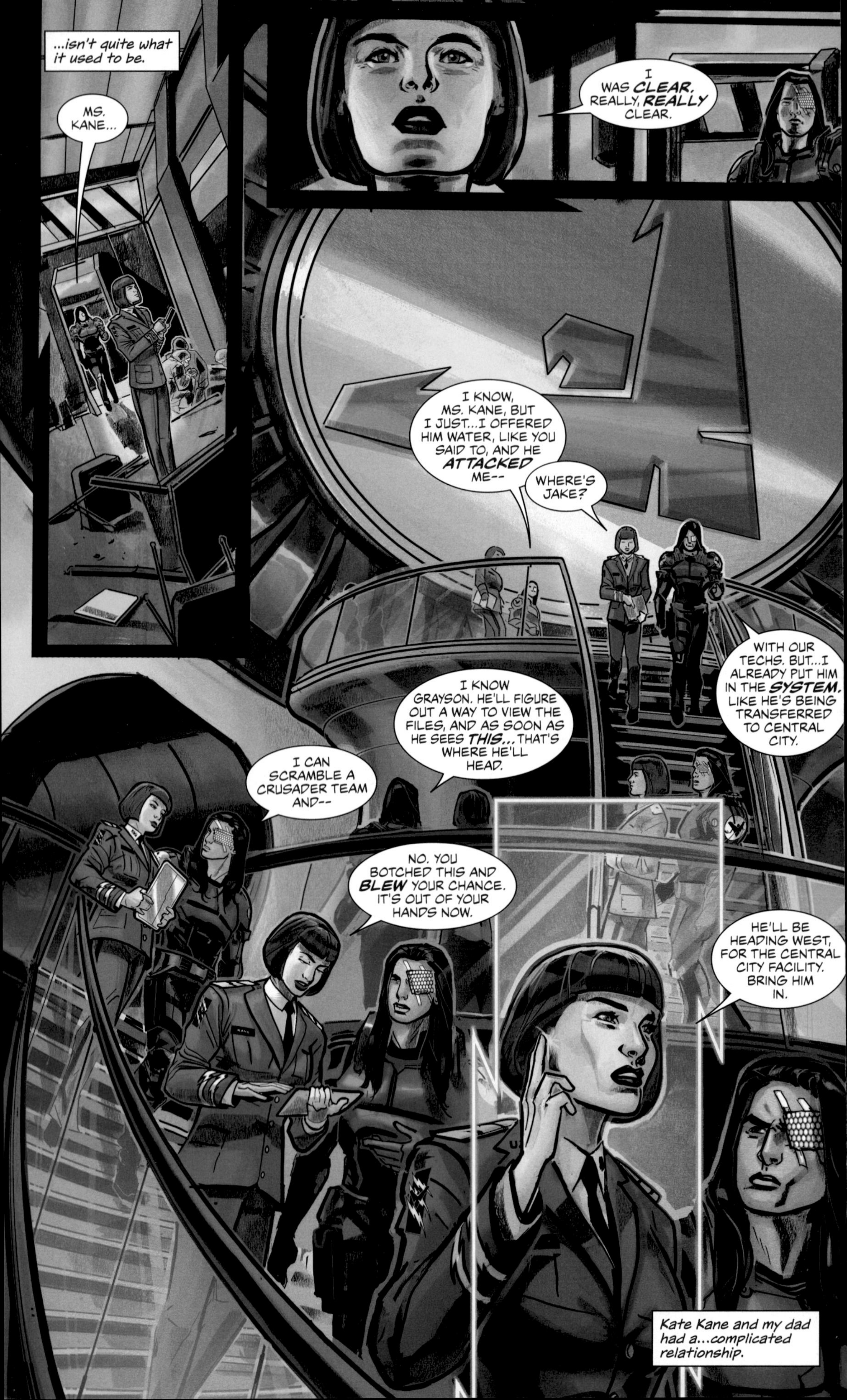
...isn't quite what it used to be.
MS. KANE...
I WAS CLEAR. REALLY, REALLY CLEAR.
I KNOW, MS. KANE, BUT I JUST...I OFFERED HIM WATER, LIKE YOU SAID TO, AND HE ATTACKED ME--
WHERE'S JAKE?
WITH OUR TECHS. BUT...I ALREADY PUT HIM IN THE SYSTEM. LIKE HE'S BEING TRANSFERRED TO CENTRAL CITY.
I KNOW GRAYSON. HE'LL FIGURE OUT A WAY TO VIEW THE FILES, AND AS SOON AS HE SEES THIS... THAT'S WHERE HE'LL HEAD.
I CAN SCRAMBLE A CRUSADER TEAM AND--
NO. YOU BOTCHED THIS AND BLEW YOUR CHANCE. IT'S OUT OF YOUR HANDS NOW.
HE'LL BE HEADING WEST, FOR THE CENTRAL CITY FACILITY. BRING HIM IN.
Kate Kane and my dad had a...complicated relationship.

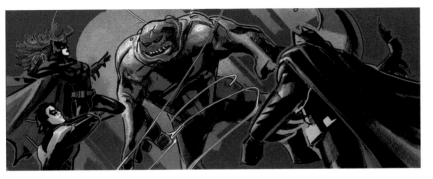

He was one of the first people to work with her when she became Batwoman.

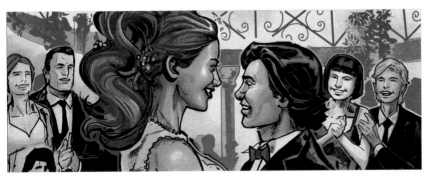

And she liked him and my mom enough to come to their wedding.

But I don't know that anyone would ever really describe them as **"close."**

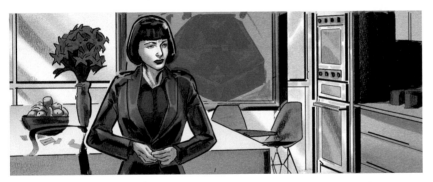

Kate had a military background and, as the years went by, she drifted more and more toward it.

As Batwoman, she'd tried being a "superhero solution" to the problems of the world. But eventually, for a variety of reasons, she started to believe that law and order came from transparency and regulation, not vigilantism.

DEPARTMENT OF DEFENSE
SECRETARIES OF DEFENSE

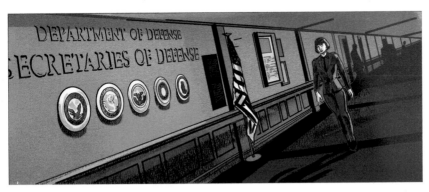

The system needed good people working **in** it, rather than **outside** it.

After her dad died... she quit the hero work altogether and joined the Pentagon.

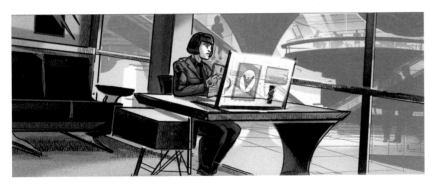

She and my dad didn't interact much until after Metropolis. When all the laws passed and the public **demanded** the Crusader program, Kate helped put it together.

And her **bosses** asked my dad to **run** it.

There was always a bit of animosity there, with my dad more or less becoming the **face** of the Crusaders.

Still, it wasn't like it was enough to warrant what she was doing now. She wasn't **that** petty.

At least, that's what my dad kept trying to tell himself.

There was something else going on here. There **had** to be.

I'M SORRY, DICK...

...BUT I CAN'T LET YOU GO ANY FARTHER.
SHE'S SENDING IN THE BIG GUNS NOW, HUH?
LOOK, THIS WHOLE THING...HAS GOTTEN VERY OUT OF HAND. KATE RECOGNIZES THAT. SHE SENT ME TO BRING YOU BACK IN, SO YOU TWO CAN TALK.
NOT SURE THERE'S MUCH TO TALK ABOUT, UNLESS SHE'S WILLING TO GUARANTEE JAKE'S SAFETY. THAT HE'LL STAY OUT OF STASIS. IS SHE WILLING TO DO THAT?
...DICK, COME ON. DON'T MAKE THIS ANY HARDER THAN--
THAT'S WHAT I THOUGHT.
GAHH!

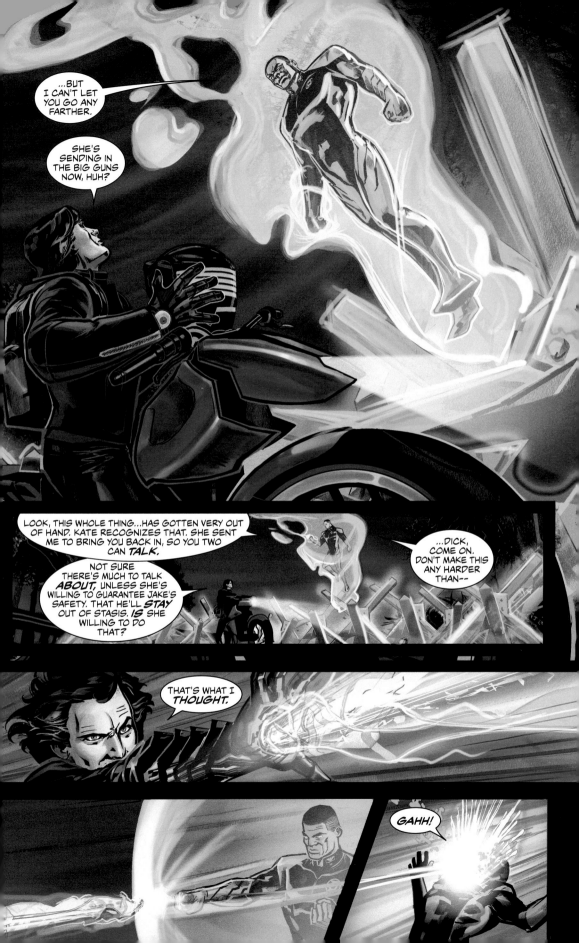

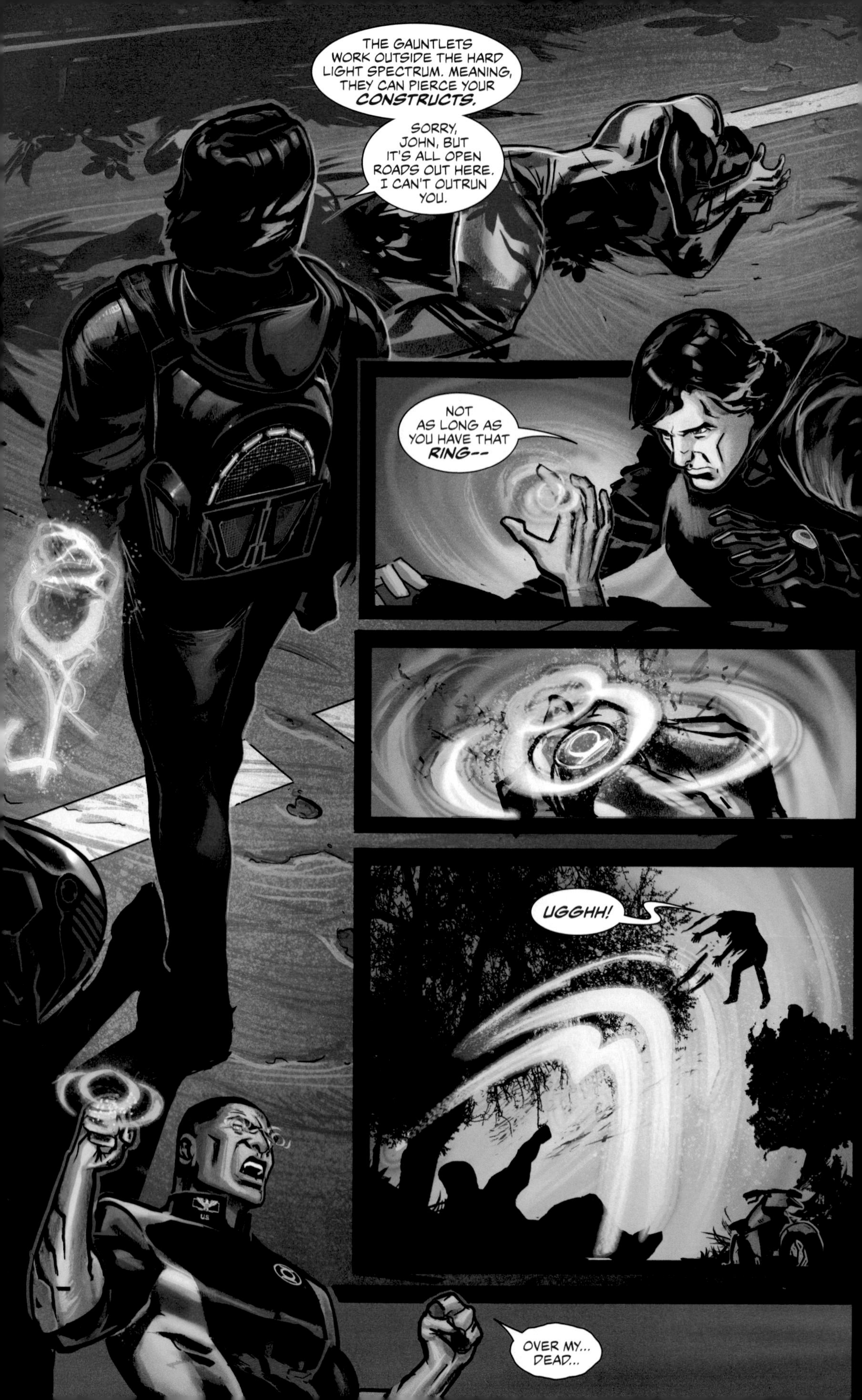
THE GAUNTLETS WORK OUTSIDE THE HARD LIGHT SPECTRUM. MEANING, THEY CAN PIERCE YOUR ***CONSTRUCTS.***
SORRY, JOHN, BUT IT'S ALL OPEN ROADS OUT HERE. I CAN'T OUTRUN YOU.
NOT AS LONG AS YOU HAVE THAT ***RING--***
UGGHH!
OVER MY... DEAD...

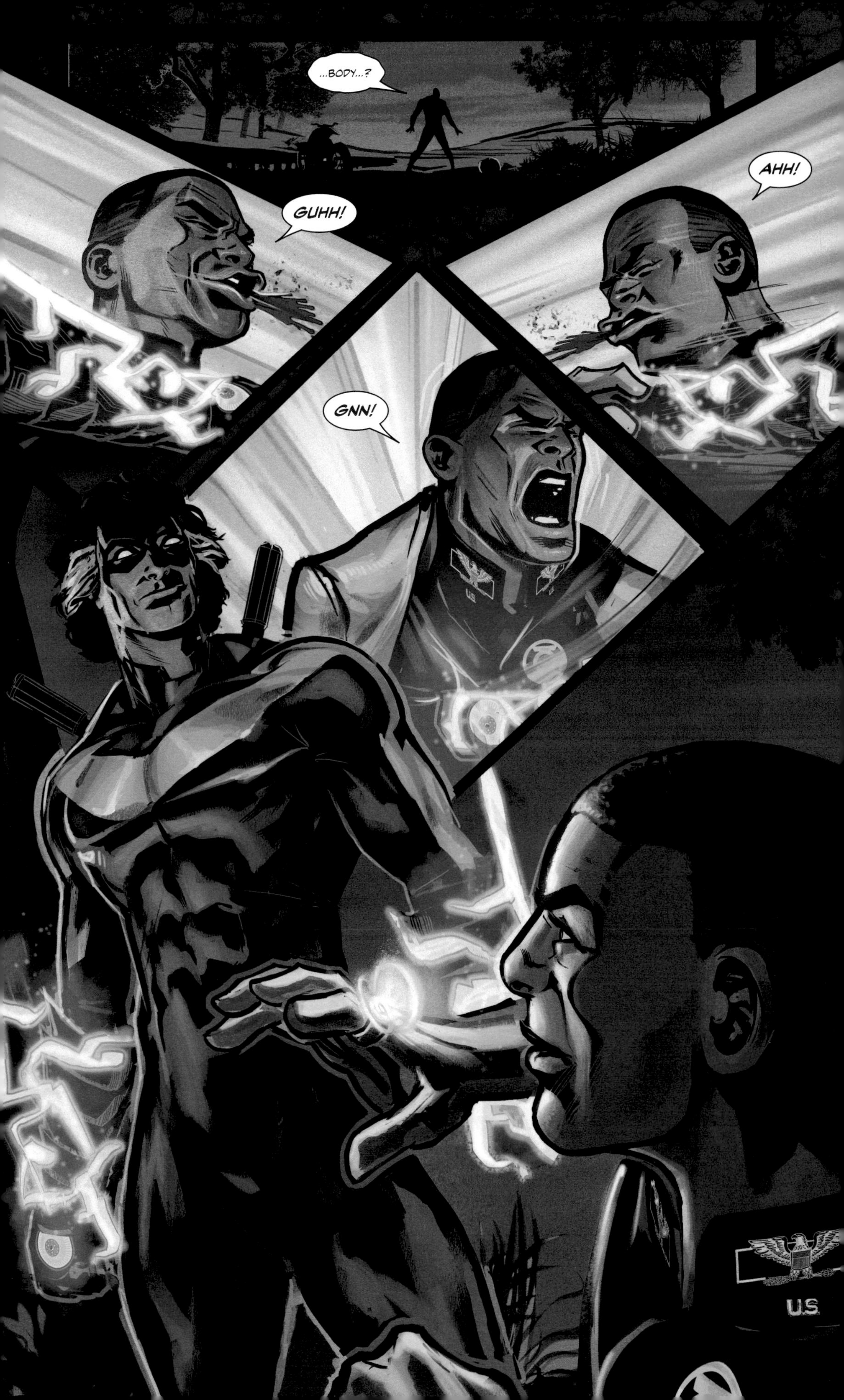
...BODY...?
GUHH!
AHH!
GNN!
U.S.
U.S.

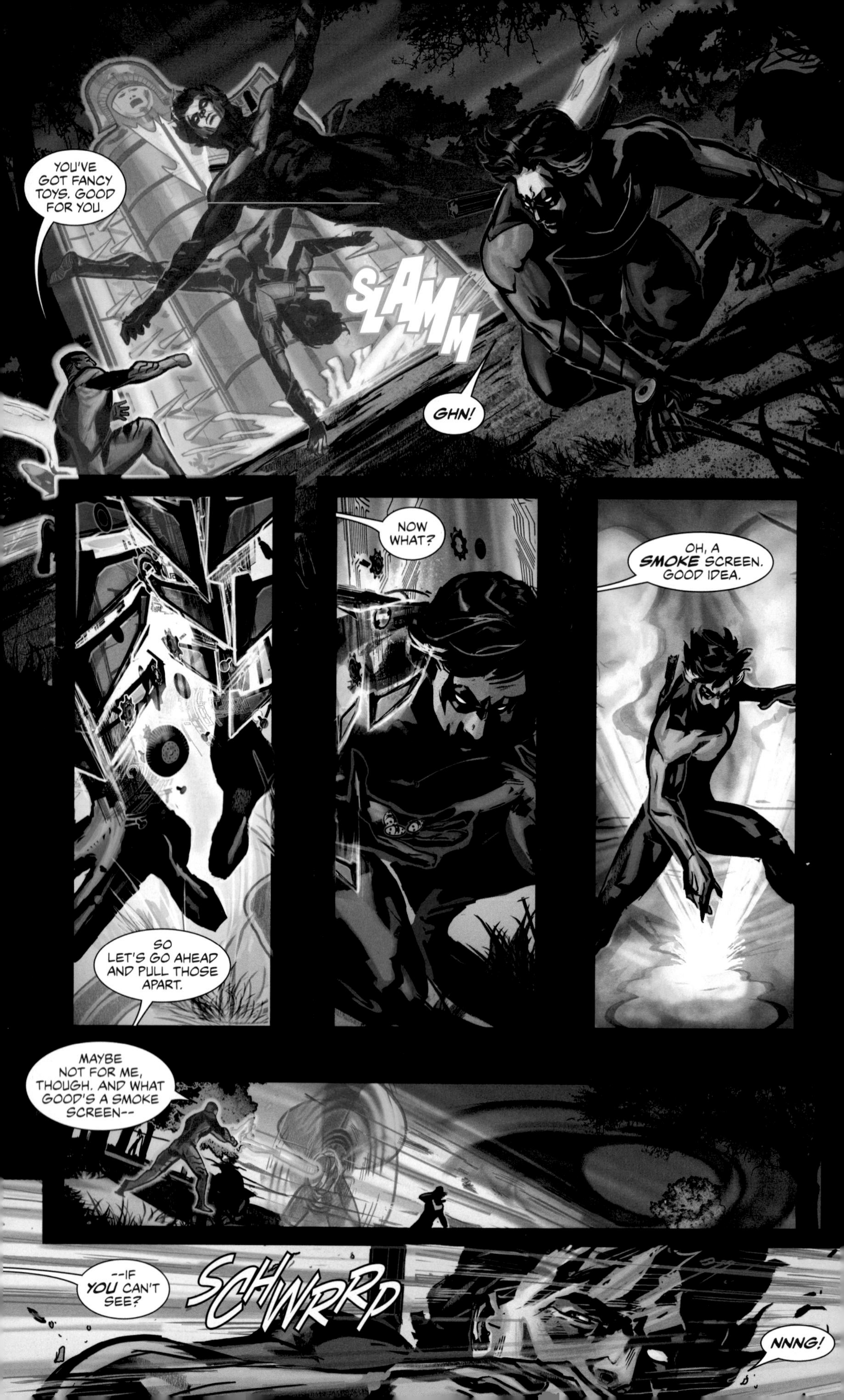
YOU'VE GOT FANCY TOYS. GOOD FOR YOU.
SLAMM
GHN!
NOW WHAT?
OH, A SMOKE SCREEN. GOOD IDEA.
SO LET'S GO AHEAD AND PULL THOSE APART.
MAYBE NOT FOR ME, THOUGH. AND WHAT GOOD'S A SMOKE SCREEN--
--IF YOU CAN'T SEE?
SCHWRRP
NNNG!

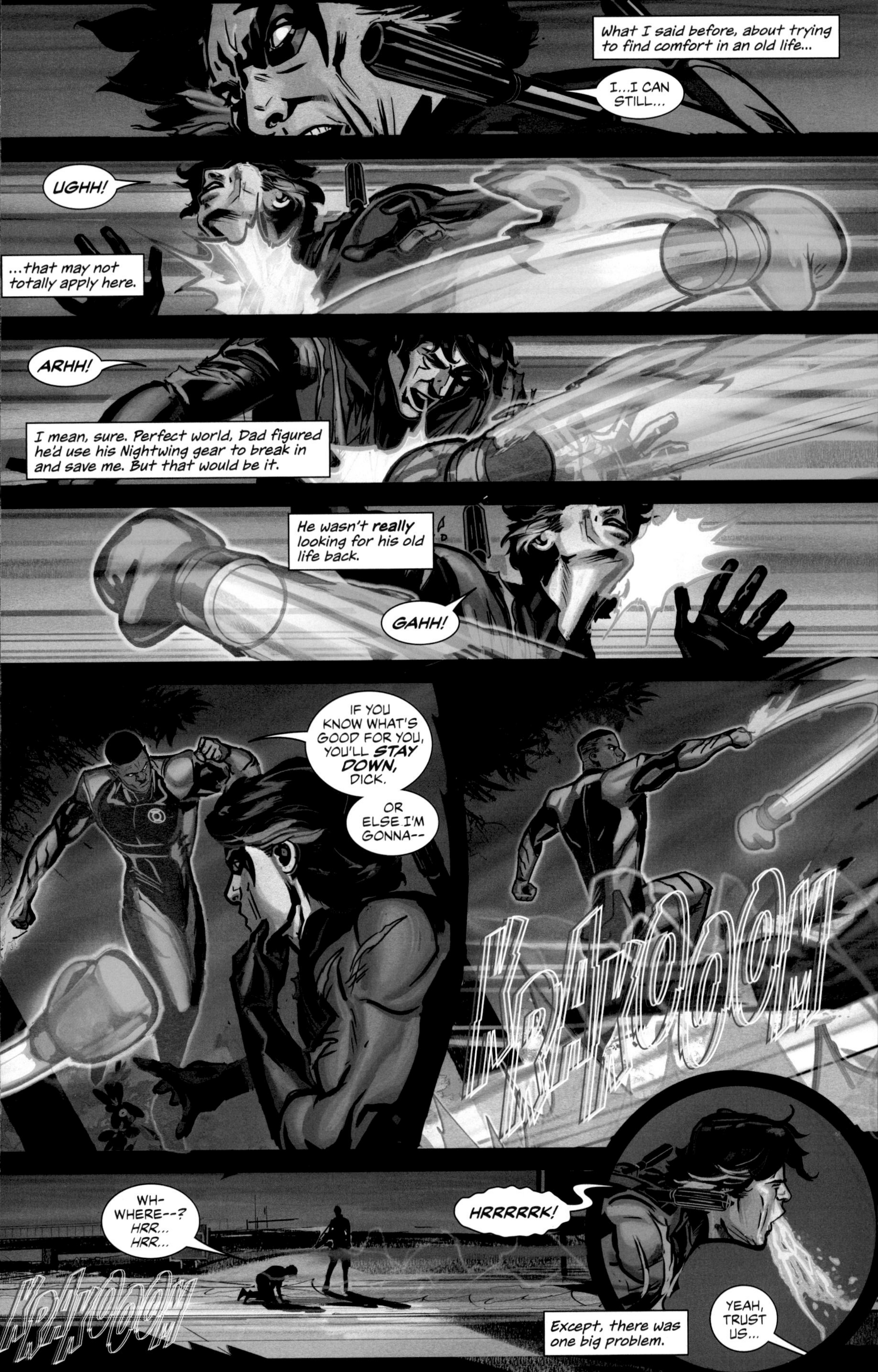
What I said before, about trying to find comfort in an old life...
I...I CAN STILL...
UGHH!
...that may not totally apply here.
ARHH!
I mean, sure. Perfect world, Dad figured he'd use his Nightwing gear to break in and save me. But that would be it.
He wasn't really looking for his old life back.
GAHH!
IF YOU KNOW WHAT'S GOOD FOR YOU, YOU'LL STAY DOWN, DICK.
OR ELSE I'M GONNA--
WH- WHERE--? HRR... HRR...
HRRRRRK!
Except, there was one big problem.
YEAH, TRUST US...

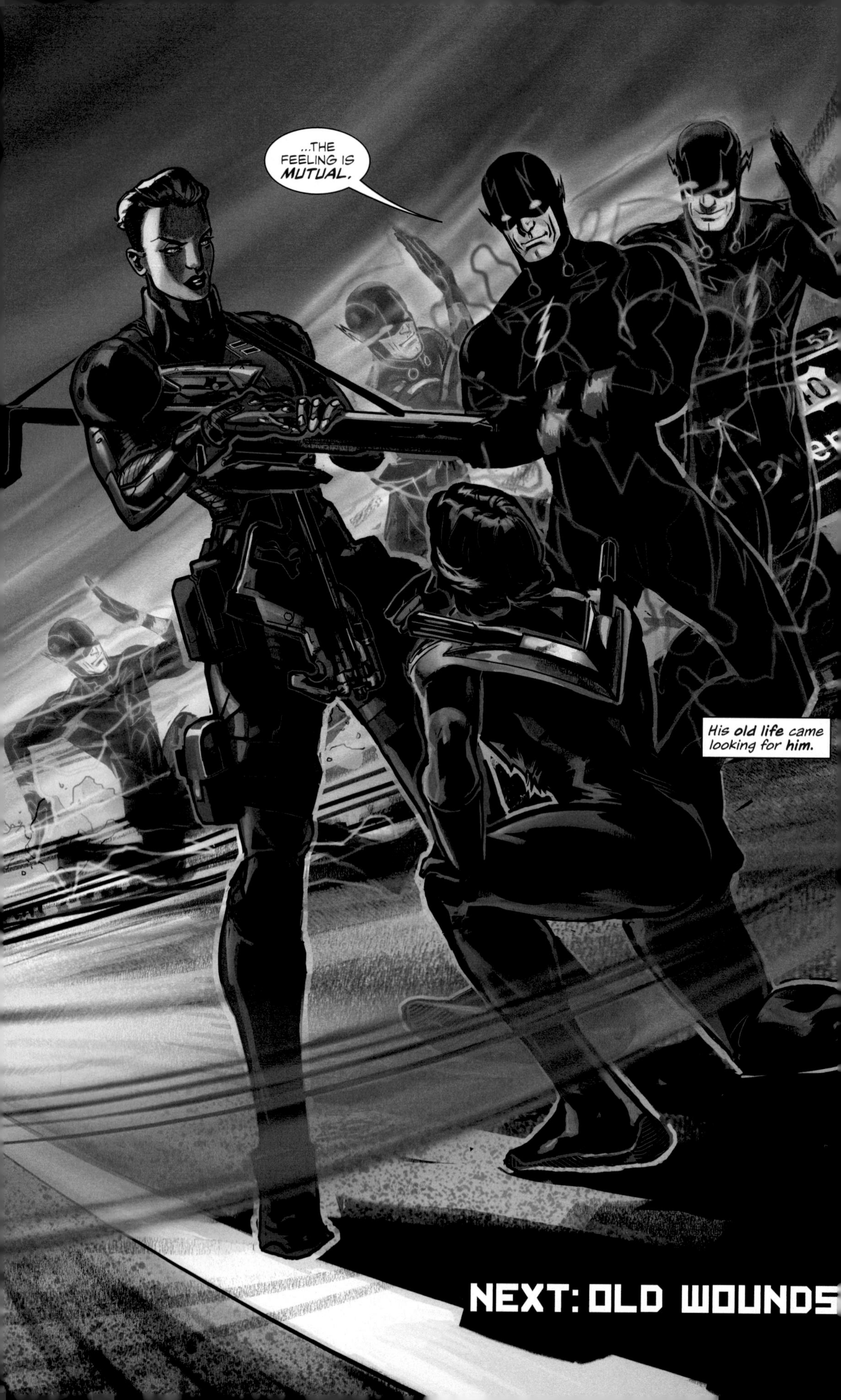

...THE FEELING IS MUTUAL.
His old life came looking for him.
NEXT: OLD WOUNDS

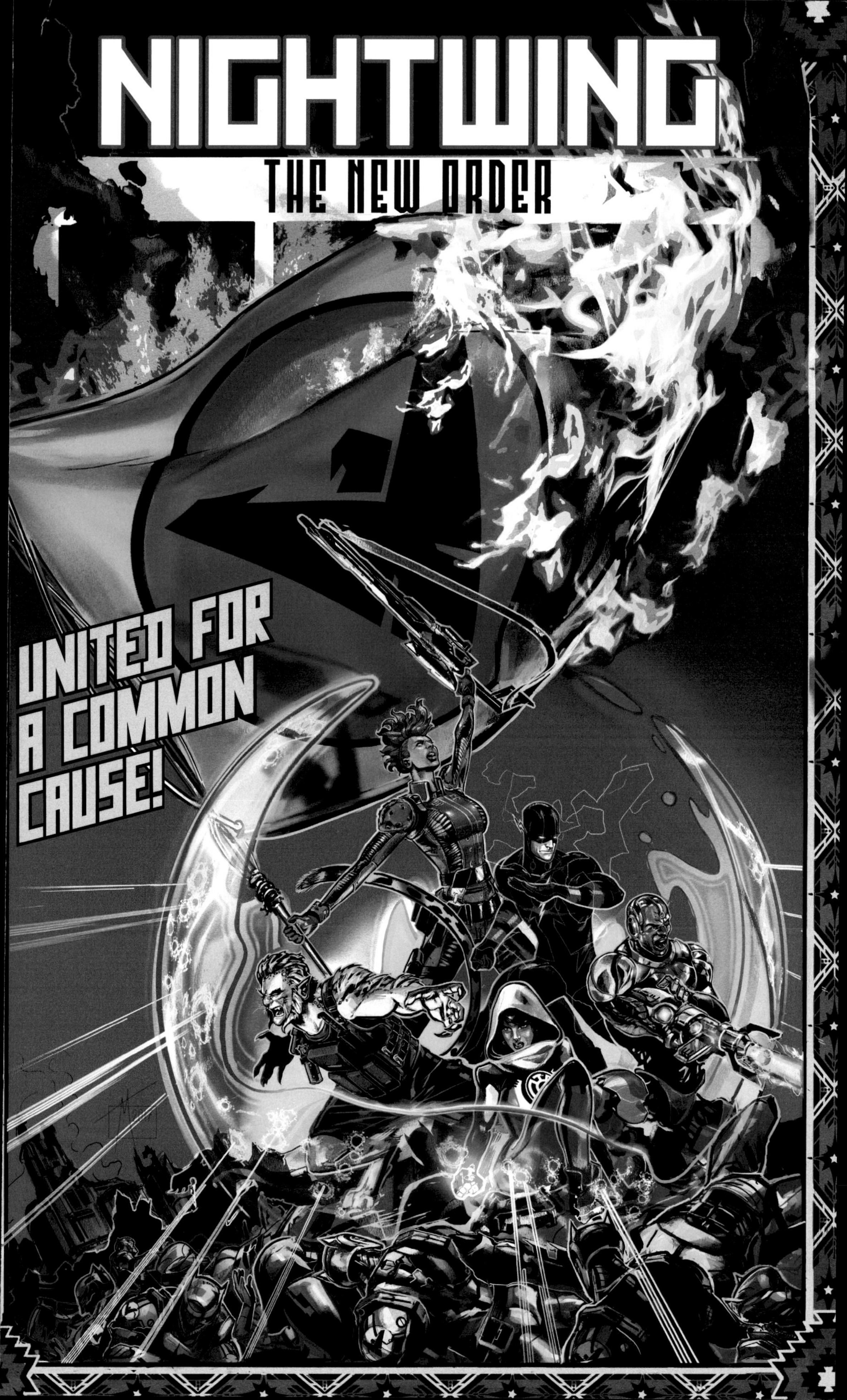
NIGHTWING
THE NEW ORDER
UNITED FOR A COMMON CAUSE!

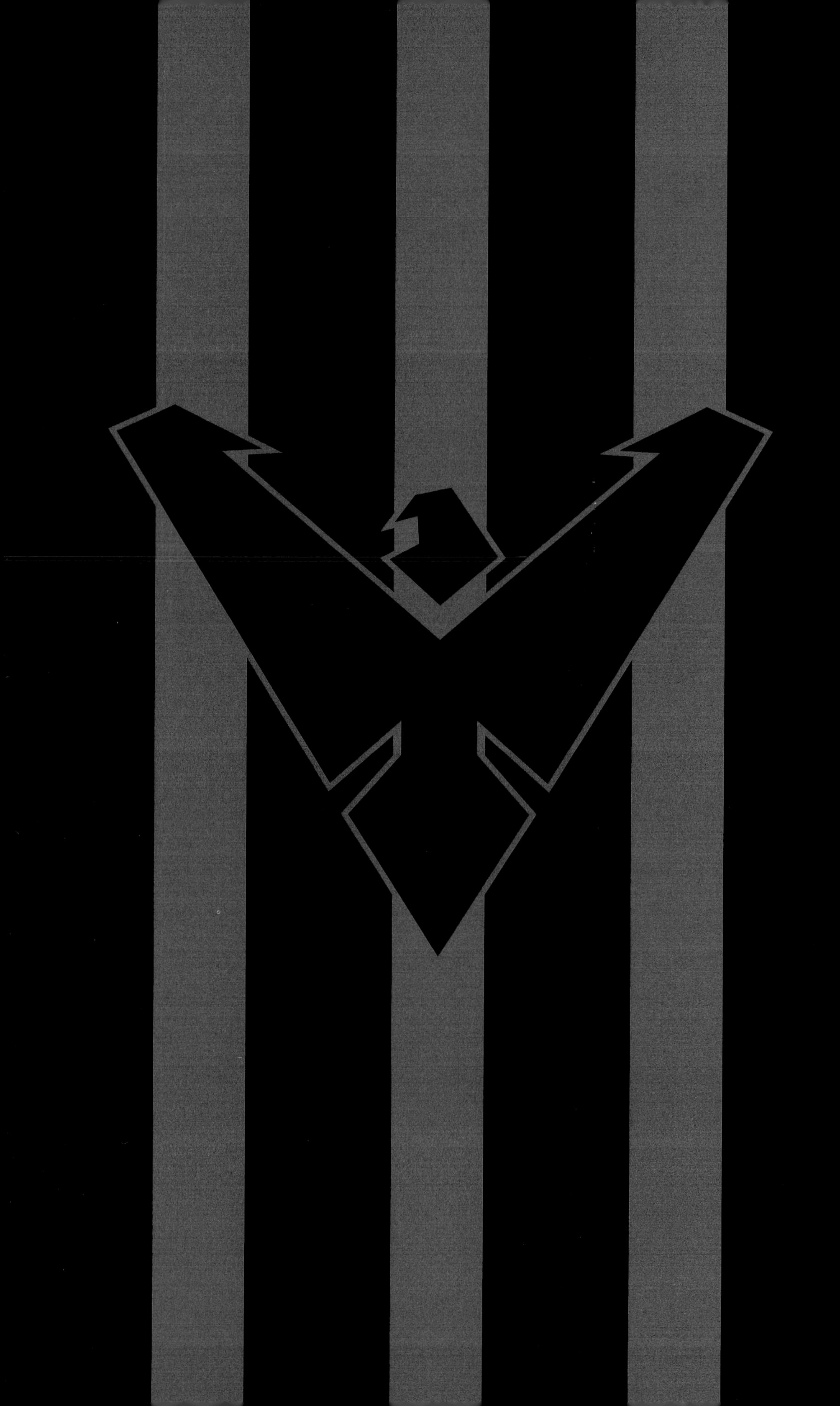

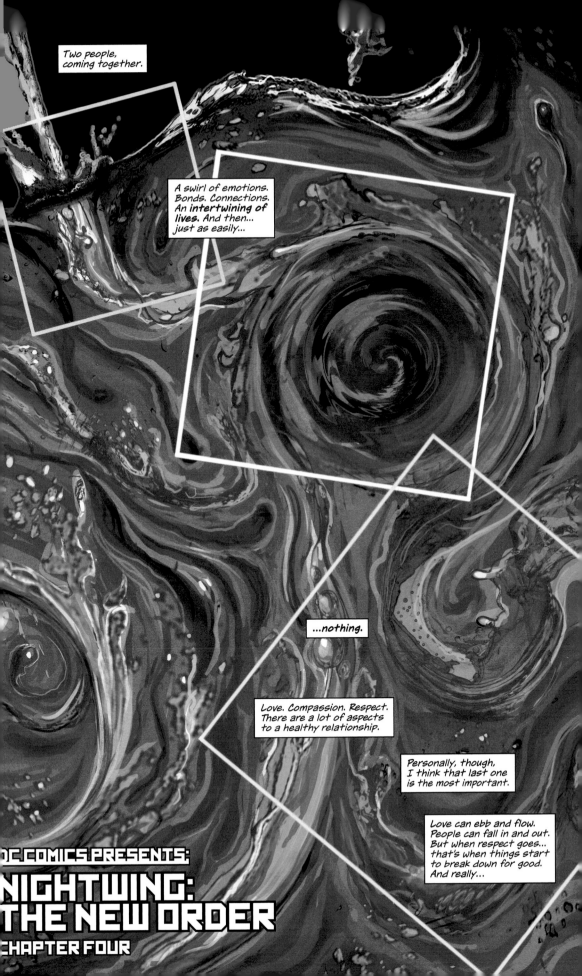

Two people,
coming together.

A swirl of emotions.
Bonds. Connections.
An *intertwining of
lives*. And then...
just as easily...

...nothing.

Love. Compassion. Respect.
There are a lot of aspects
to a healthy relationship.

Personally, though,
I think that last one
is the most important.

Love can ebb and flow.
People can fall in and out.
But when respect goes...
that's when things start
to break down for good.
And really...

DC COMICS PRESENTS:

NIGHTWING:
THE NEW ORDER

CHAPTER FOUR

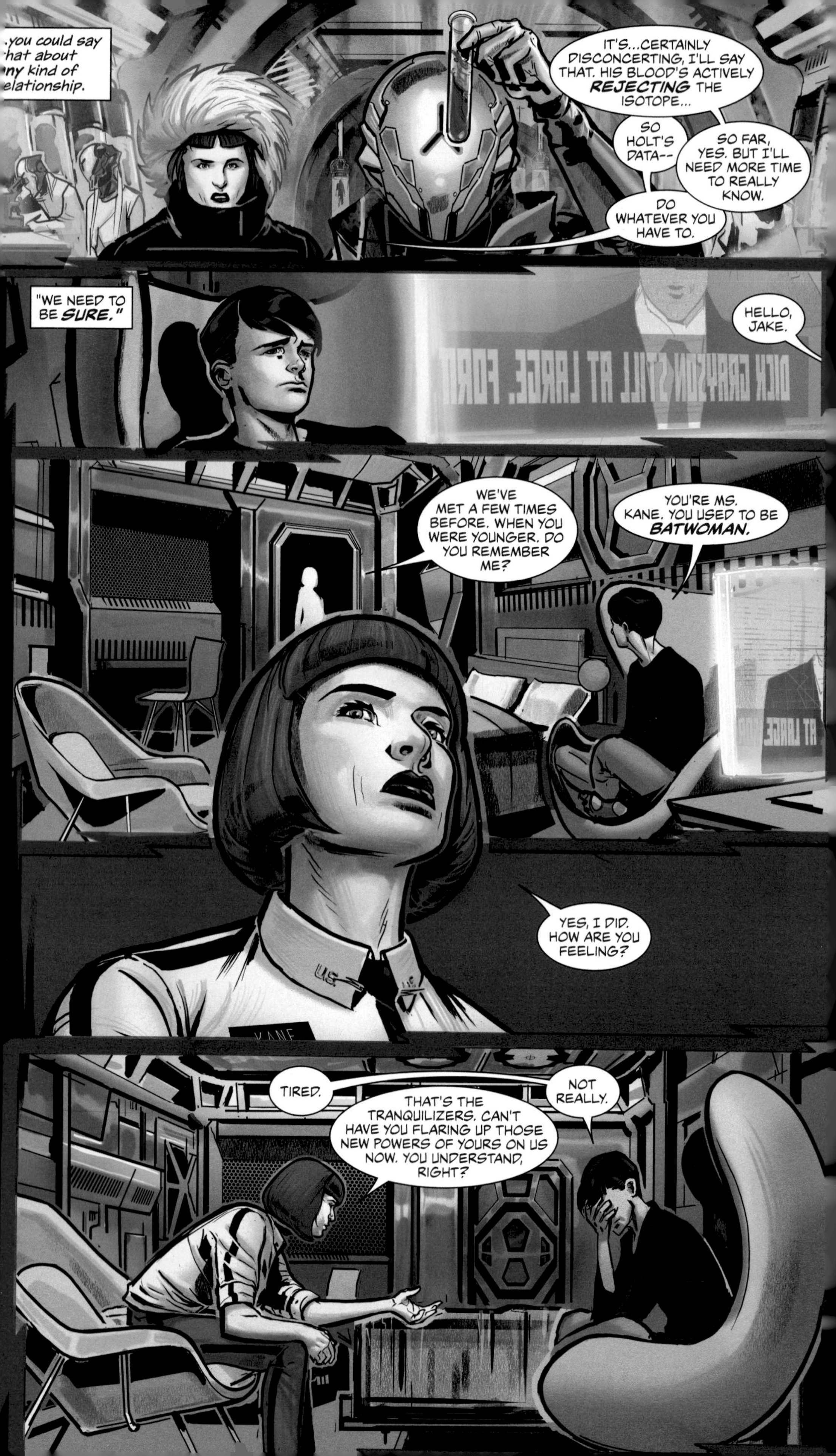
...you could say that about any kind of relationship.
IT'S...CERTAINLY DISCONCERTING, I'LL SAY THAT. HIS BLOOD'S ACTIVELY REJECTING THE ISOTOPE...
SO HOLT'S DATA--
SO FAR, YES. BUT I'LL NEED MORE TIME TO REALLY KNOW.
DO WHATEVER YOU HAVE TO.
"WE NEED TO BE SURE."
HELLO, JAKE.
DICK GRAYSON STILL AT LARGE. FORM
WE'VE MET A FEW TIMES BEFORE. WHEN YOU WERE YOUNGER. DO YOU REMEMBER ME?
YOU'RE MS. KANE. YOU USED TO BE BATWOMAN.
YES, I DID. HOW ARE YOU FEELING?
KANE
TIRED.
NOT REALLY.
THAT'S THE TRANQUILIZERS. CAN'T HAVE YOU FLARING UP THOSE NEW POWERS OF YOURS ON US NOW. YOU UNDERSTAND, RIGHT?

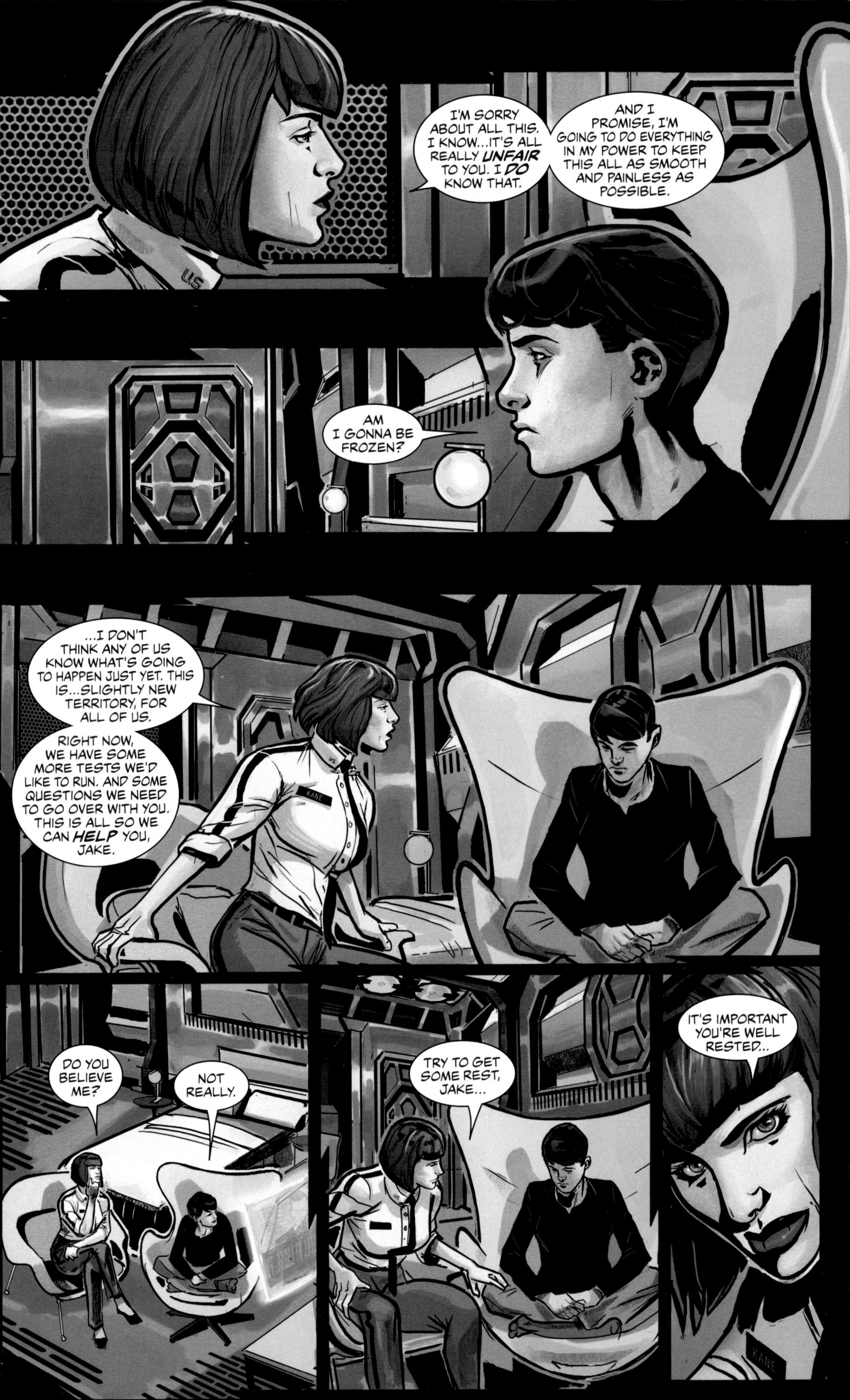
I'M SORRY ABOUT ALL THIS. I KNOW...IT'S ALL REALLY UNFAIR TO YOU. I DO KNOW THAT.
AND I PROMISE, I'M GOING TO DO EVERYTHING IN MY POWER TO KEEP THIS ALL AS SMOOTH AND PAINLESS AS POSSIBLE.
US
AM I GONNA BE FROZEN?
...I DON'T THINK ANY OF US KNOW WHAT'S GOING TO HAPPEN JUST YET. THIS IS...SLIGHTLY NEW TERRITORY, FOR ALL OF US.
RIGHT NOW, WE HAVE SOME MORE TESTS WE'D LIKE TO RUN. AND SOME QUESTIONS WE NEED TO GO OVER WITH YOU. THIS IS ALL SO WE CAN HELP YOU, JAKE.
KANE
DO YOU BELIEVE ME?
NOT REALLY.
TRY TO GET SOME REST, JAKE...
IT'S IMPORTANT YOU'RE WELL RESTED...
KANE

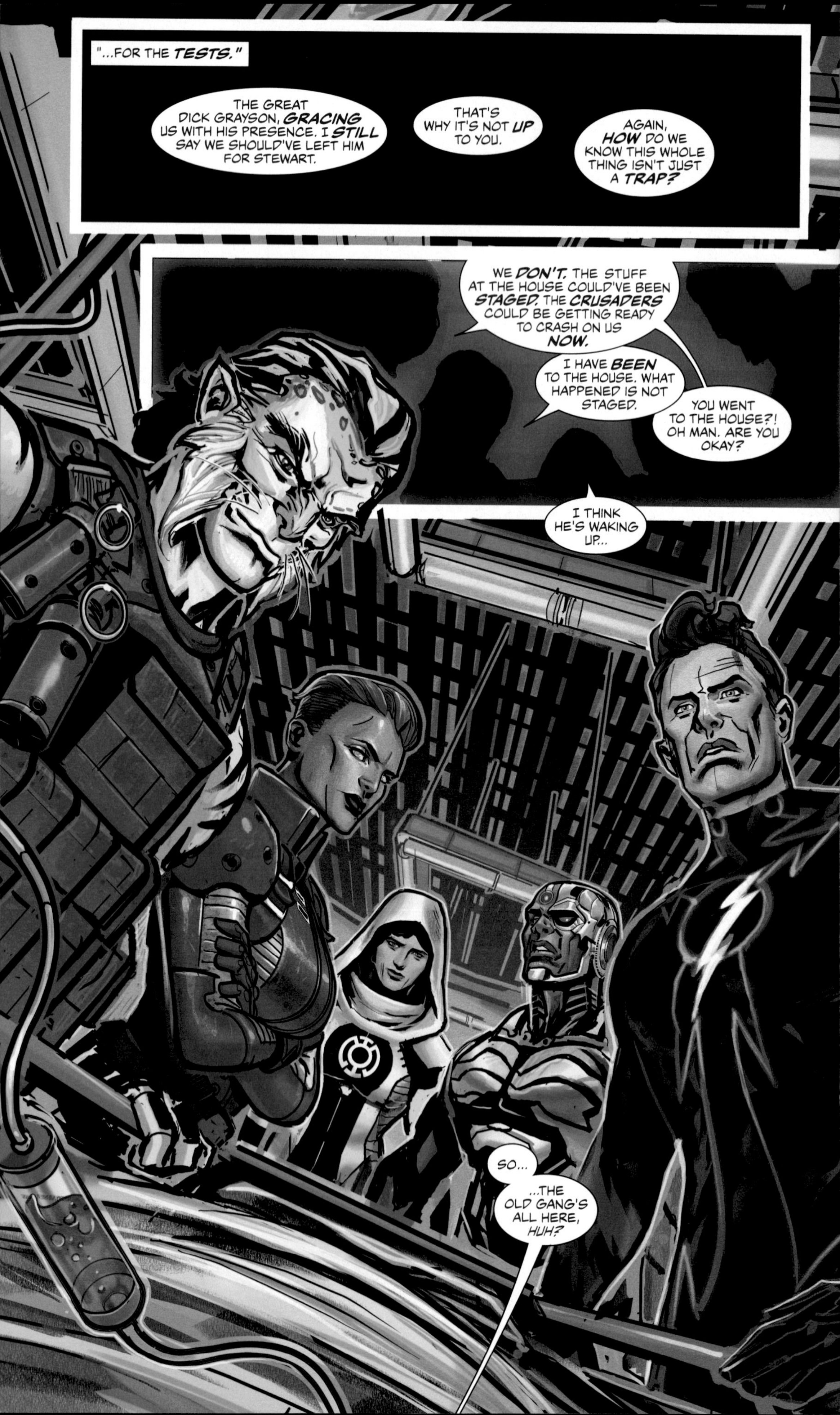
"...FOR THE TESTS."
THE GREAT DICK GRAYSON, GRACING US WITH HIS PRESENCE. I STILL SAY WE SHOULD'VE LEFT HIM FOR STEWART.
THAT'S WHY IT'S NOT UP TO YOU.
AGAIN, HOW DO WE KNOW THIS WHOLE THING ISN'T JUST A TRAP?
WE DON'T. THE STUFF AT THE HOUSE COULD'VE BEEN STAGED. THE CRUSADERS COULD BE GETTING READY TO CRASH ON US NOW.
I HAVE BEEN TO THE HOUSE. WHAT HAPPENED IS NOT STAGED.
YOU WENT TO THE HOUSE?! OH MAN. ARE YOU OKAY?
I THINK HE'S WAKING UP...
SO...
...THE OLD GANG'S ALL HERE, HUH?

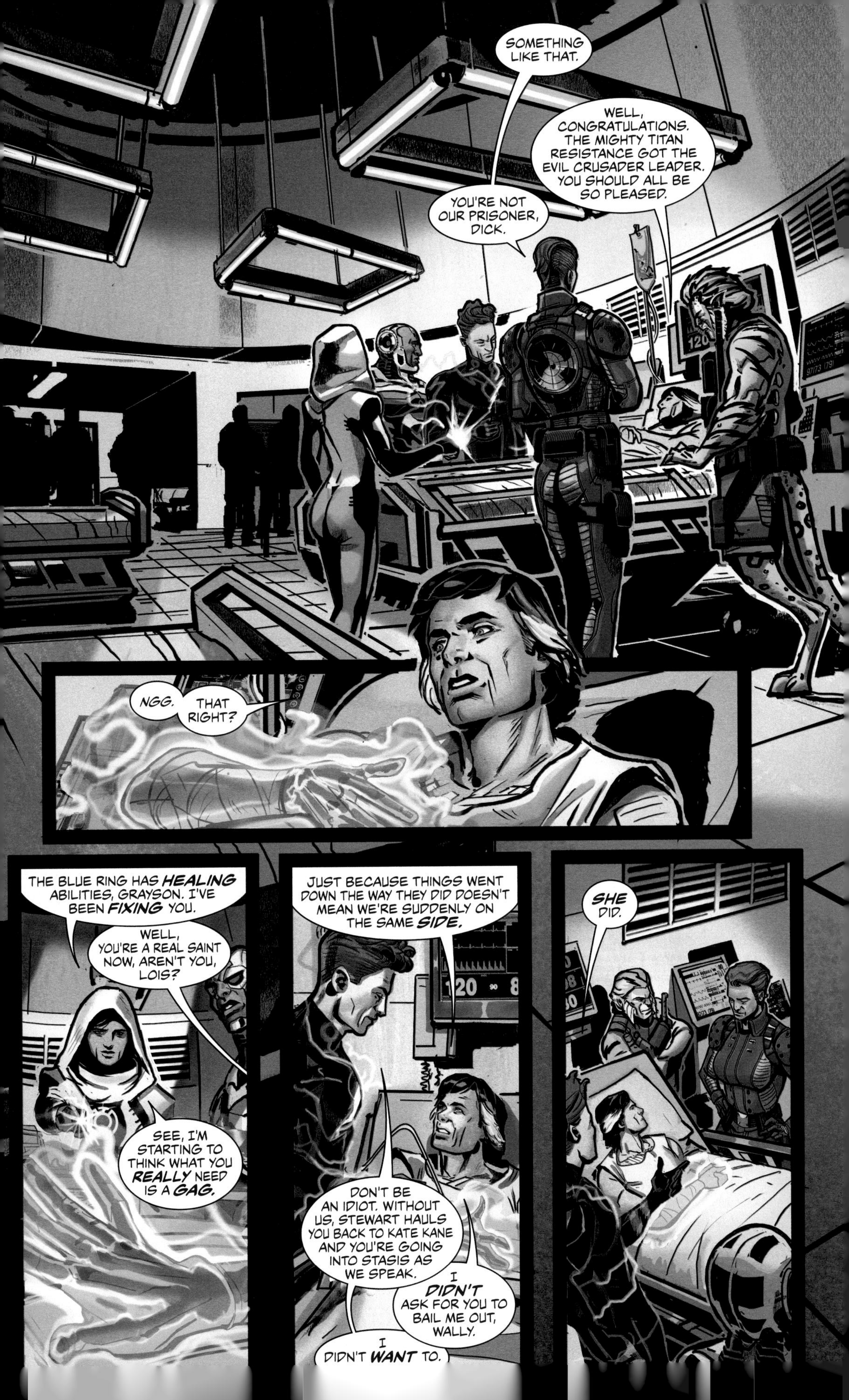

SOMETHING LIKE THAT.
WELL, CONGRATULATIONS. THE MIGHTY TITAN RESISTANCE GOT THE EVIL CRUSADER LEADER. YOU SHOULD ALL BE SO PLEASED.
YOU'RE NOT OUR PRISONER, DICK.
NGG.
THAT RIGHT?
THE BLUE RING HAS HEALING ABILITIES, GRAYSON. I'VE BEEN FIXING YOU.
WELL, YOU'RE A REAL SAINT NOW, AREN'T YOU, LOIS?
SEE, I'M STARTING TO THINK WHAT YOU REALLY NEED IS A GAG.
JUST BECAUSE THINGS WENT DOWN THE WAY THEY DID DOESN'T MEAN WE'RE SUDDENLY ON THE SAME SIDE.
DON'T BE AN IDIOT. WITHOUT US, STEWART HAULS YOU BACK TO KATE KANE AND YOU'RE GOING INTO STASIS AS WE SPEAK.
I DIDN'T ASK FOR YOU TO BAIL ME OUT, WALLY.
I DIDN'T WANT TO.
SHE DID.

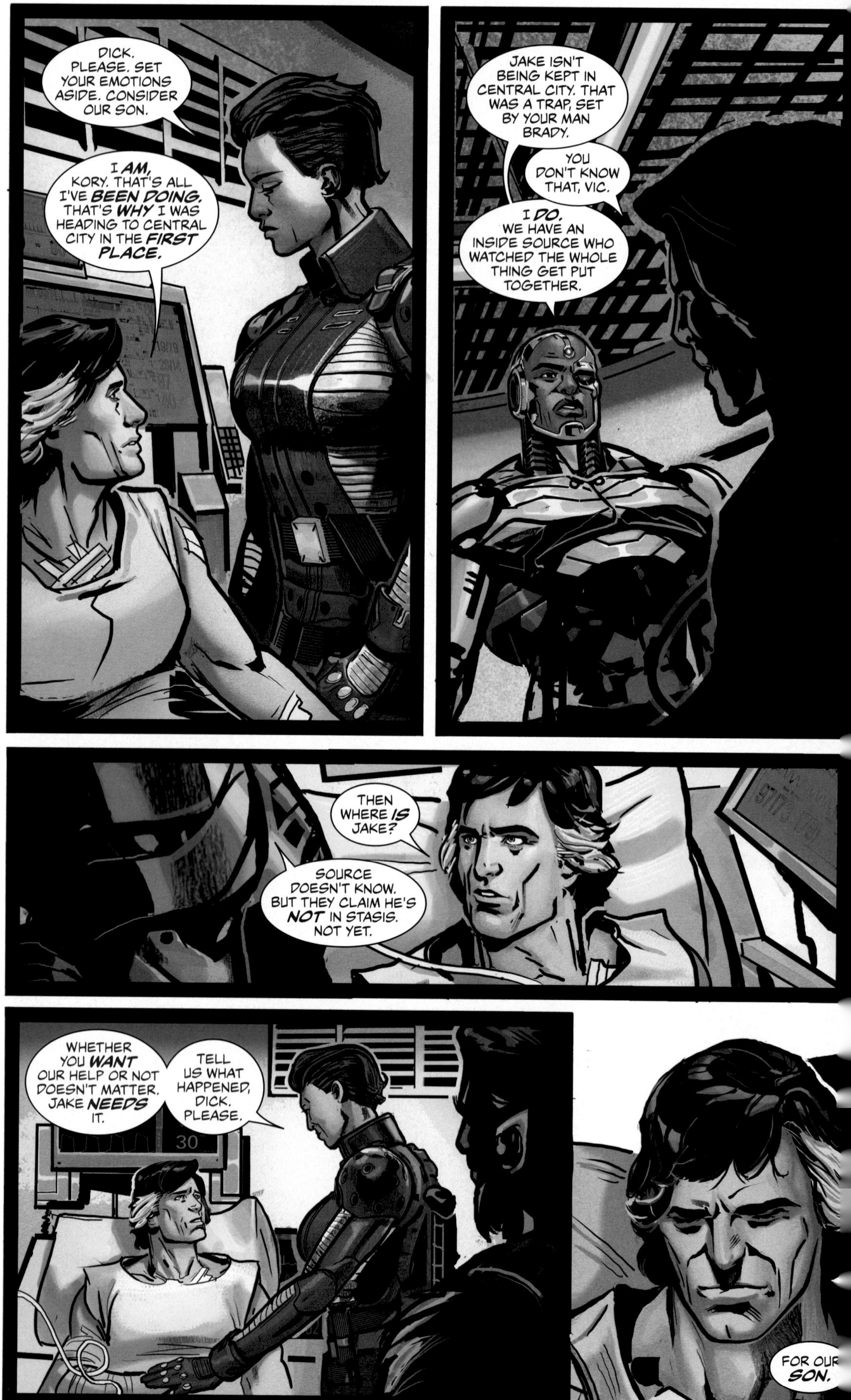
DICK. PLEASE. SET YOUR EMOTIONS ASIDE. CONSIDER OUR SON.
I AM, KORY. THAT'S ALL I'VE BEEN DOING. THAT'S WHY I WAS HEADING TO CENTRAL CITY IN THE FIRST PLACE.
JAKE ISN'T BEING KEPT IN CENTRAL CITY. THAT WAS A TRAP, SET BY YOUR MAN BRADY.
YOU DON'T KNOW THAT, VIC.
I DO. WE HAVE AN INSIDE SOURCE WHO WATCHED THE WHOLE THING GET PUT TOGETHER.
THEN WHERE IS JAKE?
SOURCE DOESN'T KNOW. BUT THEY CLAIM HE'S NOT IN STASIS. NOT YET.
WHETHER YOU WANT OUR HELP OR NOT DOESN'T MATTER. JAKE NEEDS IT.
TELL US WHAT HAPPENED, DICK. PLEASE.
FOR OUR SON.

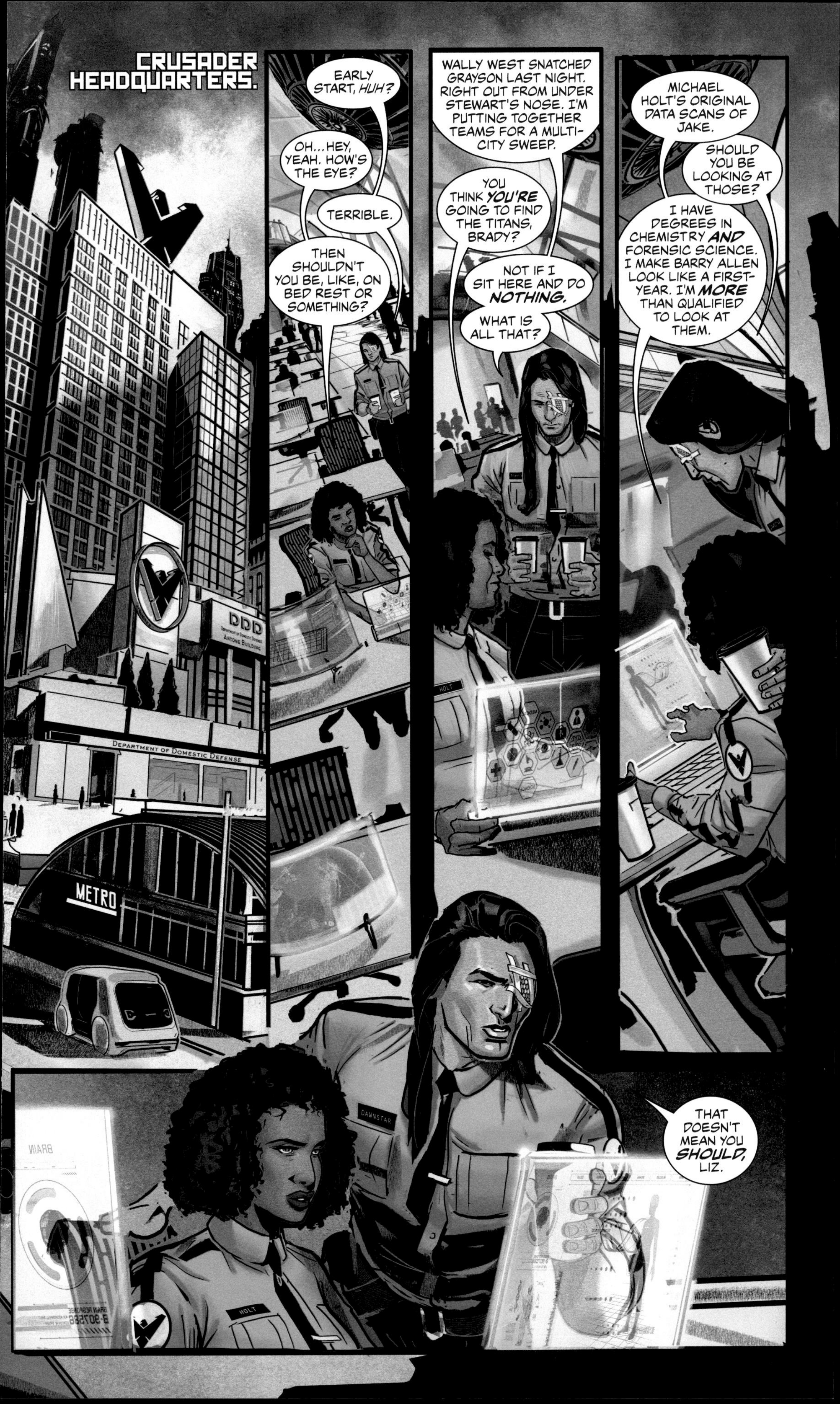
CRUSADER HEADQUARTERS.
DEPARTMENT OF DOMESTIC DEFENSE
METRO
EARLY START, HUH?
OH...HEY, YEAH. HOW'S THE EYE?
TERRIBLE.
THEN SHOULDN'T YOU BE, LIKE, ON BED REST OR SOMETHING?
WALLY WEST SNATCHED GRAYSON LAST NIGHT. RIGHT OUT FROM UNDER STEWART'S NOSE. I'M PUTTING TOGETHER TEAMS FOR A MULTI-CITY SWEEP.
YOU THINK YOU'RE GOING TO FIND THE TITANS, BRADY?
NOT IF I SIT HERE AND DO NOTHING.
WHAT IS ALL THAT?
MICHAEL HOLT'S ORIGINAL DATA SCANS OF JAKE.
SHOULD YOU BE LOOKING AT THOSE?
I HAVE DEGREES IN CHEMISTRY AND FORENSIC SCIENCE. I MAKE BARRY ALLEN LOOK LIKE A FIRST-YEAR. I'M MORE THAN QUALIFIED TO LOOK AT THEM.
DAWNSTAR
HOLT
THAT DOESN'T MEAN YOU SHOULD, LIZ.

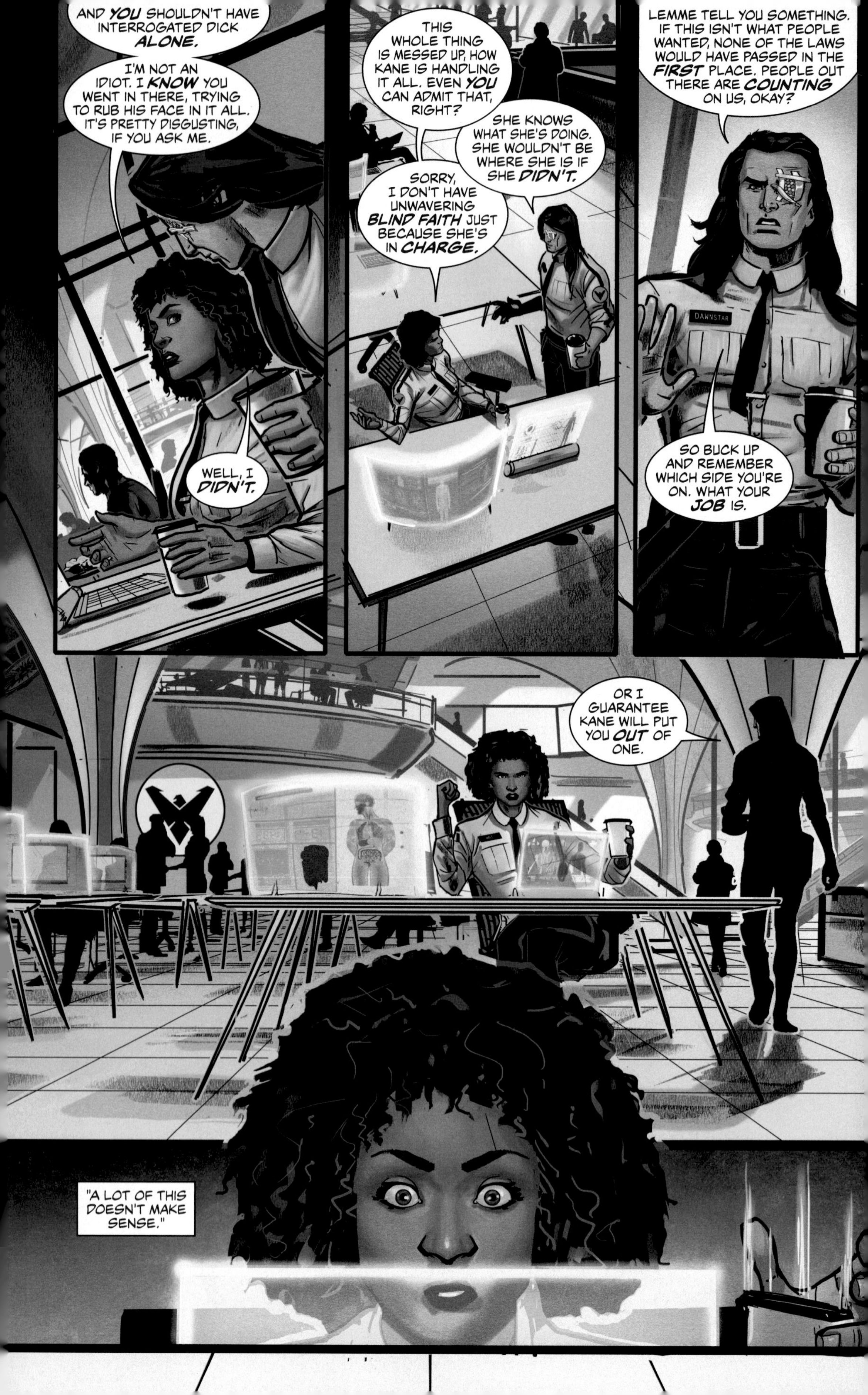
AND YOU SHOULDN'T HAVE INTERROGATED DICK ALONE.
I'M NOT AN IDIOT. I KNOW YOU WENT IN THERE, TRYING TO RUB HIS FACE IN IT ALL. IT'S PRETTY DISGUSTING, IF YOU ASK ME.
WELL, I DIDN'T.
THIS WHOLE THING IS MESSED UP, HOW KANE IS HANDLING IT ALL. EVEN YOU CAN ADMIT THAT, RIGHT?
SHE KNOWS WHAT SHE'S DOING. SHE WOULDN'T BE WHERE SHE IS IF SHE DIDN'T.
SORRY, I DON'T HAVE UNWAVERING BLIND FAITH JUST BECAUSE SHE'S IN CHARGE.
LEMME TELL YOU SOMETHING. IF THIS ISN'T WHAT PEOPLE WANTED, NONE OF THE LAWS WOULD HAVE PASSED IN THE FIRST PLACE. PEOPLE OUT THERE ARE COUNTING ON US, OKAY?
DAWNSTAR
SO BUCK UP AND REMEMBER WHICH SIDE YOU'RE ON. WHAT YOUR JOB IS.
OR I GUARANTEE KANE WILL PUT YOU OUT OF ONE.
"A LOT OF THIS DOESN'T MAKE SENSE."

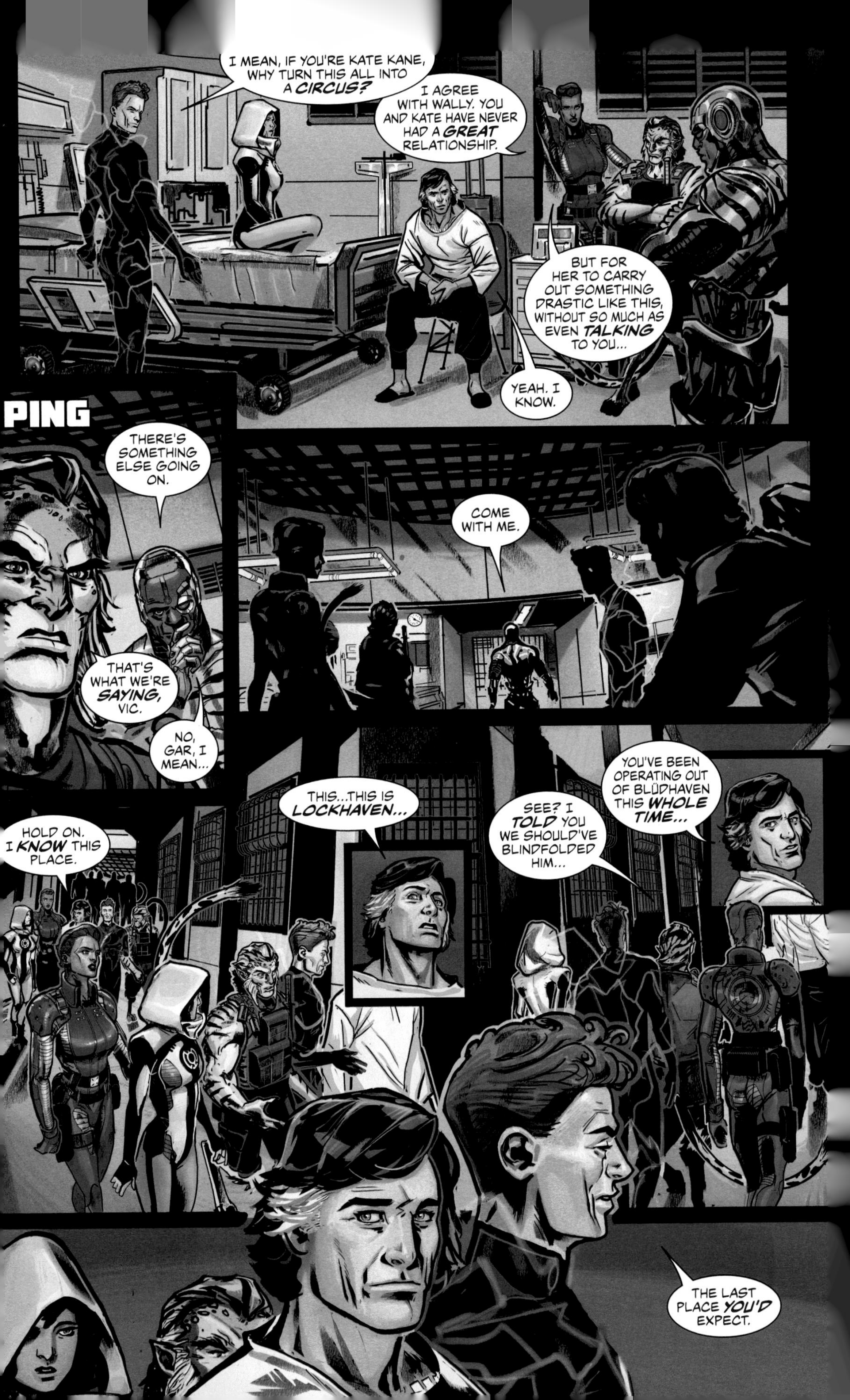

I MEAN, IF YOU'RE KATE KANE, WHY TURN THIS ALL INTO A *CIRCUS?*
I AGREE WITH WALLY. YOU AND KATE HAVE NEVER HAD A *GREAT* RELATIONSHIP.
BUT FOR HER TO CARRY OUT SOMETHING DRASTIC LIKE THIS, WITHOUT SO MUCH AS EVEN *TALKING* TO YOU...
YEAH. I KNOW.
PING
THERE'S SOMETHING ELSE GOING ON.
THAT'S WHAT WE'RE *SAYING,* VIC.
NO, GAR, I MEAN...
COME WITH ME.
HOLD ON. I *KNOW* THIS PLACE.
THIS...THIS IS *LOCKHAVEN...*
SEE? I *TOLD* YOU WE SHOULD'VE BLINDFOLDED HIM...
YOU'VE BEEN OPERATING OUT OF BLÜDHAVEN THIS *WHOLE TIME...*
THE LAST PLACE *YOU'D* EXPECT.

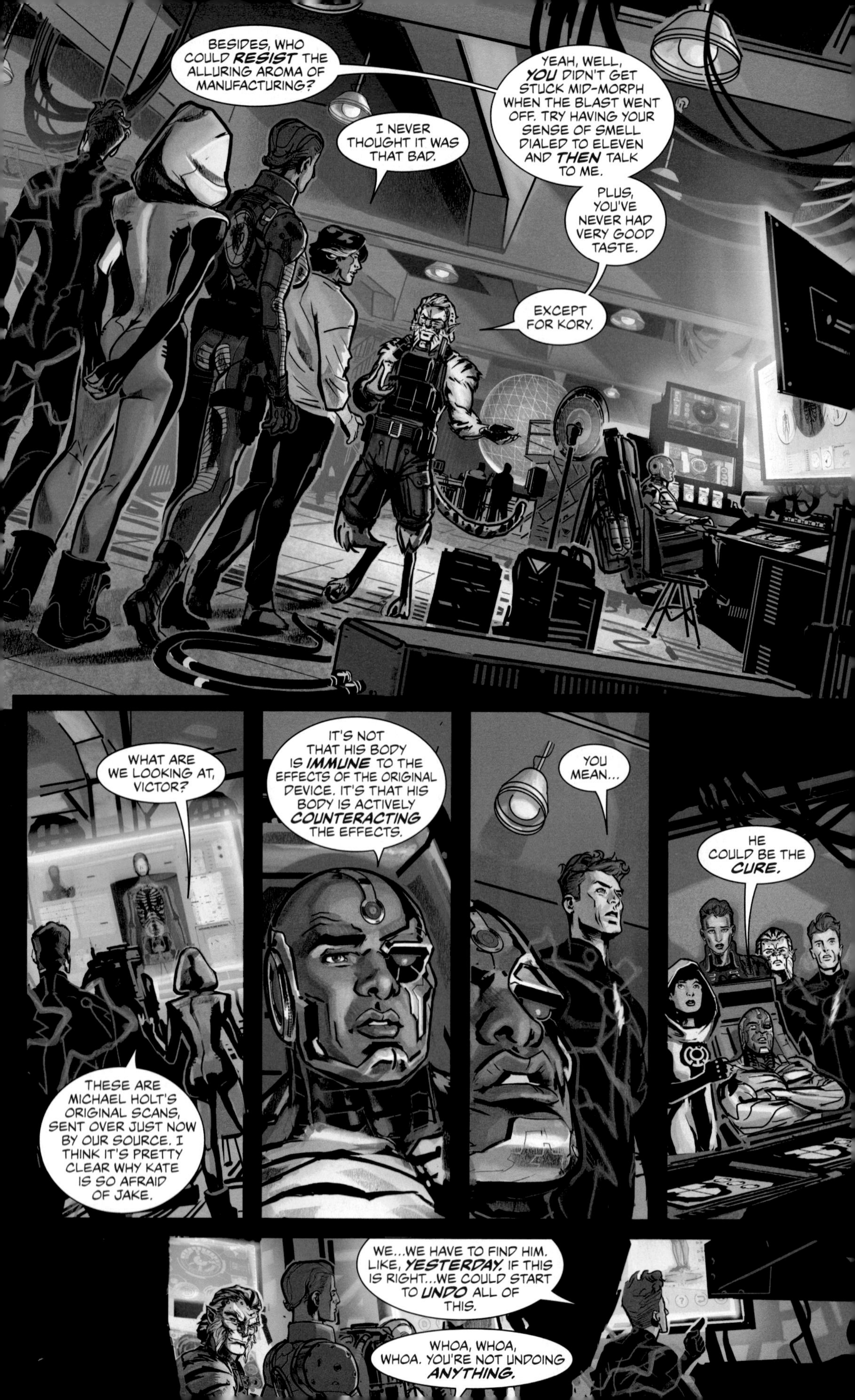
BESIDES, WHO COULD RESIST THE ALLURING AROMA OF MANUFACTURING?
I NEVER THOUGHT IT WAS THAT BAD.
YEAH, WELL, YOU DIDN'T GET STUCK MID-MORPH WHEN THE BLAST WENT OFF. TRY HAVING YOUR SENSE OF SMELL DIALED TO ELEVEN AND THEN TALK TO ME.
PLUS, YOU'VE NEVER HAD VERY GOOD TASTE.
EXCEPT FOR KORY.
WHAT ARE WE LOOKING AT, VICTOR?
THESE ARE MICHAEL HOLT'S ORIGINAL SCANS, SENT OVER JUST NOW BY OUR SOURCE. I THINK IT'S PRETTY CLEAR WHY KATE IS SO AFRAID OF JAKE.
IT'S NOT THAT HIS BODY IS IMMUNE TO THE EFFECTS OF THE ORIGINAL DEVICE. IT'S THAT HIS BODY IS ACTIVELY COUNTERACTING THE EFFECTS.
YOU MEAN...
HE COULD BE THE CURE.
WE...WE HAVE TO FIND HIM. LIKE, YESTERDAY. IF THIS IS RIGHT...WE COULD START TO UNDO ALL OF THIS.
WHOA, WHOA, WHOA. YOU'RE NOT UNDOING ANYTHING.

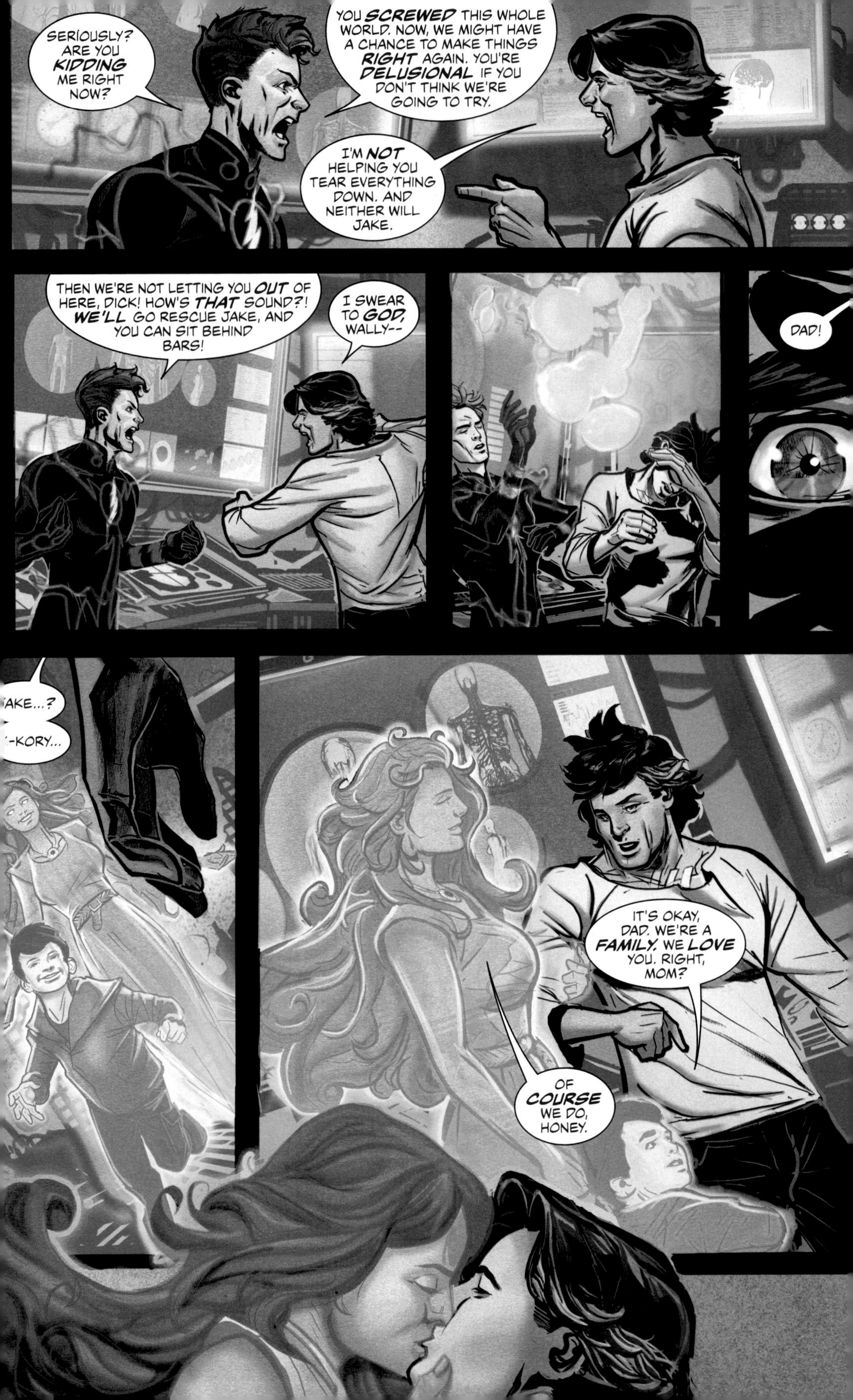
SERIOUSLY? ARE YOU KIDDING ME RIGHT NOW?
YOU SCREWED THIS WHOLE WORLD. NOW, WE MIGHT HAVE A CHANCE TO MAKE THINGS RIGHT AGAIN. YOU'RE DELUSIONAL IF YOU DON'T THINK WE'RE GOING TO TRY.
I'M NOT HELPING YOU TEAR EVERYTHING DOWN. AND NEITHER WILL JAKE.
THEN WE'RE NOT LETTING YOU OUT OF HERE, DICK! HOW'S THAT SOUND?! WE'LL GO RESCUE JAKE, AND YOU CAN SIT BEHIND BARS!
I SWEAR TO GOD, WALLY--
DAD!
IT'S OKAY, DAD. WE'RE A FAMILY. WE LOVE YOU. RIGHT, MOM?
OF COURSE WE DO, HONEY.

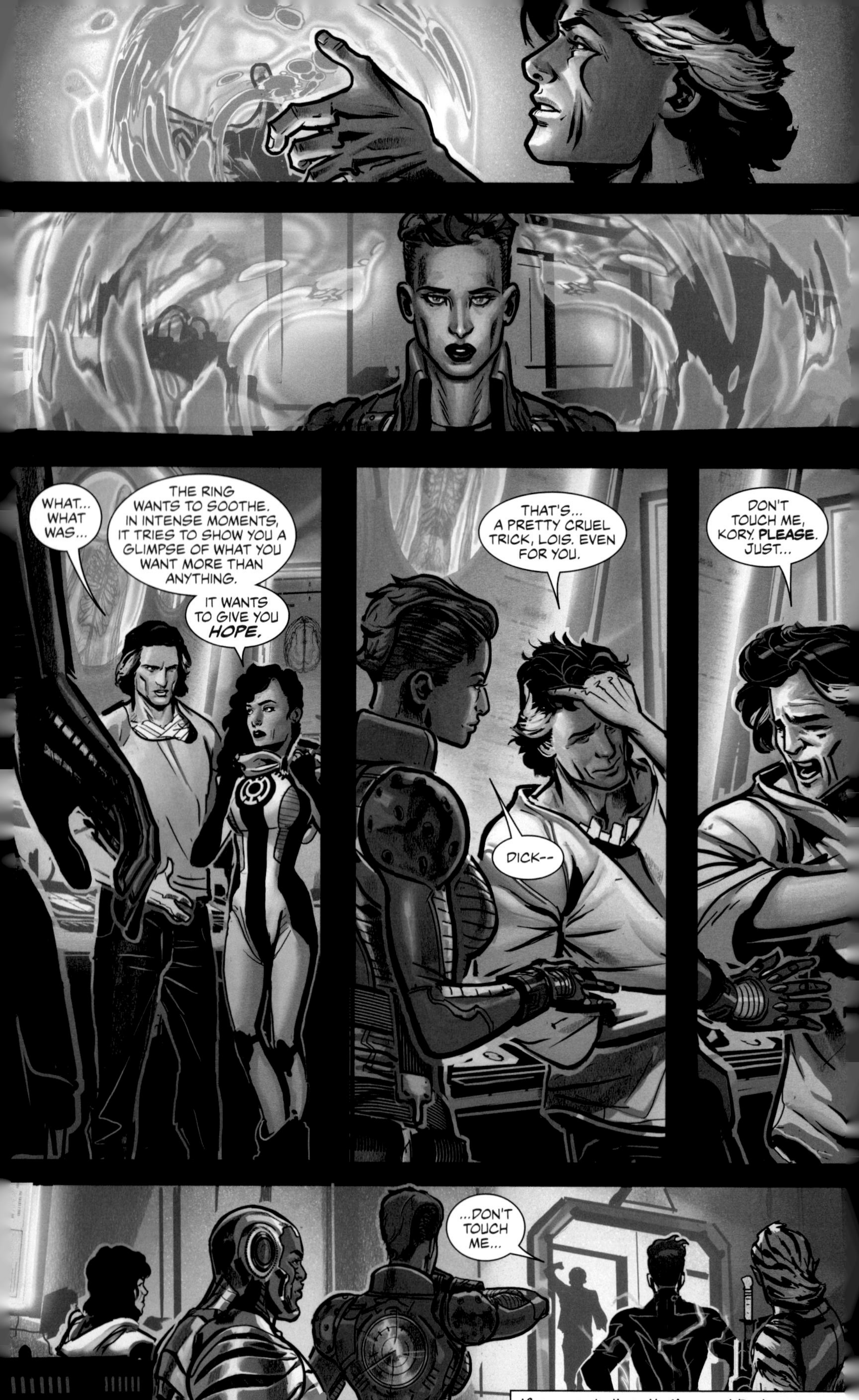
WHAT... WHAT WAS...
THE RING WANTS TO SOOTHE. IN INTENSE MOMENTS, IT TRIES TO SHOW YOU A GLIMPSE OF WHAT YOU WANT MORE THAN ANYTHING.
IT WANTS TO GIVE YOU ***HOPE.***
THAT'S... A PRETTY CRUEL TRICK, LOIS. EVEN FOR YOU.
DICK--
DON'T TOUCH ME, KORY. **PLEASE**. JUST...
...DON'T TOUCH ME...

If you can believe it, Mom and Dad were

She was born and raised
on the planet Tamaran,
where she was supposed
to grow up to be queen.

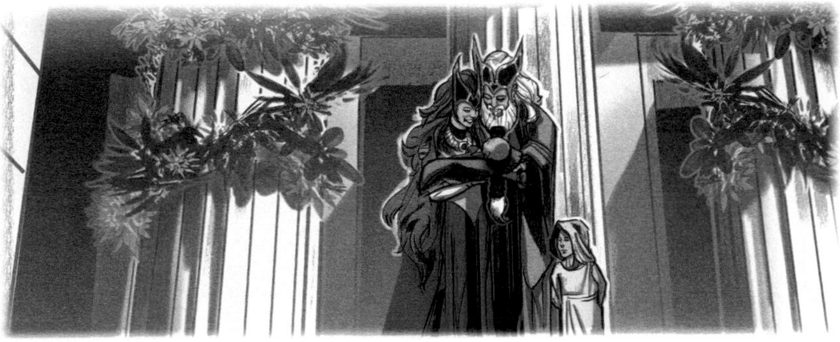

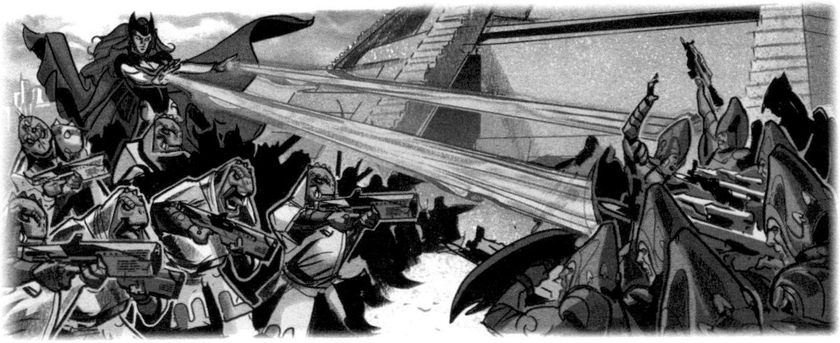

Instead, her older sister
became really jealous.
Betrayed the family, sold
secrets to the bad guys,
and helped them conquer
the planet.

When it was done, Mom
was sold into slavery--
purchased by an empire
called "The Citadel."

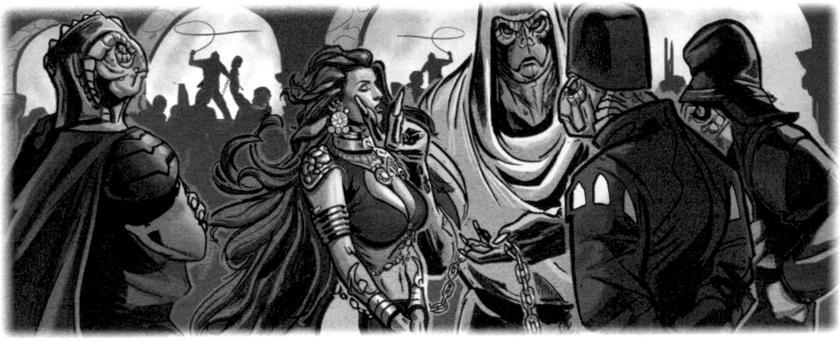

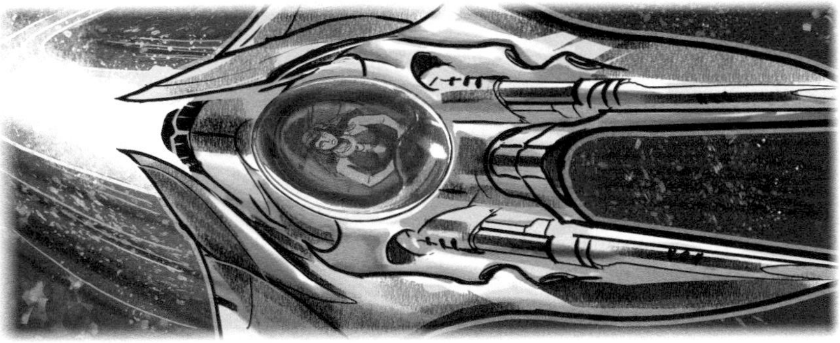

It took years, but she
eventually escaped.
Hijacked the first ship
she could, and made her
way to the first **planet**
she could.

he kids who would become
the Teen Titans were
actually some of the first
people she met.

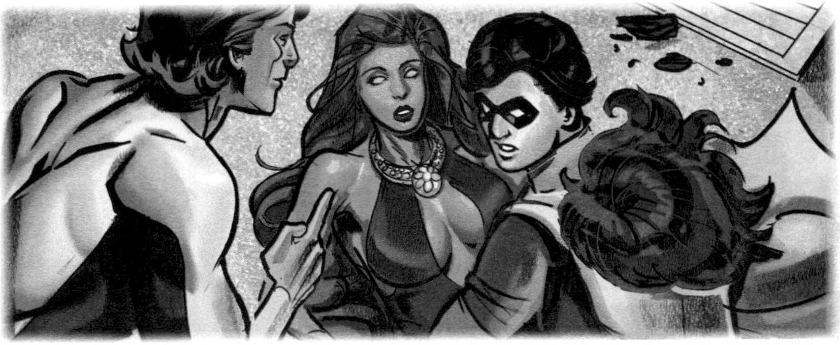

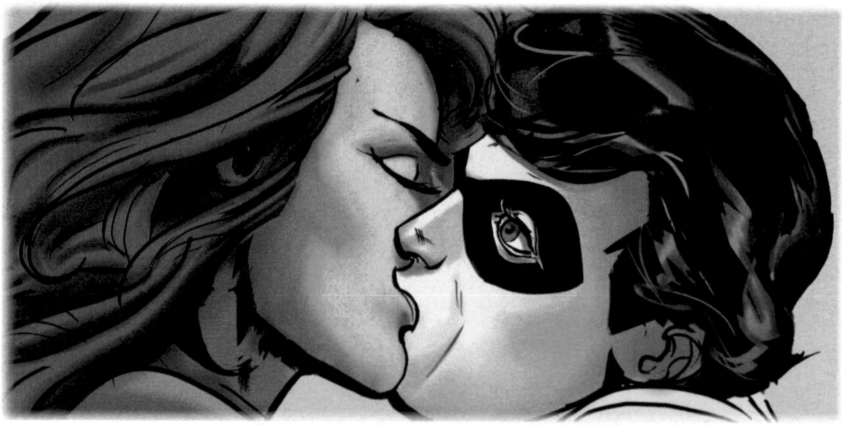

Like I said--pretty much literally love at first sight.

But, you know, things and people and relationships all change.

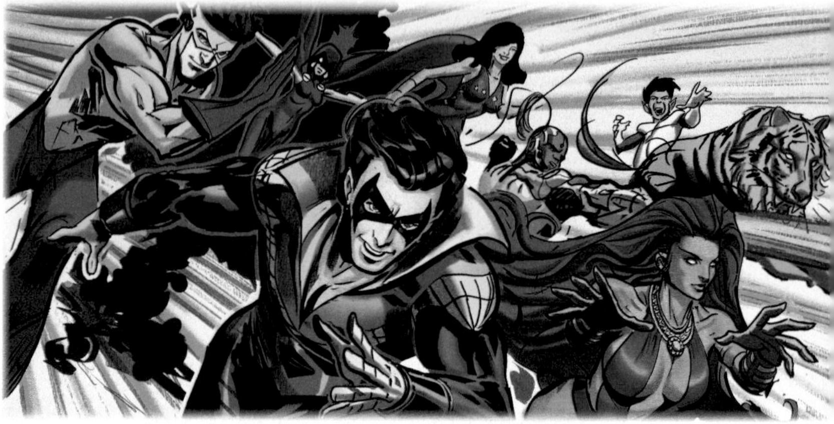

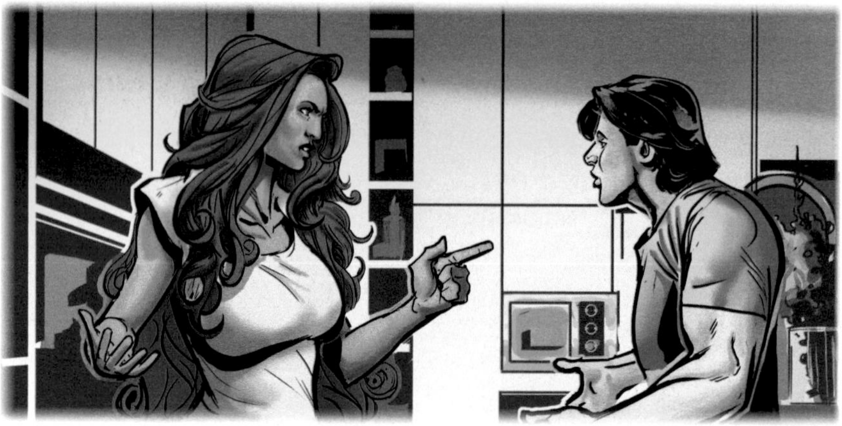

They had their share o ups and downs, like any couple. Much less a ***superhero couple.***

But, time and time again, they worked through things. Because they ***loved*** *each other. And that was enough.*

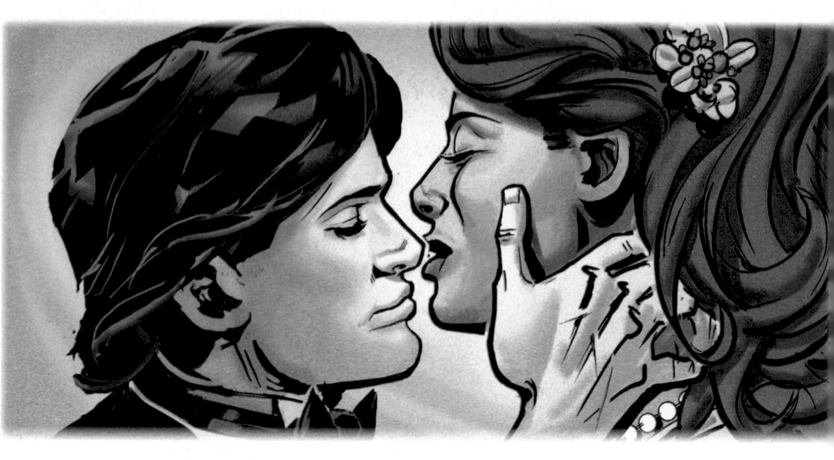

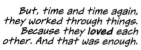

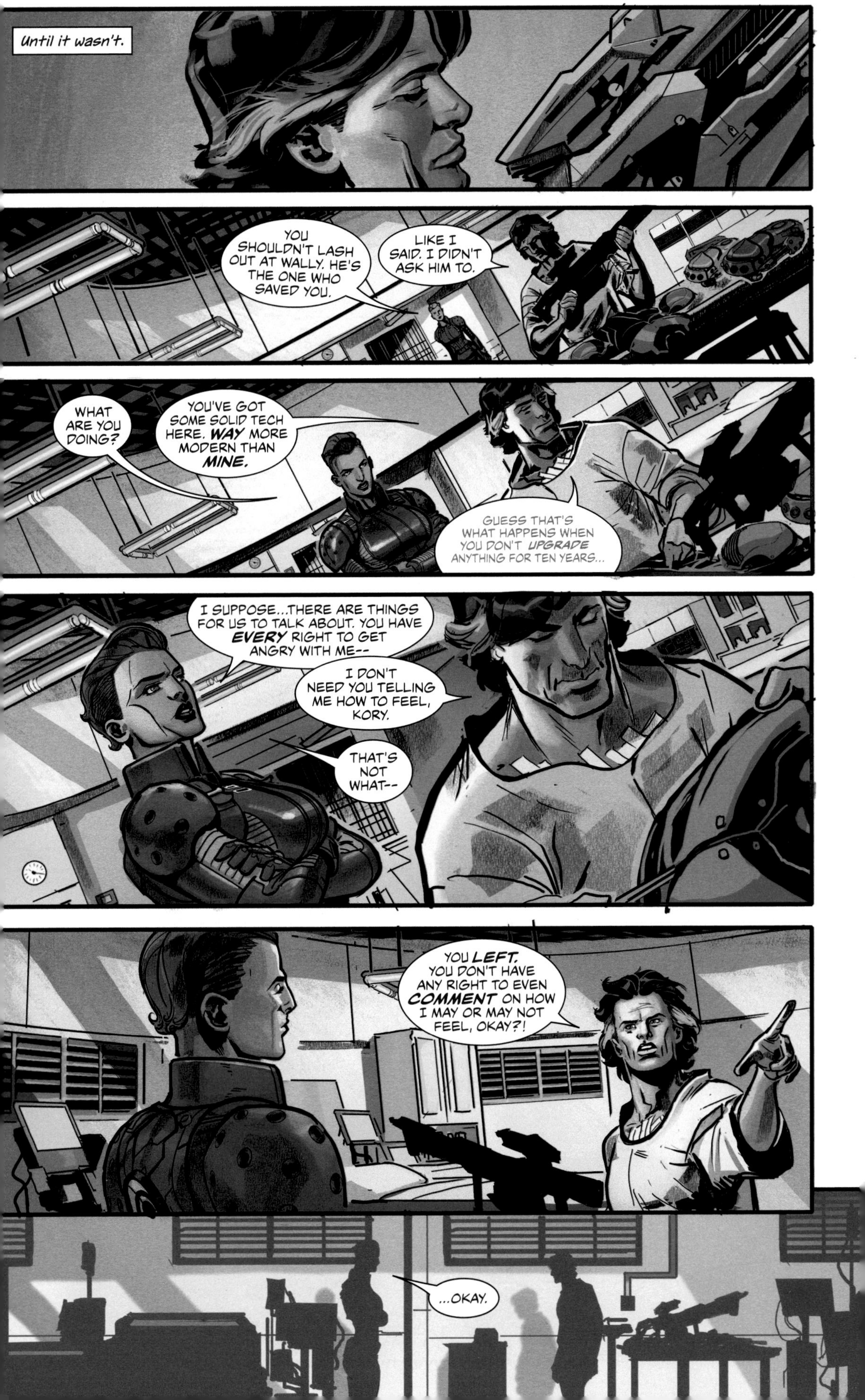
Until it wasn't.
YOU SHOULDN'T LASH OUT AT WALLY. HE'S THE ONE WHO SAVED YOU.
LIKE I SAID. I DIDN'T ASK HIM TO.
WHAT ARE YOU DOING?
YOU'VE GOT SOME SOLID TECH HERE. WAY MORE MODERN THAN MINE.
GUESS THAT'S WHAT HAPPENS WHEN YOU DON'T UPGRADE ANYTHING FOR TEN YEARS...
I SUPPOSE...THERE ARE THINGS FOR US TO TALK ABOUT. YOU HAVE EVERY RIGHT TO GET ANGRY WITH ME--
I DON'T NEED YOU TELLING ME HOW TO FEEL, KORY.
THAT'S NOT WHAT--
YOU LEFT. YOU DON'T HAVE ANY RIGHT TO EVEN COMMENT ON HOW I MAY OR MAY NOT FEEL, OKAY?!
...OKAY.

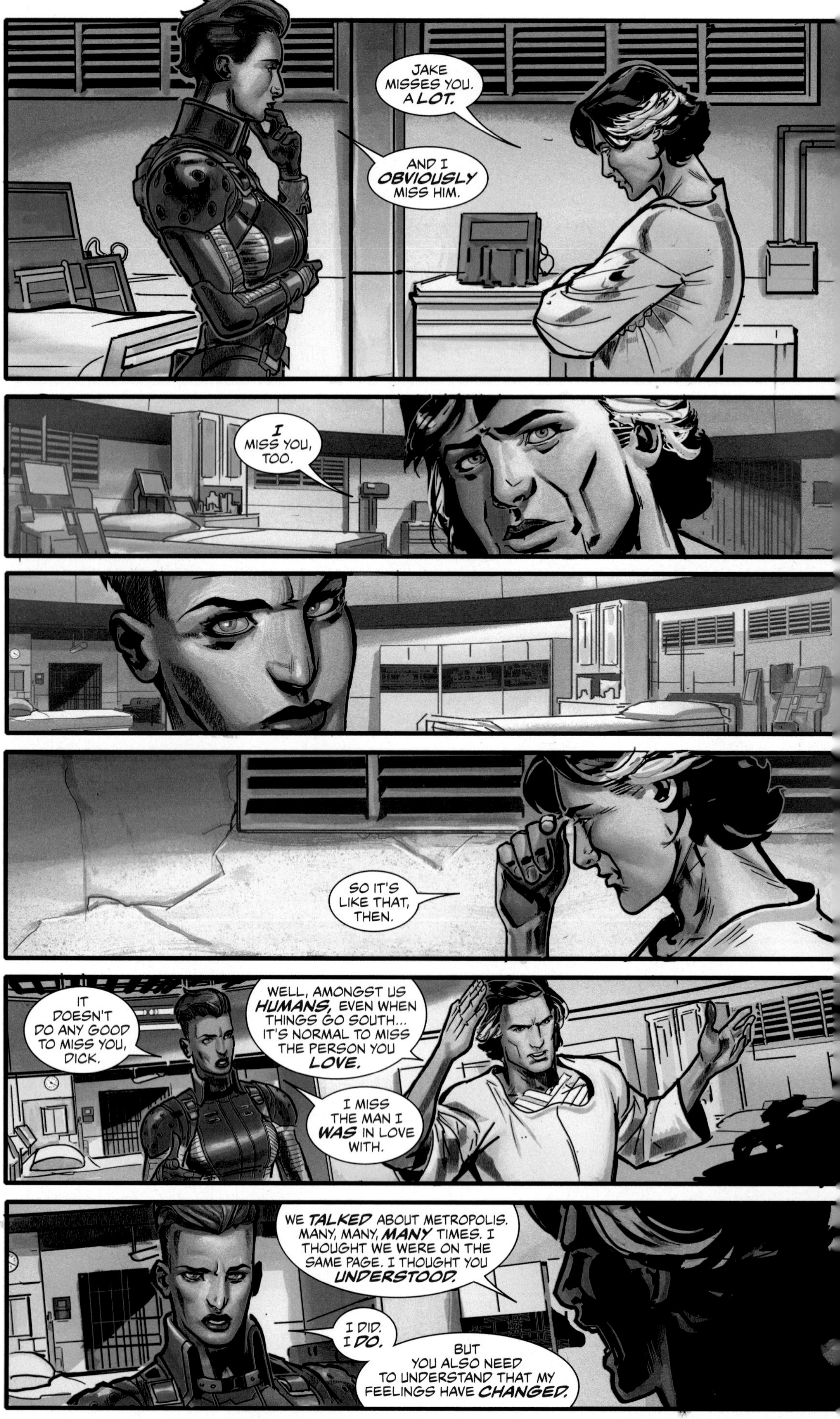
JAKE MISSES YOU. A LOT.
AND I OBVIOUSLY MISS HIM.
I MISS YOU, TOO.
SO IT'S LIKE THAT, THEN.
IT DOESN'T DO ANY GOOD TO MISS YOU, DICK.
WELL, AMONGST US HUMANS, EVEN WHEN THINGS GO SOUTH... IT'S NORMAL TO MISS THE PERSON YOU LOVE.
I MISS THE MAN I WAS IN LOVE WITH.
WE TALKED ABOUT METROPOLIS. MANY, MANY, MANY TIMES. I THOUGHT WE WERE ON THE SAME PAGE. I THOUGHT YOU UNDERSTOOD.
I DID. I DO.
BUT YOU ALSO NEED TO UNDERSTAND THAT MY FEELINGS HAVE CHANGED.

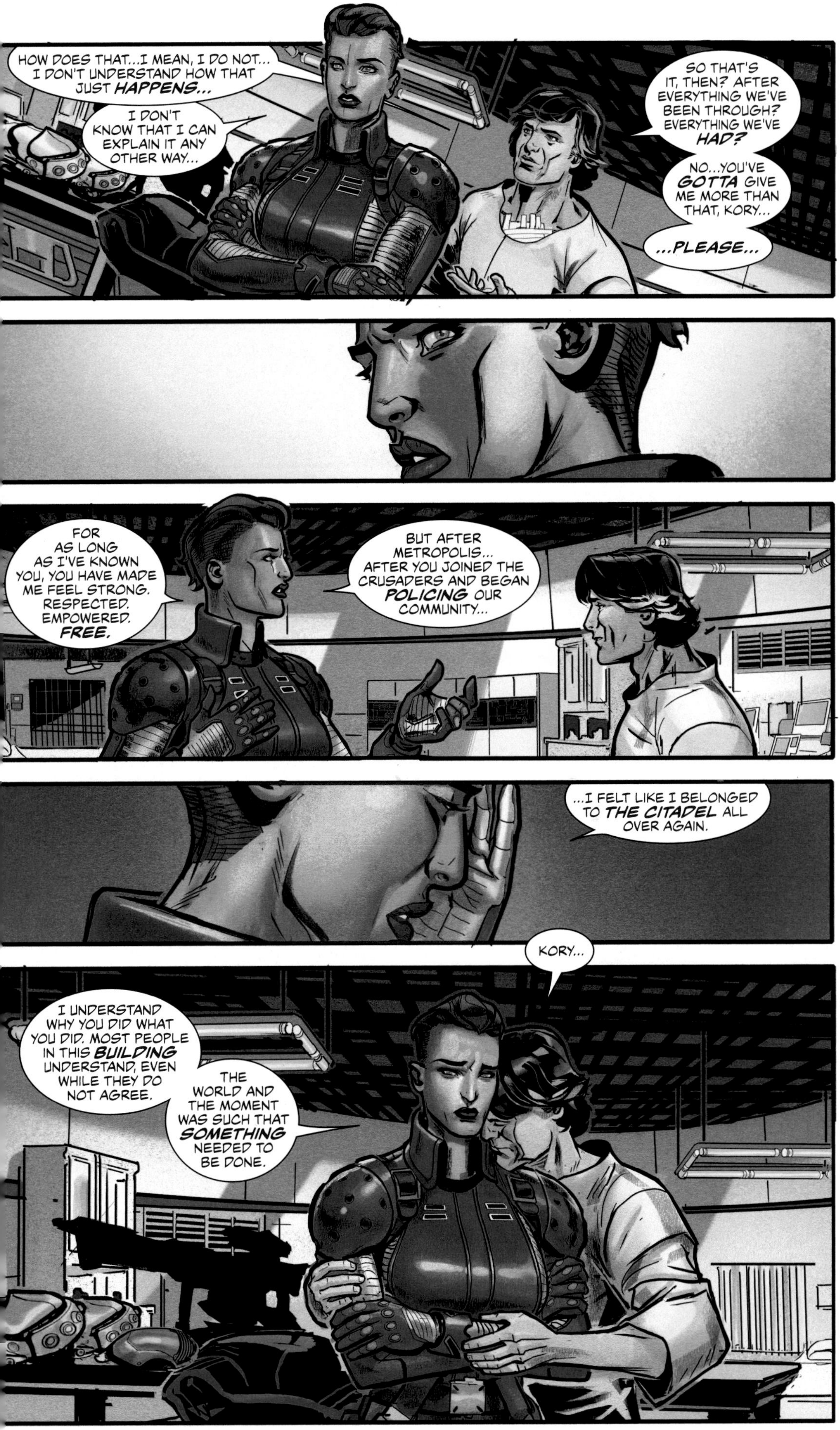

HOW DOES THAT...I MEAN, I DO NOT... I DON'T UNDERSTAND HOW THAT JUST HAPPENS...
I DON'T KNOW THAT I CAN EXPLAIN IT ANY OTHER WAY...
SO THAT'S IT, THEN? AFTER EVERYTHING WE'VE BEEN THROUGH? EVERYTHING WE'VE HAD?
NO...YOU'VE GOTTA GIVE ME MORE THAN THAT, KORY...
...PLEASE...
FOR AS LONG AS I'VE KNOWN YOU, YOU HAVE MADE ME FEEL STRONG. RESPECTED. EMPOWERED. FREE.
BUT AFTER METROPOLIS... AFTER YOU JOINED THE CRUSADERS AND BEGAN POLICING OUR COMMUNITY...
...I FELT LIKE I BELONGED TO THE CITADEL ALL OVER AGAIN.
KORY...
I UNDERSTAND WHY YOU DID WHAT YOU DID. MOST PEOPLE IN THIS BUILDING UNDERSTAND, EVEN WHILE THEY DO NOT AGREE.
THE WORLD AND THE MOMENT WAS SUCH THAT SOMETHING NEEDED TO BE DONE.

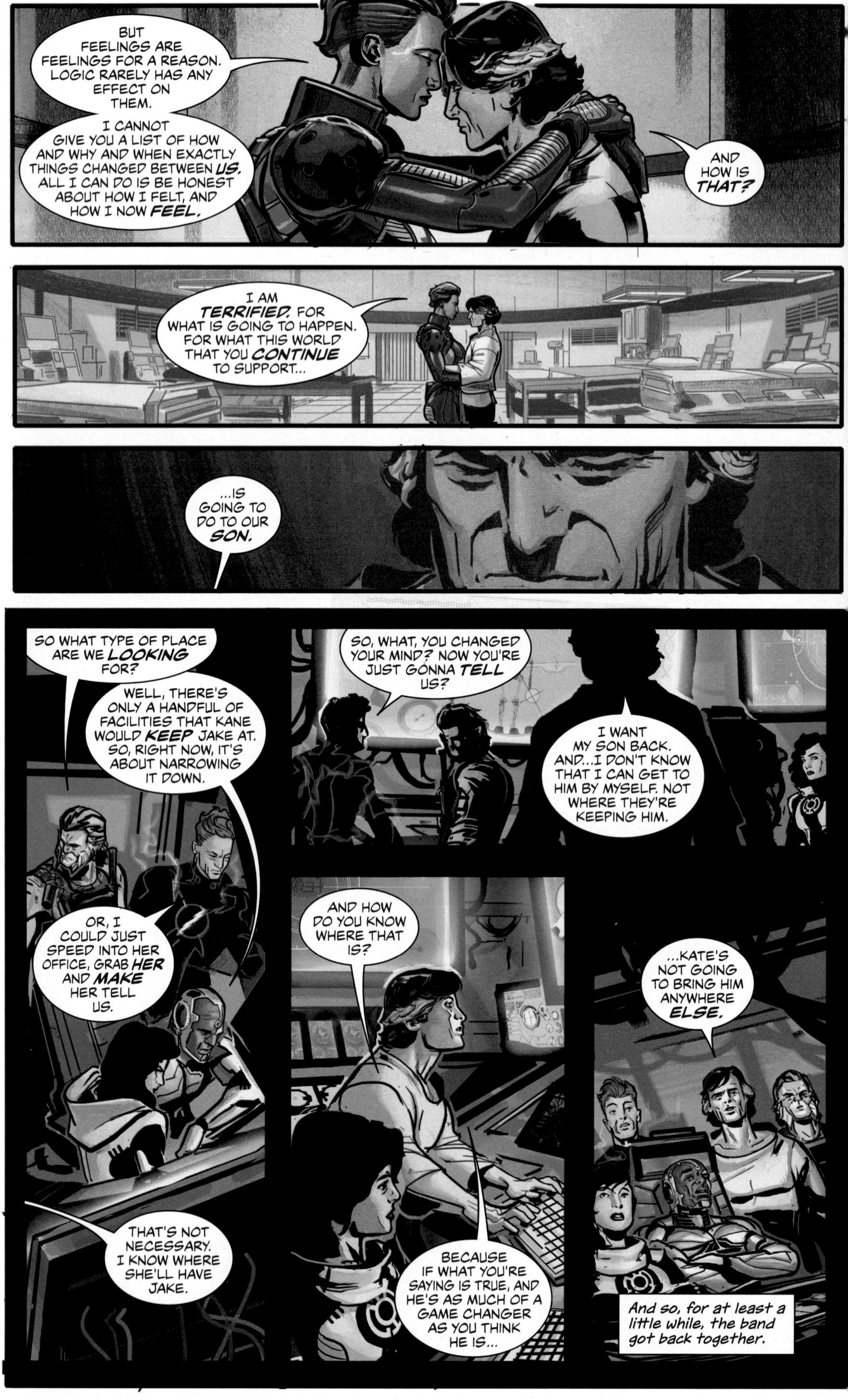
BUT FEELINGS ARE FEELINGS FOR A REASON. LOGIC RARELY HAS ANY EFFECT ON THEM.
I CANNOT GIVE YOU A LIST OF HOW AND WHY AND WHEN EXACTLY THINGS CHANGED BETWEEN US. ALL I CAN DO IS BE HONEST ABOUT HOW I FELT, AND HOW I NOW FEEL.
AND HOW IS THAT?
I AM TERRIFIED. FOR WHAT IS GOING TO HAPPEN. FOR WHAT THIS WORLD THAT YOU CONTINUE TO SUPPORT...
...IS GOING TO DO TO OUR SON.
SO WHAT TYPE OF PLACE ARE WE LOOKING FOR?
WELL, THERE'S ONLY A HANDFUL OF FACILITIES THAT KANE WOULD KEEP JAKE AT. SO, RIGHT NOW, IT'S ABOUT NARROWING IT DOWN.
OR, I COULD JUST SPEED INTO HER OFFICE, GRAB HER AND MAKE HER TELL US.
THAT'S NOT NECESSARY. I KNOW WHERE SHE'LL HAVE JAKE.
SO, WHAT, YOU CHANGED YOUR MIND? NOW YOU'RE JUST GONNA TELL US?
I WANT MY SON BACK. AND...I DON'T KNOW THAT I CAN GET TO HIM BY MYSELF. NOT WHERE THEY'RE KEEPING HIM.
AND HOW DO YOU KNOW WHERE THAT IS?
BECAUSE IF WHAT YOU'RE SAYING IS TRUE, AND HE'S AS MUCH OF A GAME CHANGER AS YOU THINK HE IS...
...KATE'S NOT GOING TO BRING HIM ANYWHERE ELSE.
And so, for at least a little while, the band got back together.

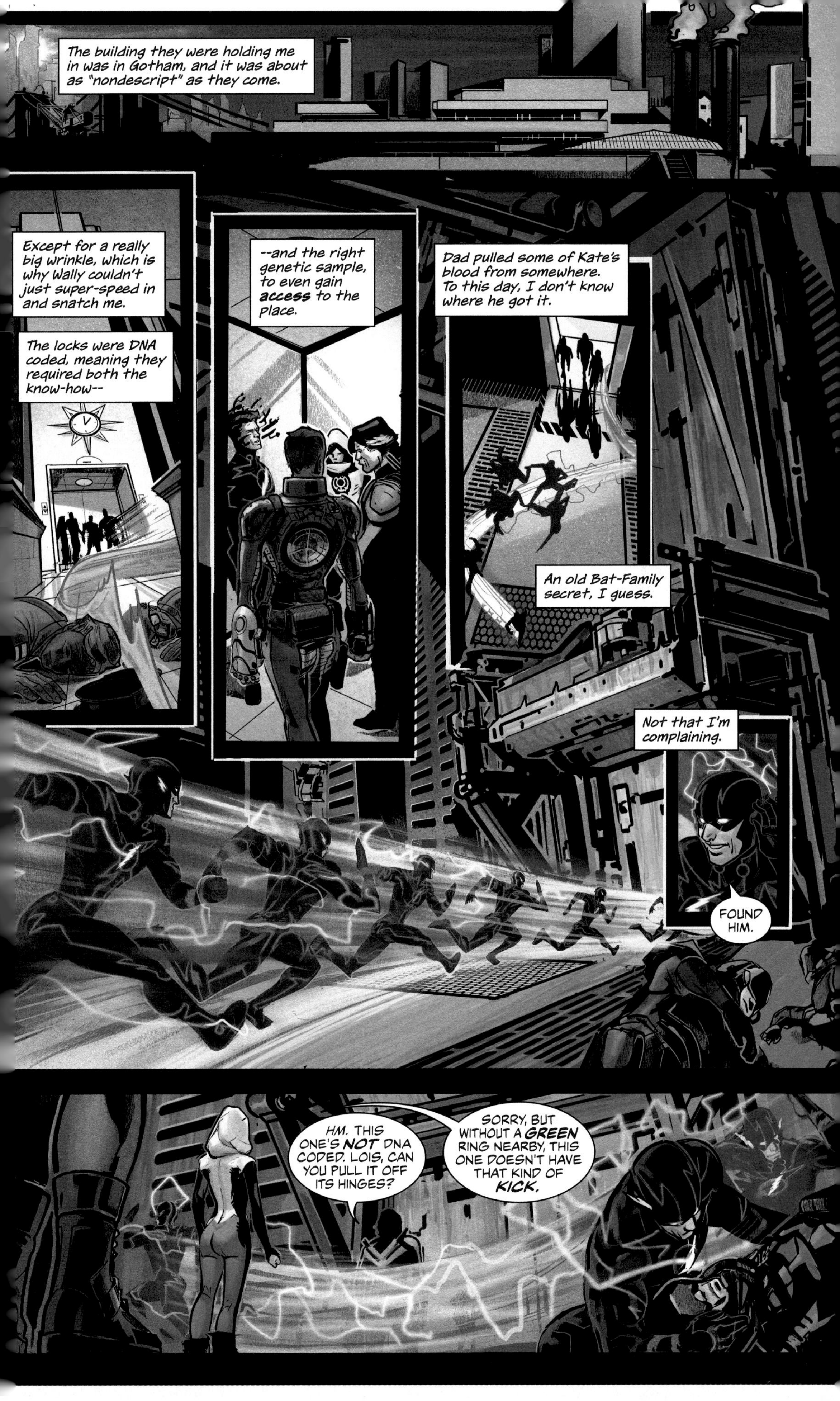
The building they were holding me in was in Gotham, and it was about as "nondescript" as they come.
Except for a really big wrinkle, which is why Wally couldn't just super-speed in and snatch me.
The locks were DNA coded, meaning they required both the know-how--
--and the right genetic sample, to even gain access to the place.
Dad pulled some of Kate's blood from somewhere. To this day, I don't know where he got it.
An old Bat-Family secret, I guess.
Not that I'm complaining.
FOUND HIM.
HM. THIS ONE'S NOT DNA CODED. LOIS, CAN YOU PULL IT OFF ITS HINGES?
SORRY, BUT WITHOUT A GREEN RING NEARBY, THIS ONE DOESN'T HAVE THAT KIND OF KICK.

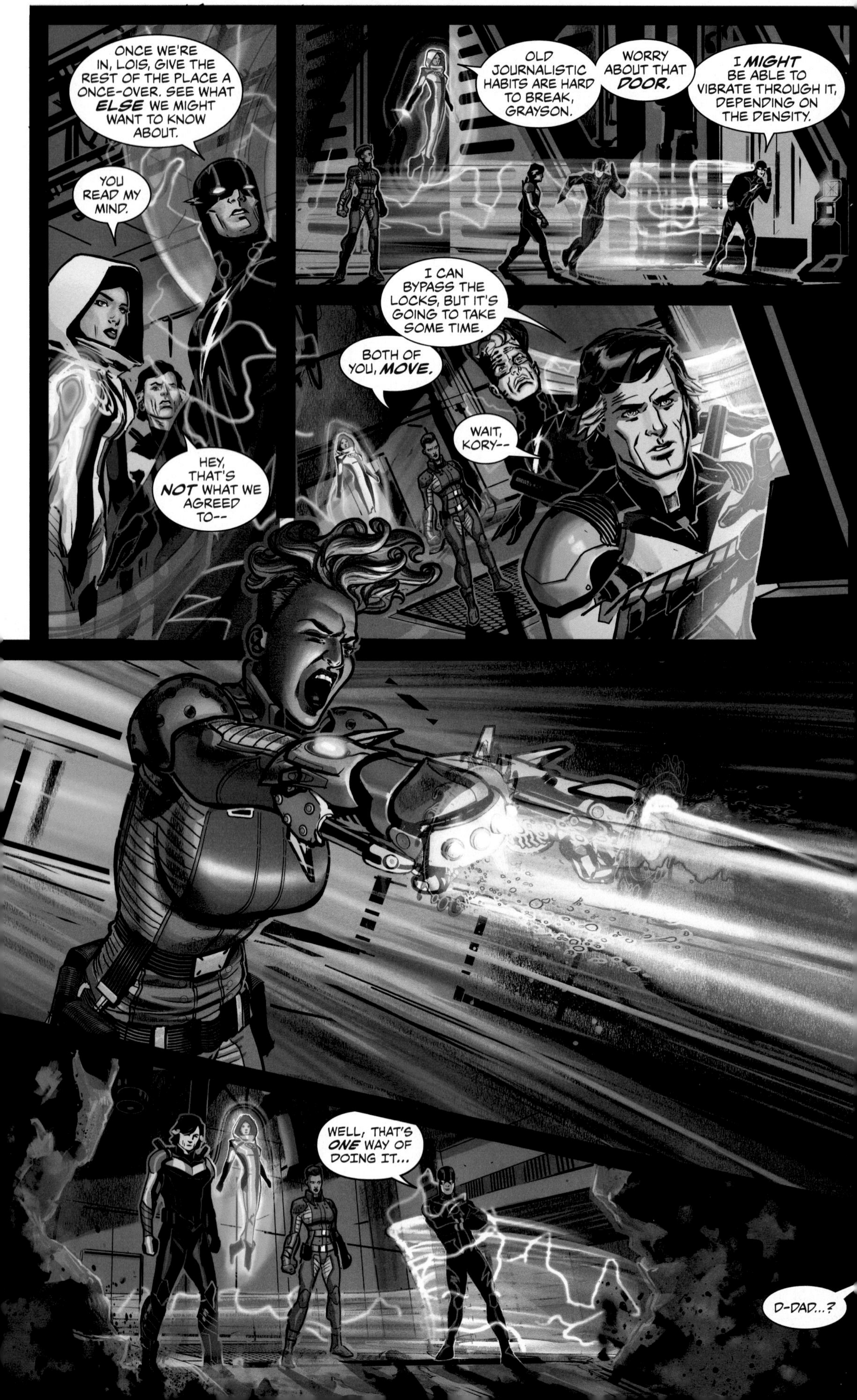
ONCE WE'RE IN, LOIS, GIVE THE REST OF THE PLACE A ONCE-OVER. SEE WHAT ELSE WE MIGHT WANT TO KNOW ABOUT.
YOU READ MY MIND.
HEY, THAT'S NOT WHAT WE AGREED TO--
OLD JOURNALISTIC HABITS ARE HARD TO BREAK, GRAYSON.
WORRY ABOUT THAT DOOR.
I MIGHT BE ABLE TO VIBRATE THROUGH IT, DEPENDING ON THE DENSITY.
I CAN BYPASS THE LOCKS, BUT IT'S GOING TO TAKE SOME TIME.
BOTH OF YOU, MOVE.
WAIT, KORY--
WELL, THAT'S ONE WAY OF DOING IT...
D-DAD...?

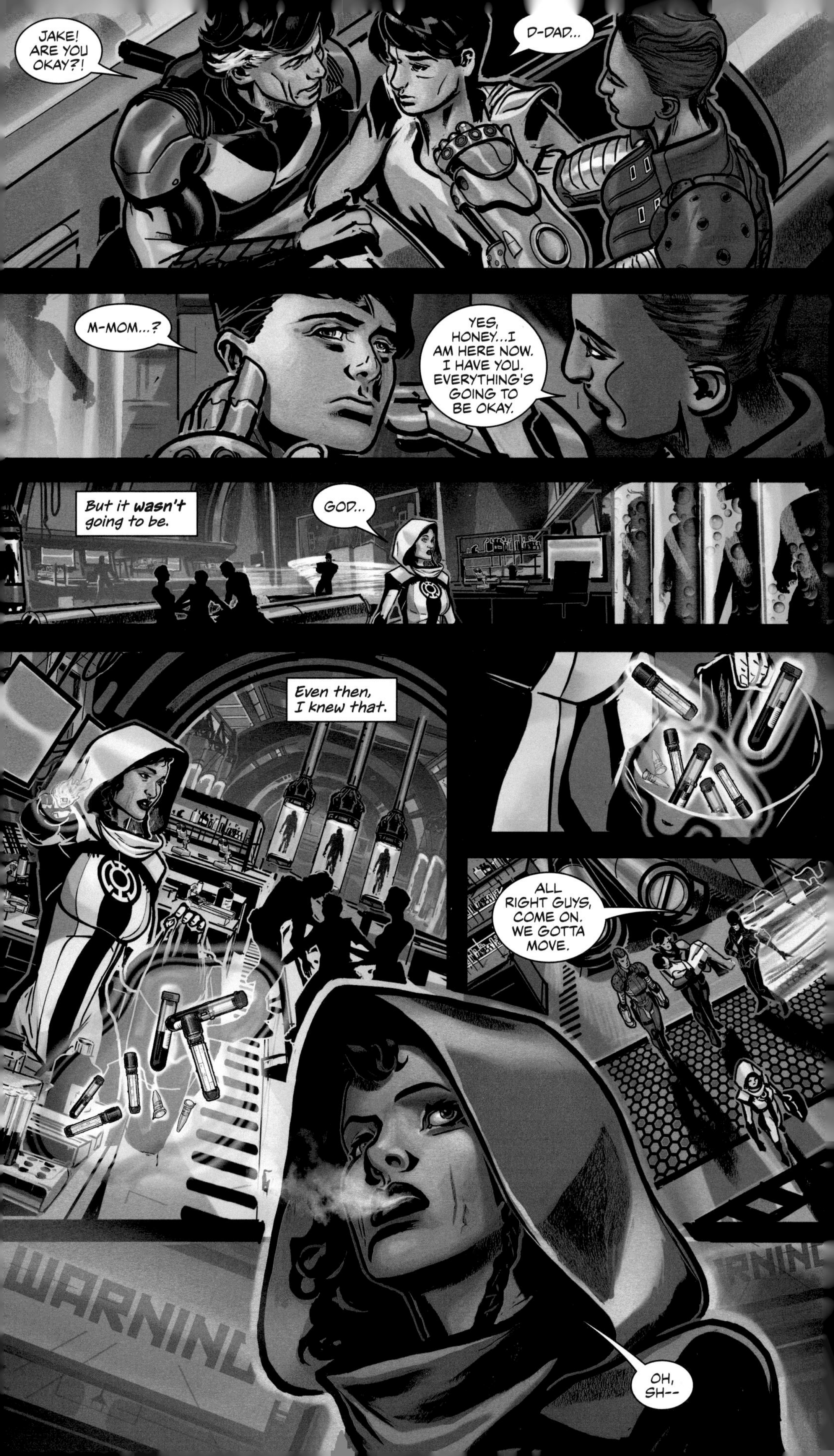
JAKE! ARE YOU OKAY?!
D-DAD...
M-MOM...?
YES, HONEY...I AM HERE NOW. I HAVE YOU. EVERYTHING'S GOING TO BE OKAY.
But it wasn't going to be.
GOD...
Even then, I knew that.
ALL RIGHT GUYS, COME ON. WE GOTTA MOVE.
WARNING
WARNING
OH, SH--

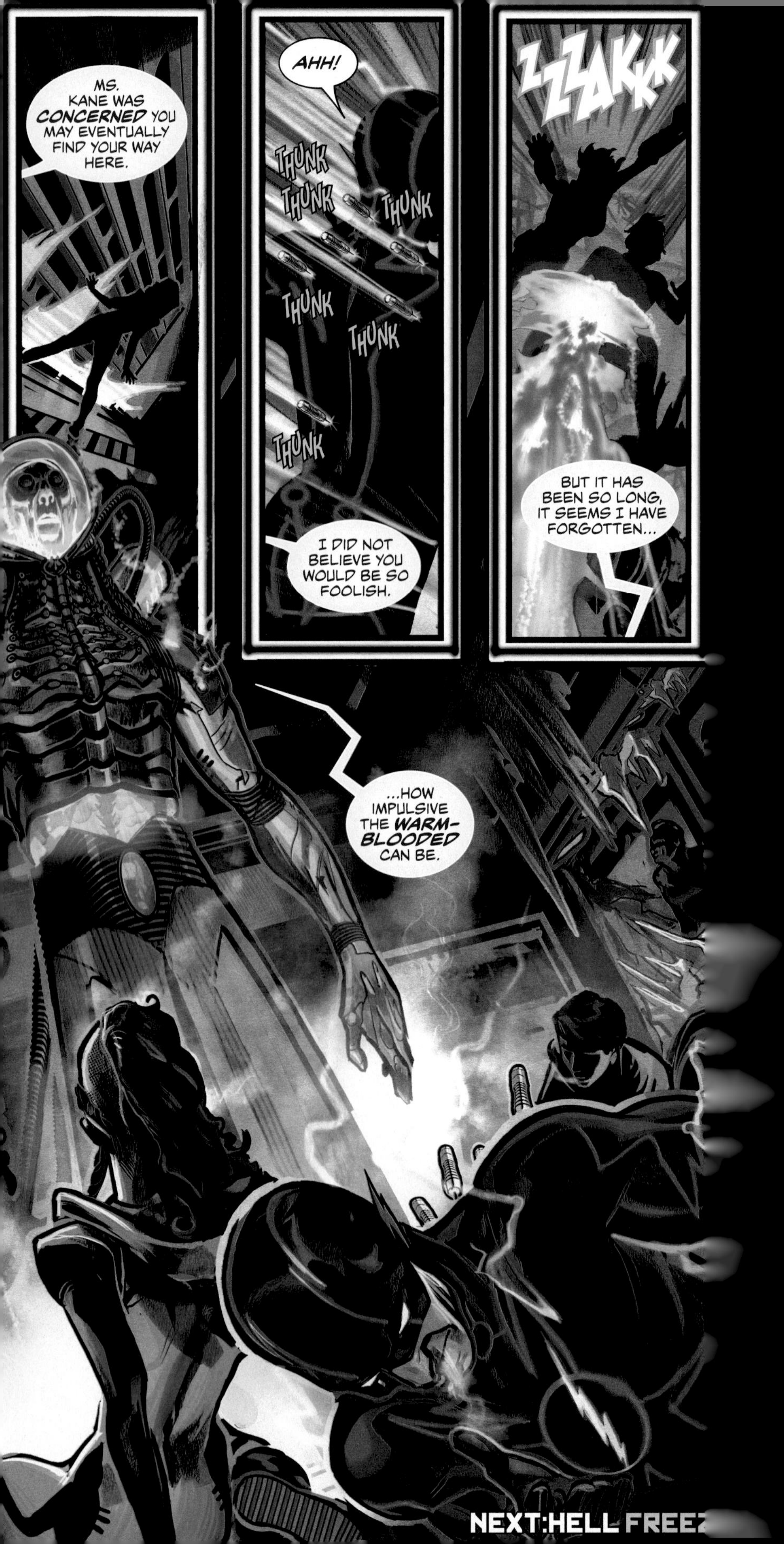
MS. KANE WAS CONCERNED YOU MAY EVENTUALLY FIND YOUR WAY HERE.
AHH!
THUNK
THUNK
THUNK
THUNK
THUNK
THUNK
I DID NOT BELIEVE YOU WOULD BE SO FOOLISH.
ZZZAKKK
BUT IT HAS BEEN SO LONG, IT SEEMS I HAVE FORGOTTEN...
...HOW IMPULSIVE THE WARM-BLOODED CAN BE.
NEXT: HELL FREEZ

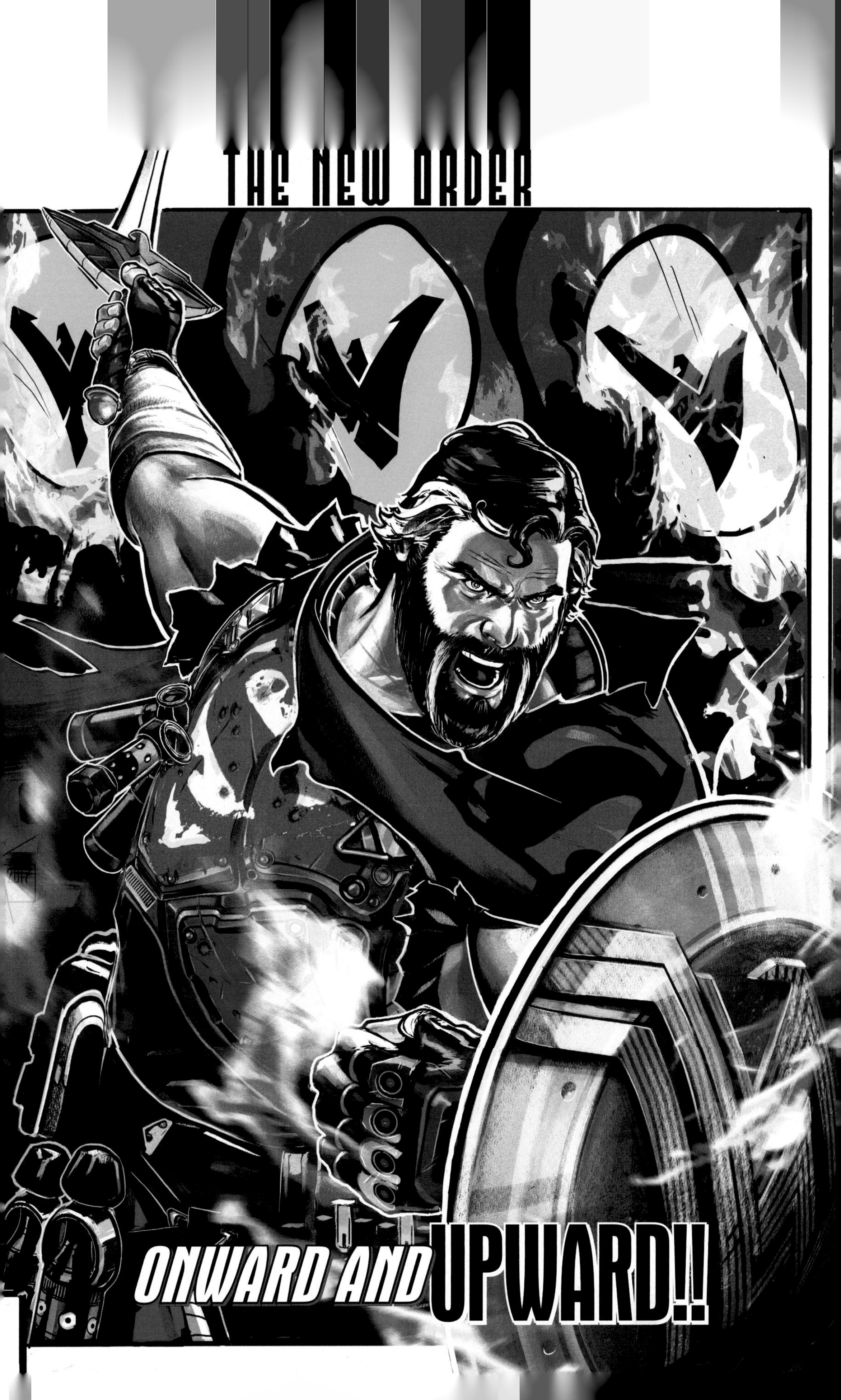
THE NEW ORDER
ONWARD AND UPWARD!!

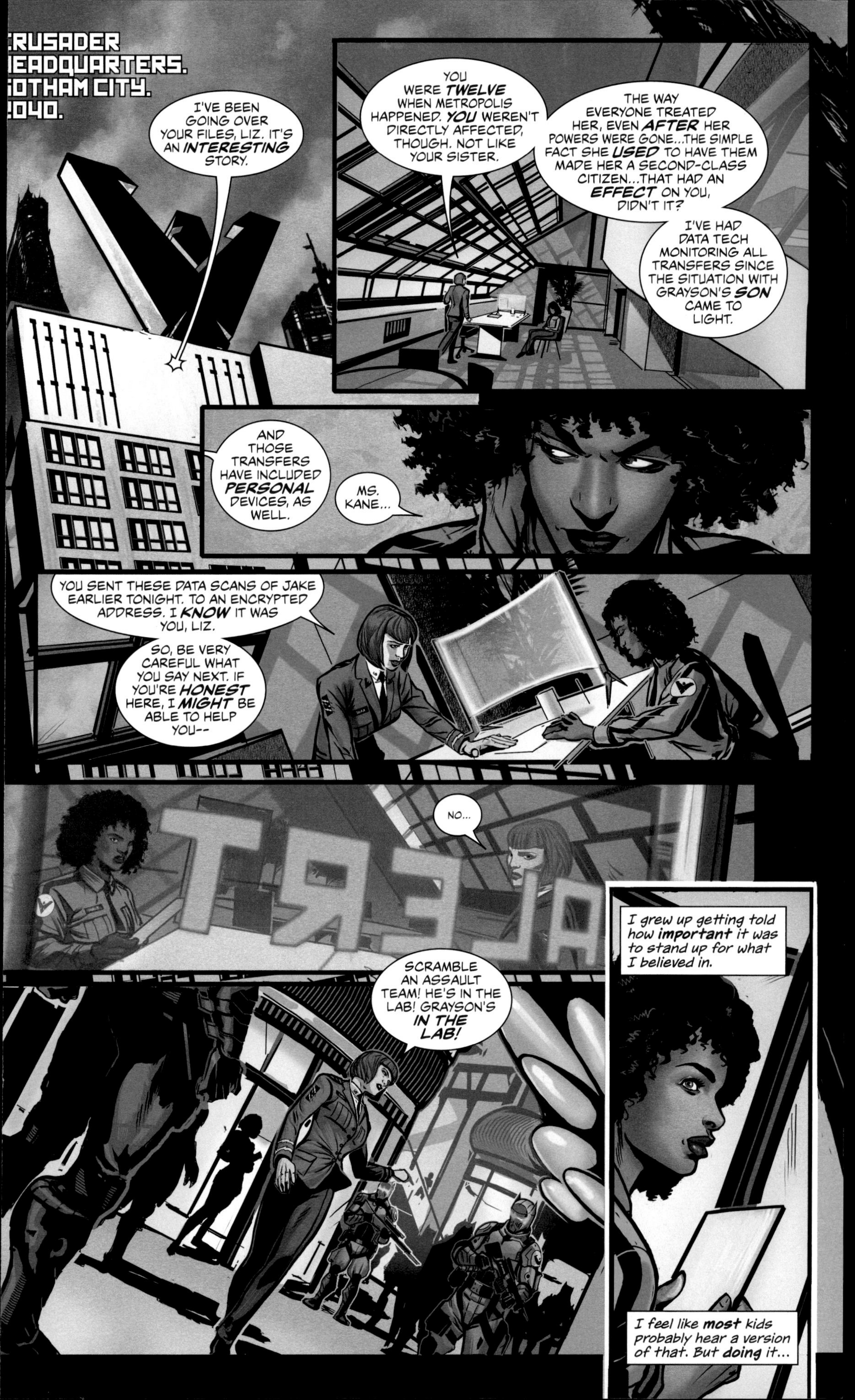

RUSADER
EADQUARTERS.
OTHAM CITY.
040.
I'VE BEEN GOING OVER YOUR FILES, LIZ. IT'S AN INTERESTING STORY.
YOU WERE TWELVE WHEN METROPOLIS HAPPENED. YOU WEREN'T DIRECTLY AFFECTED, THOUGH. NOT LIKE YOUR SISTER.
THE WAY EVERYONE TREATED HER, EVEN AFTER HER POWERS WERE GONE...THE SIMPLE FACT SHE USED TO HAVE THEM MADE HER A SECOND-CLASS CITIZEN...THAT HAD AN EFFECT ON YOU, DIDN'T IT?
I'VE HAD DATA TECH MONITORING ALL TRANSFERS SINCE THE SITUATION WITH GRAYSON'S SON CAME TO LIGHT.
AND THOSE TRANSFERS HAVE INCLUDED PERSONAL DEVICES, AS WELL.
MS. KANE...
YOU SENT THESE DATA SCANS OF JAKE EARLIER TONIGHT. TO AN ENCRYPTED ADDRESS. I KNOW IT WAS YOU, LIZ.
SO, BE VERY CAREFUL WHAT YOU SAY NEXT. IF YOU'RE HONEST HERE, I MIGHT BE ABLE TO HELP YOU--
NO...
SCRAMBLE AN ASSAULT TEAM! HE'S IN THE LAB! GRAYSON'S IN THE LAB!
I grew up getting told how important it was to stand up for what I believed in.
I feel like most kids probably hear a version of that. But doing it...

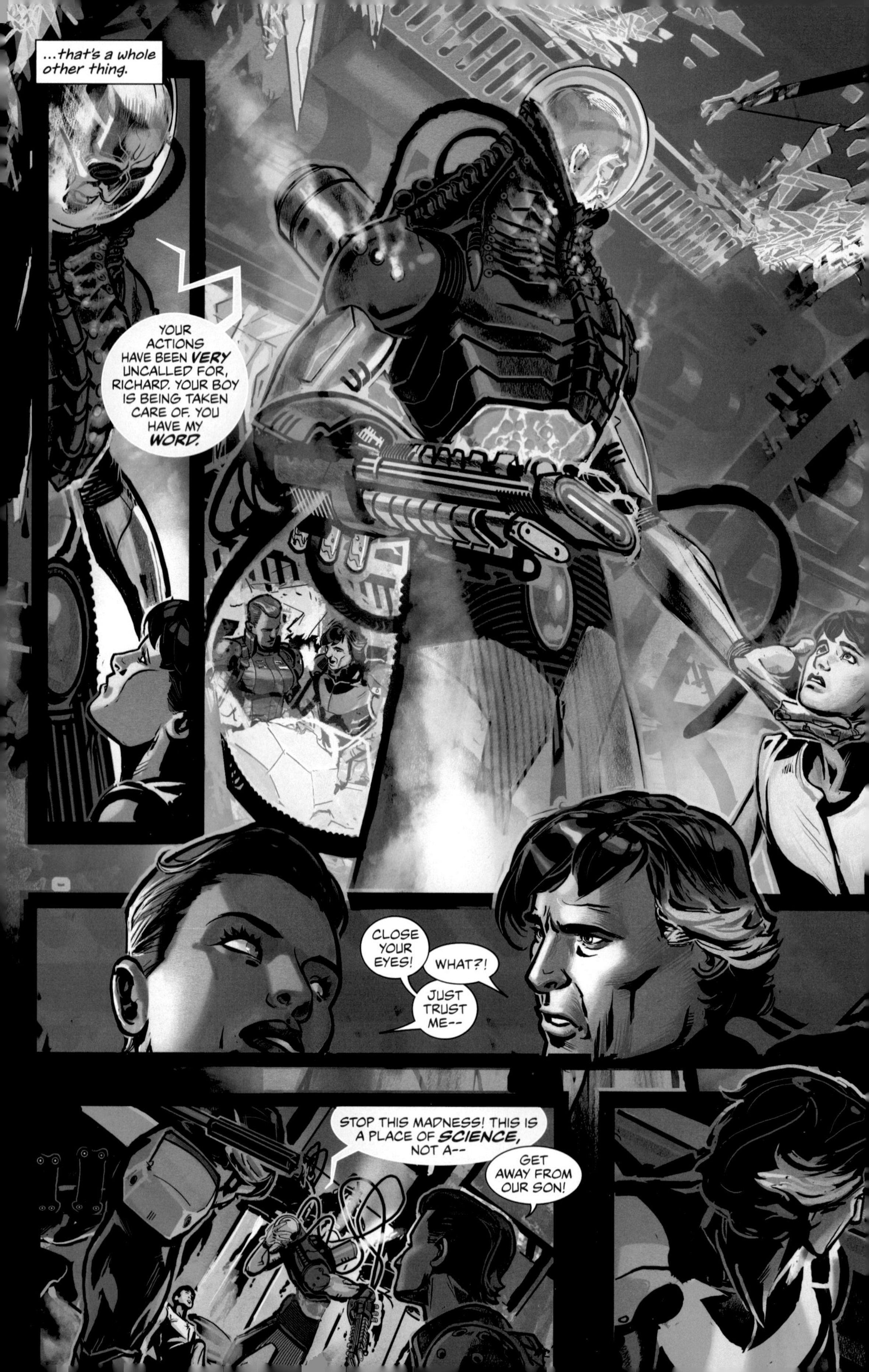
...that's a whole other thing.
YOUR ACTIONS HAVE BEEN VERY UNCALLED FOR, RICHARD. YOUR BOY IS BEING TAKEN CARE OF. YOU HAVE MY WORD.
CLOSE YOUR EYES!
WHAT?!
JUST TRUST ME--
STOP THIS MADNESS! THIS IS A PLACE OF SCIENCE, NOT A--
GET AWAY FROM OUR SON!

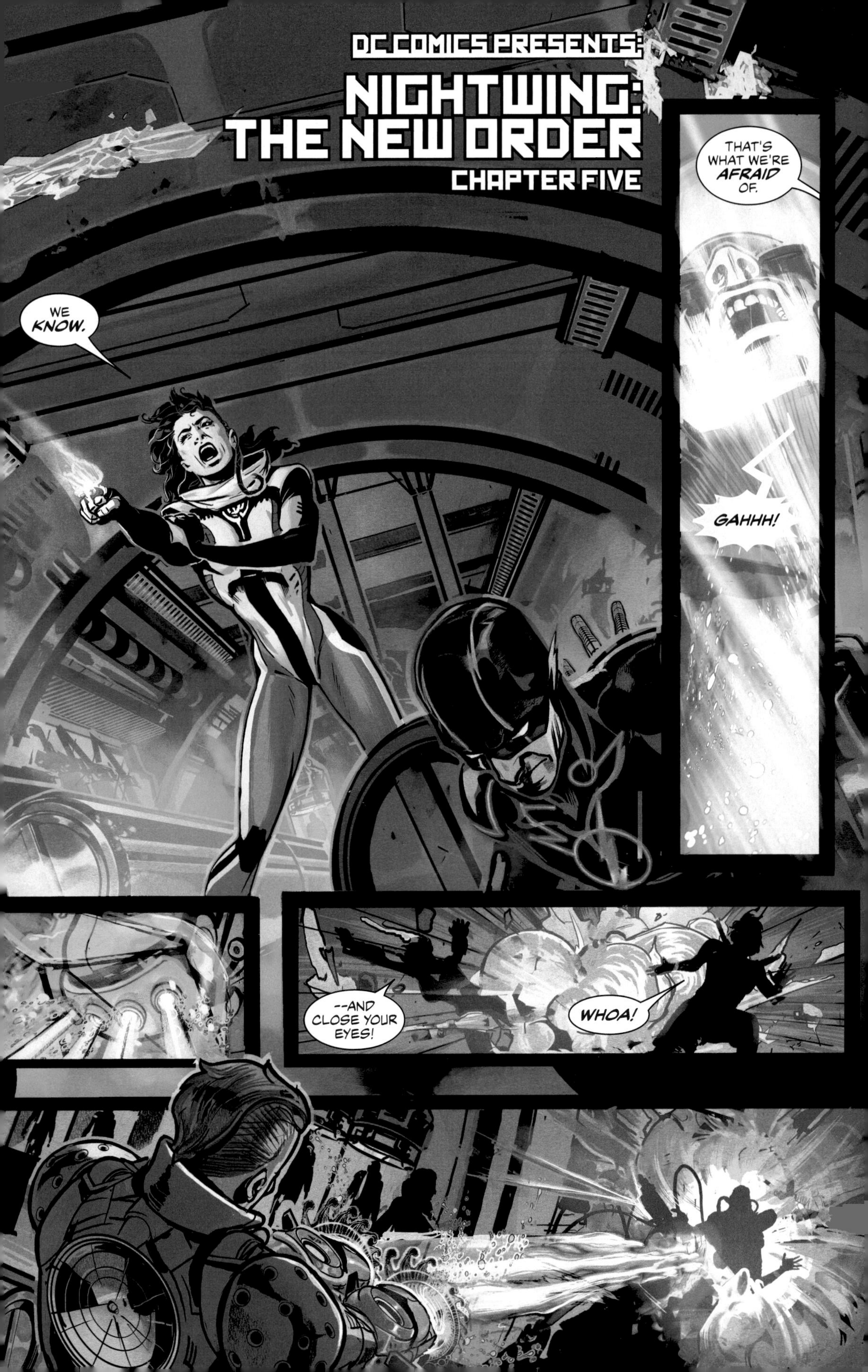
DC COMICS PRESENTS:
NIGHTWING: THE NEW ORDER
CHAPTER FIVE
WE KNOW.
THAT'S WHAT WE'RE AFRAID OF.
GAHHH!
--AND CLOSE YOUR EYES!
WHOA!

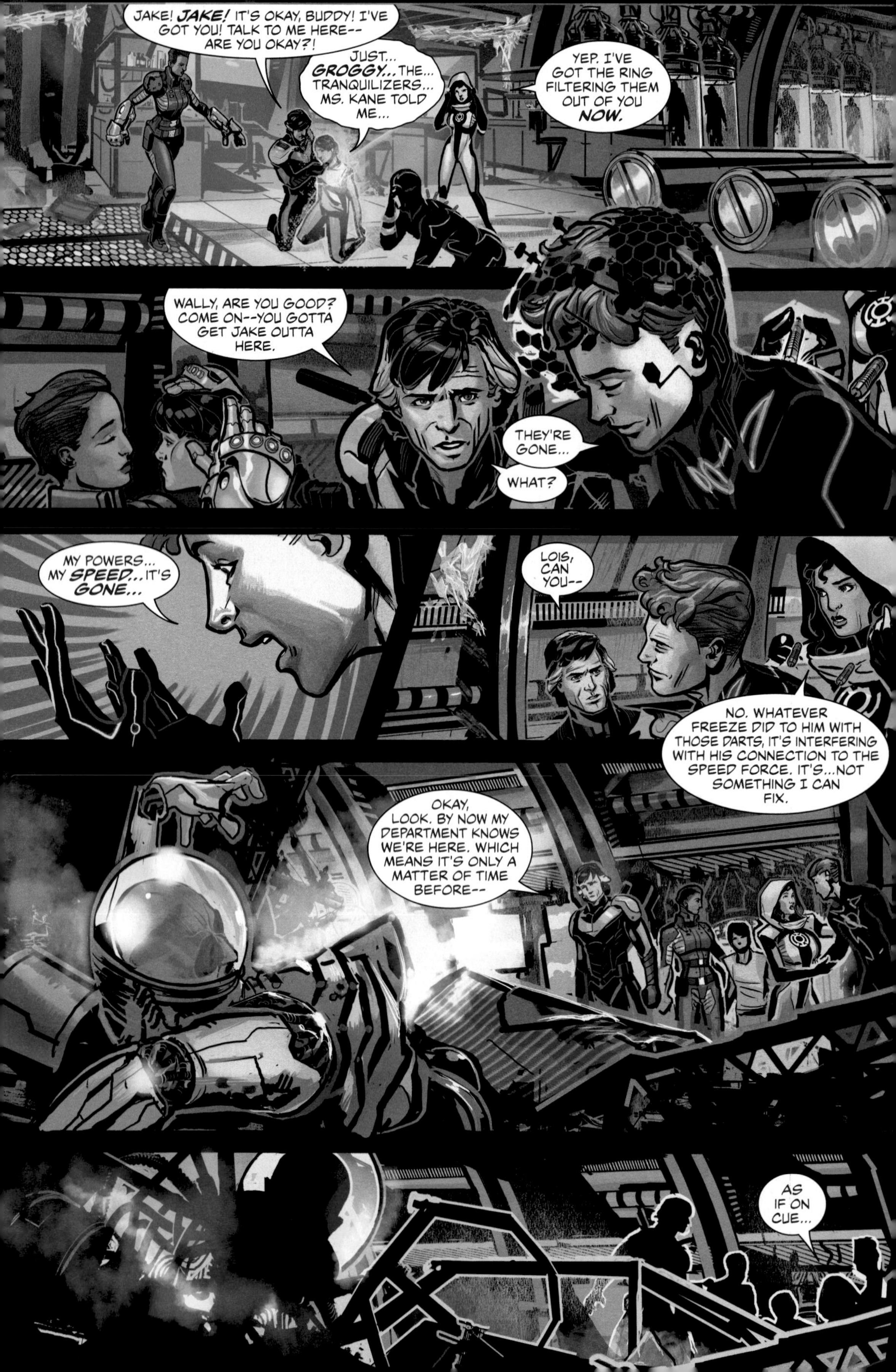
JAKE! JAKE! IT'S OKAY, BUDDY! I'VE GOT YOU! TALK TO ME HERE-- ARE YOU OKAY?!
JUST... GROGGY... THE... TRANQUILIZERS... MS. KANE TOLD ME...
YEP. I'VE GOT THE RING FILTERING THEM OUT OF YOU NOW.
WALLY, ARE YOU GOOD? COME ON--YOU GOTTA GET JAKE OUTTA HERE.
THEY'RE GONE...
WHAT?
MY POWERS... MY SPEED... IT'S GONE...
LOIS, CAN YOU--
NO. WHATEVER FREEZE DID TO HIM WITH THOSE DARTS, IT'S INTERFERING WITH HIS CONNECTION TO THE SPEED FORCE. IT'S...NOT SOMETHING I CAN FIX.
OKAY, LOOK. BY NOW MY DEPARTMENT KNOWS WE'RE HERE. WHICH MEANS IT'S ONLY A MATTER OF TIME BEFORE--
AS IF ON CUE...

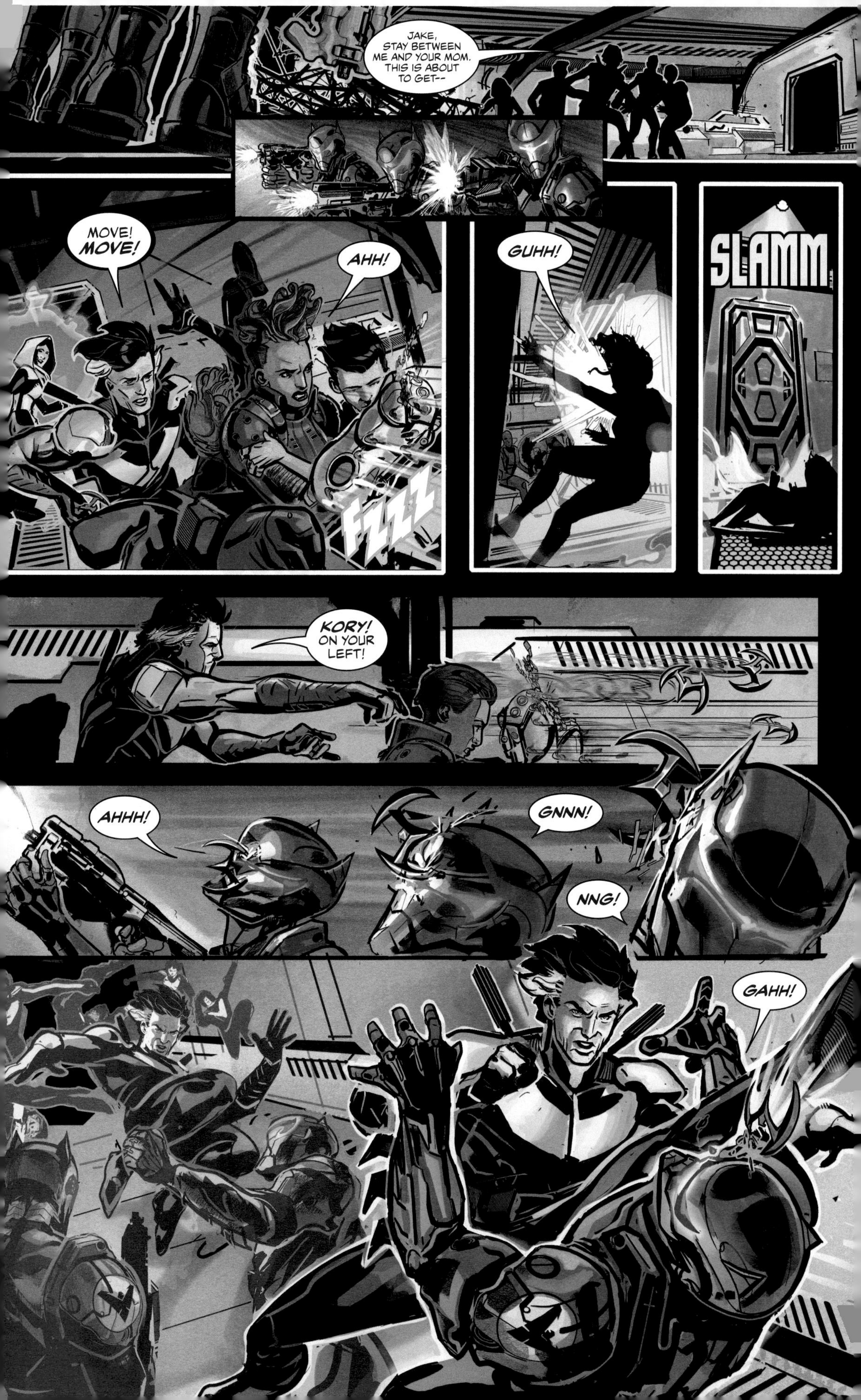
JAKE, STAY BETWEEN ME AND YOUR MOM. THIS IS ABOUT TO GET--
MOVE! MOVE!
AHH!
FZZZ
GUHH!
SLAMM
KORY! ON YOUR LEFT!
AHHH!
GNNN!
NNG!
GAHH!

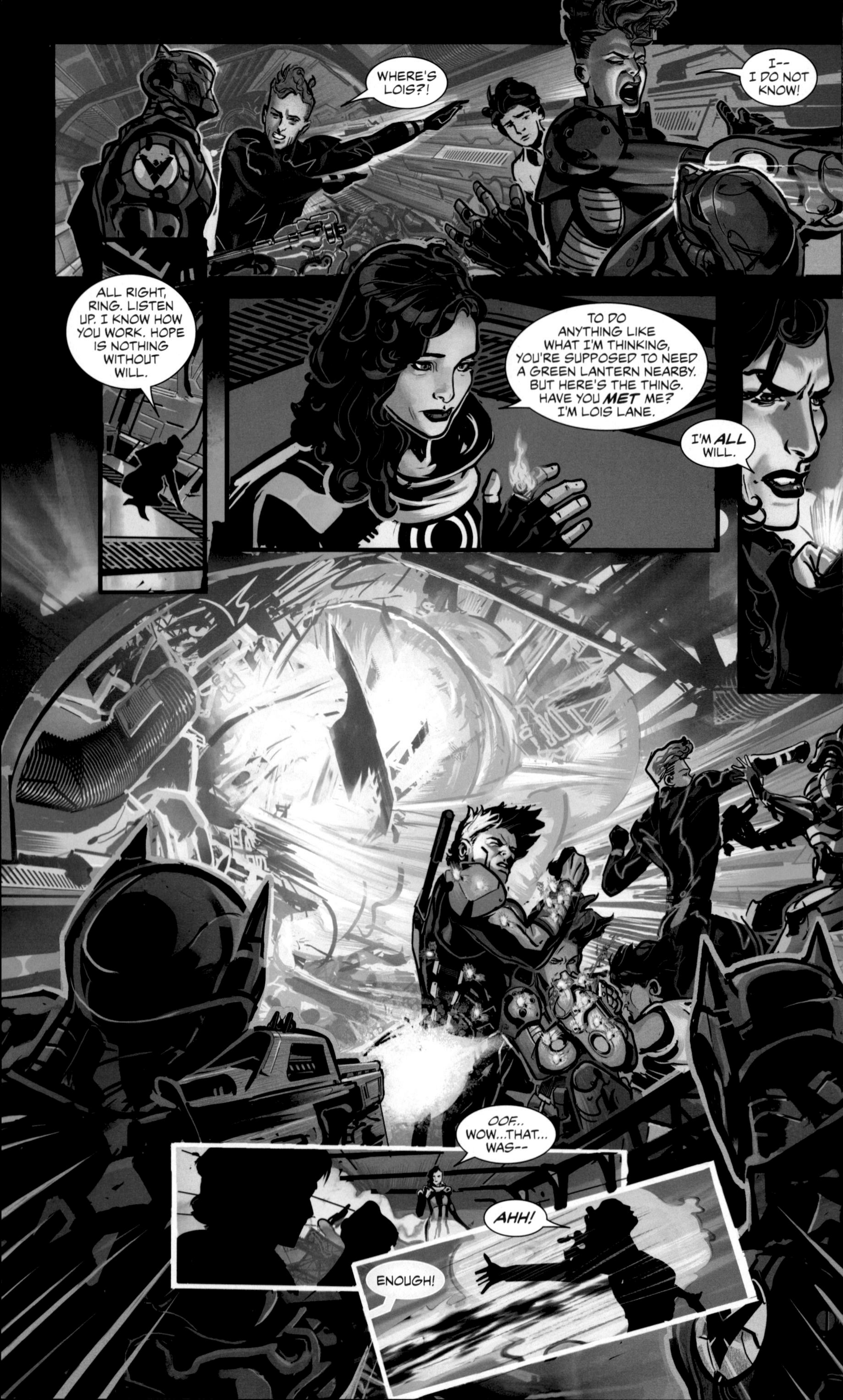
WHERE'S LOIS?!
I-- I DO NOT KNOW!
ALL RIGHT, RING. LISTEN UP. I KNOW HOW YOU WORK. HOPE IS NOTHING WITHOUT WILL.
TO DO ANYTHING LIKE WHAT I'M THINKING, YOU'RE SUPPOSED TO NEED A GREEN LANTERN NEARBY. BUT HERE'S THE THING. HAVE YOU MET ME? I'M LOIS LANE.
I'M ALL WILL.
OOF... WOW...THAT... WAS--
AHH!
ENOUGH!

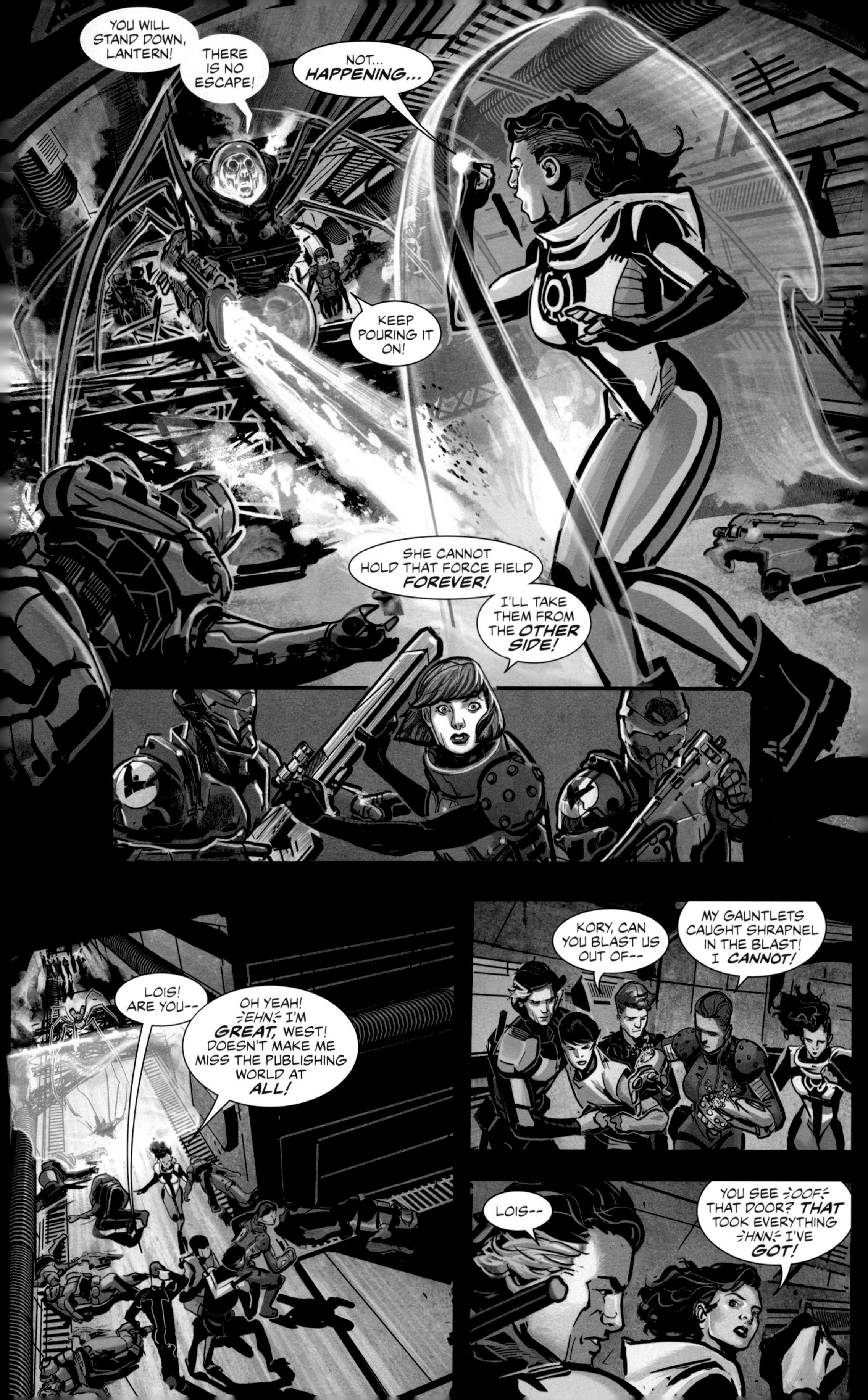

YOU WILL STAND DOWN, LANTERN!
THERE IS NO ESCAPE!
NOT... HAPPENING...
KEEP POURING IT ON!
SHE CANNOT HOLD THAT FORCE FIELD FOREVER!
I'LL TAKE THEM FROM THE OTHER SIDE!
LOIS! ARE YOU--
OH YEAH! -EHN- I'M GREAT, WEST! DOESN'T MAKE ME MISS THE PUBLISHING WORLD AT ALL!
KORY, CAN YOU BLAST US OUT OF--
MY GAUNTLETS CAUGHT SHRAPNEL IN THE BLAST! I CANNOT!
LOIS--
YOU SEE -OOF- THAT DOOR? THAT TOOK EVERYTHING -HNN- I'VE GOT!

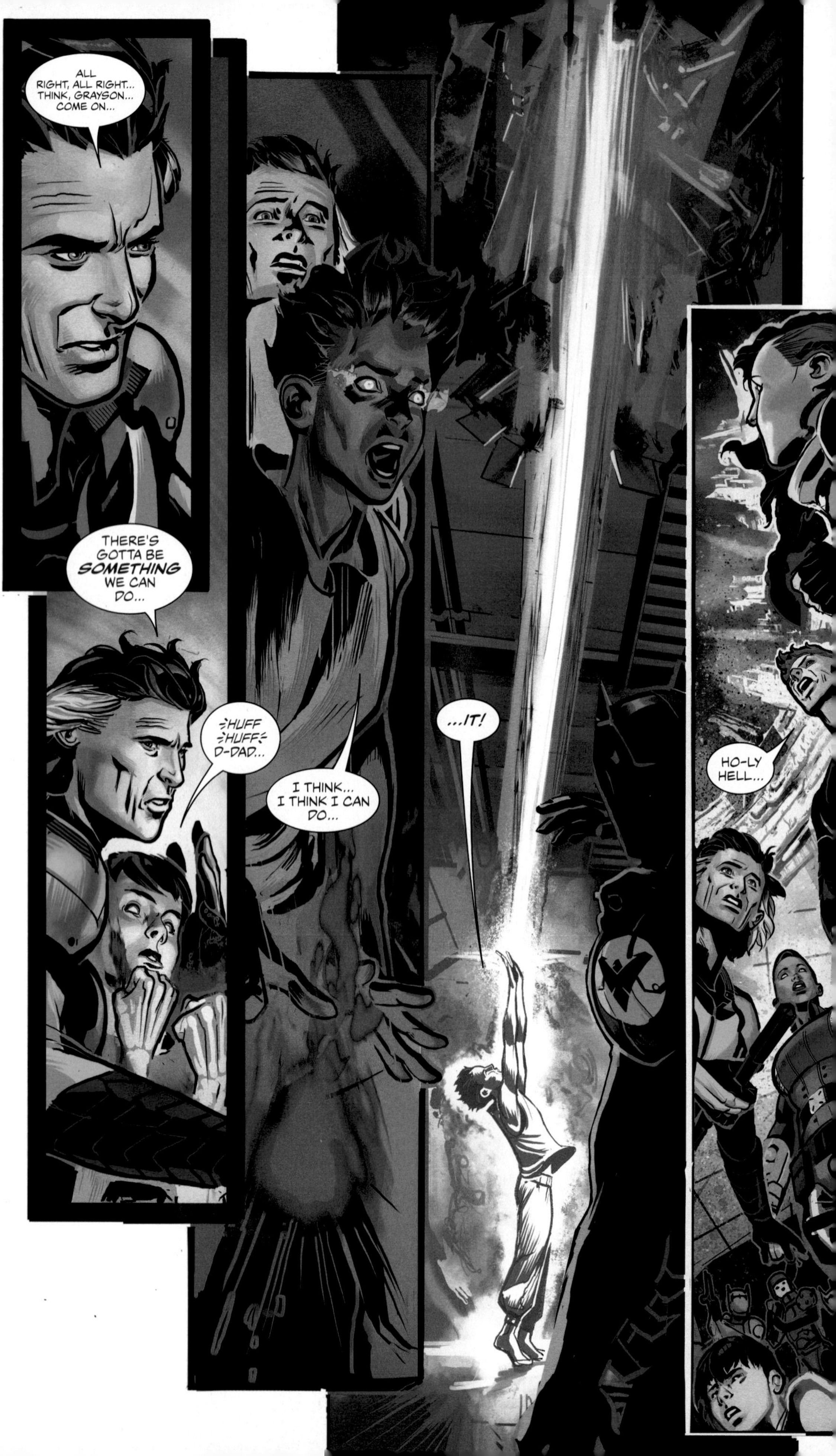

ALL RIGHT, ALL RIGHT... THINK, GRAYSON... COME ON...
THERE'S GOTTA BE **SOMETHING** WE CAN DO...
HUFF HUFF D-DAD...
I THINK... I THINK I CAN DO...
...IT!
HO-LY HELL...

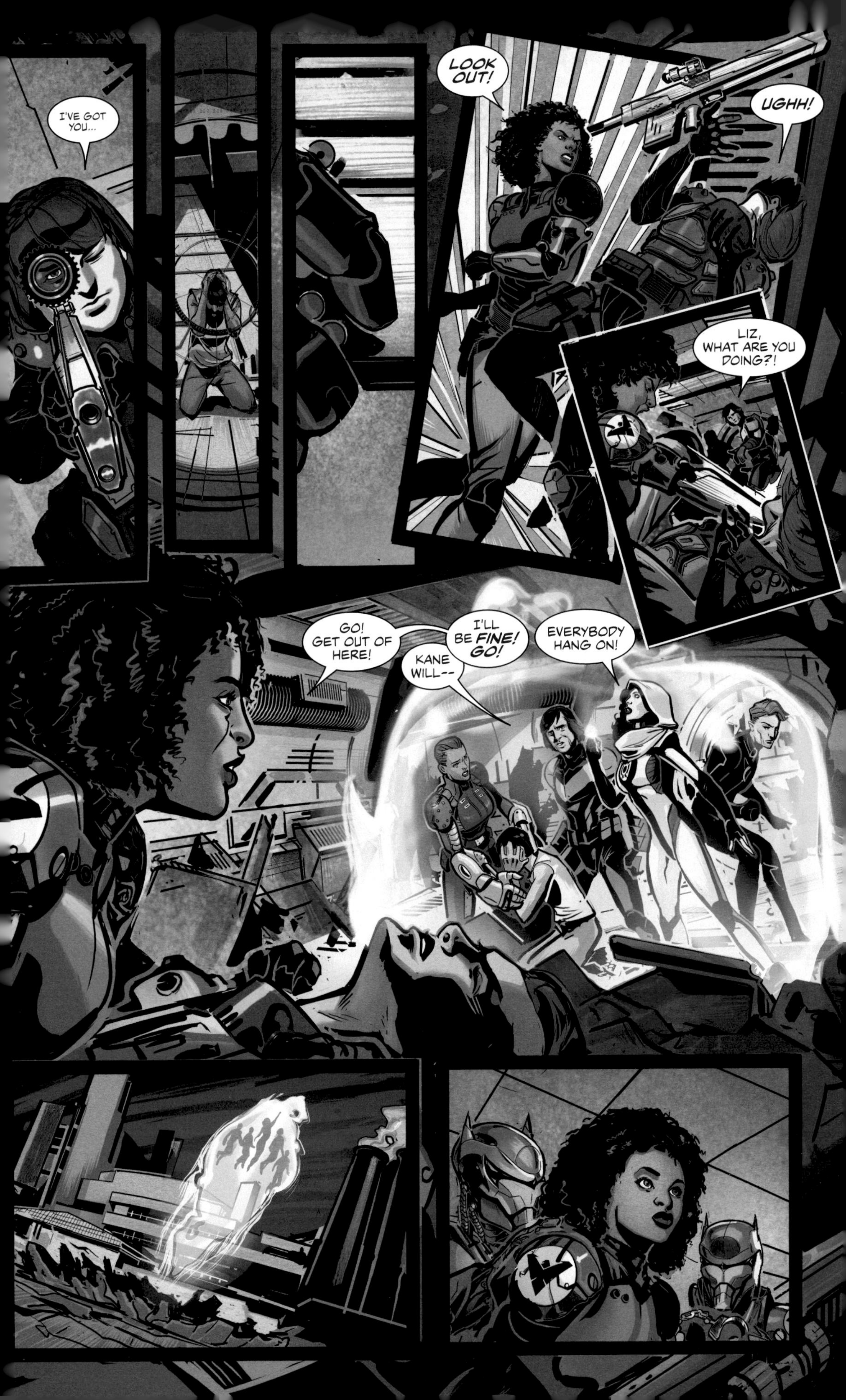
I'VE GOT YOU...
LOOK OUT!
UGHH!
LIZ, WHAT ARE YOU DOING?!
GO! GET OUT OF HERE!
I'LL BE FINE! GO!
KANE WILL--
EVERYBODY HANG ON!

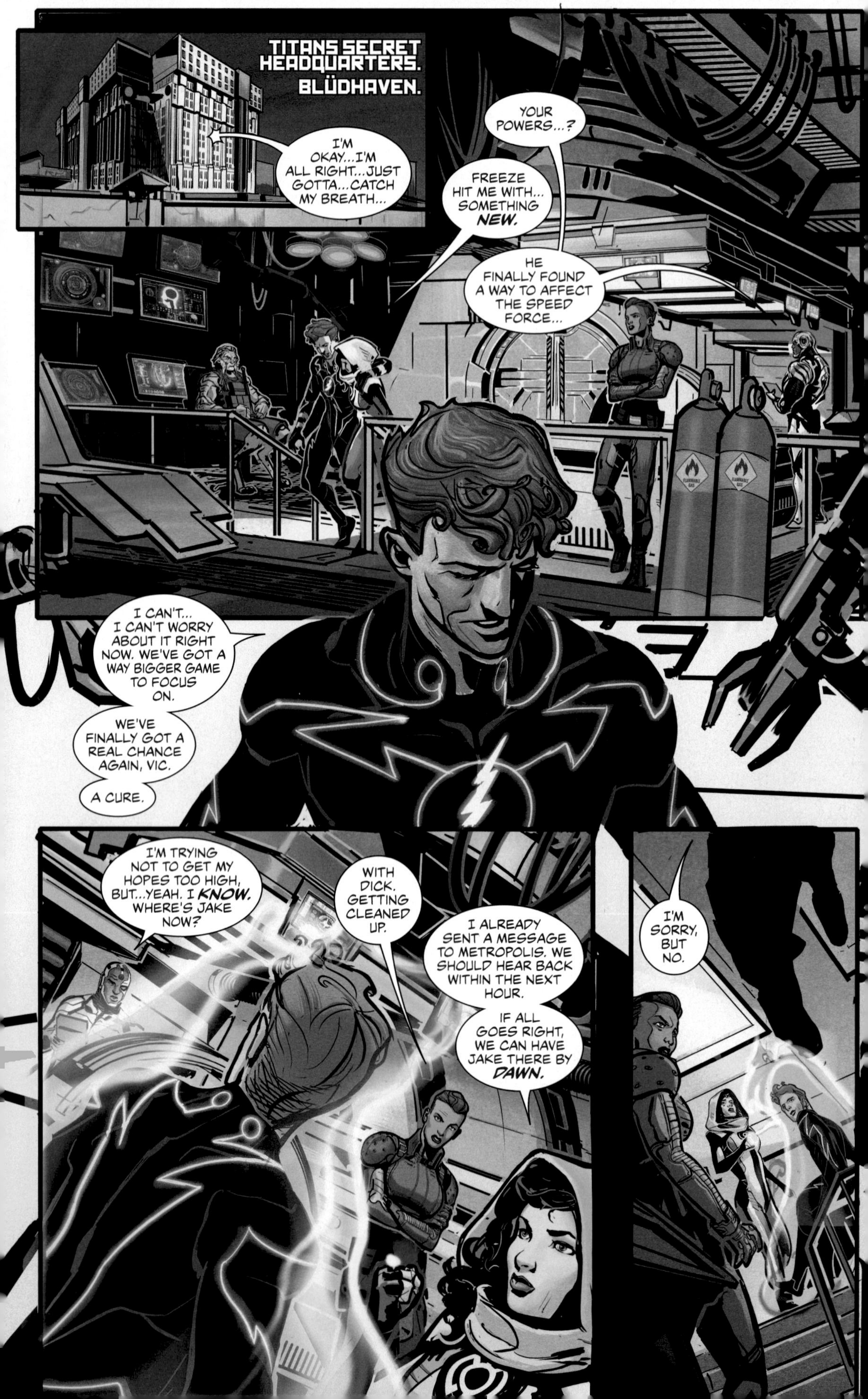
TITANS SECRET HEADQUARTERS.
BLÜDHAVEN.
I'M OKAY...I'M ALL RIGHT...JUST GOTTA...CATCH MY BREATH...
YOUR POWERS...?
FREEZE HIT ME WITH... SOMETHING *NEW.*
HE FINALLY FOUND A WAY TO AFFECT THE SPEED FORCE...
I CAN'T... I CAN'T WORRY ABOUT IT RIGHT NOW. WE'VE GOT A WAY BIGGER GAME TO FOCUS ON.
WE'VE FINALLY GOT A REAL CHANCE AGAIN, VIC.
A CURE.
I'M TRYING NOT TO GET MY HOPES TOO HIGH, BUT...YEAH. I *KNOW.* WHERE'S JAKE NOW?
WITH DICK. GETTING CLEANED UP.
I ALREADY SENT A MESSAGE TO METROPOLIS. WE SHOULD HEAR BACK WITHIN THE NEXT HOUR.
IF ALL GOES RIGHT, WE CAN HAVE JAKE THERE BY *DAWN.*
I'M SORRY, BUT NO.

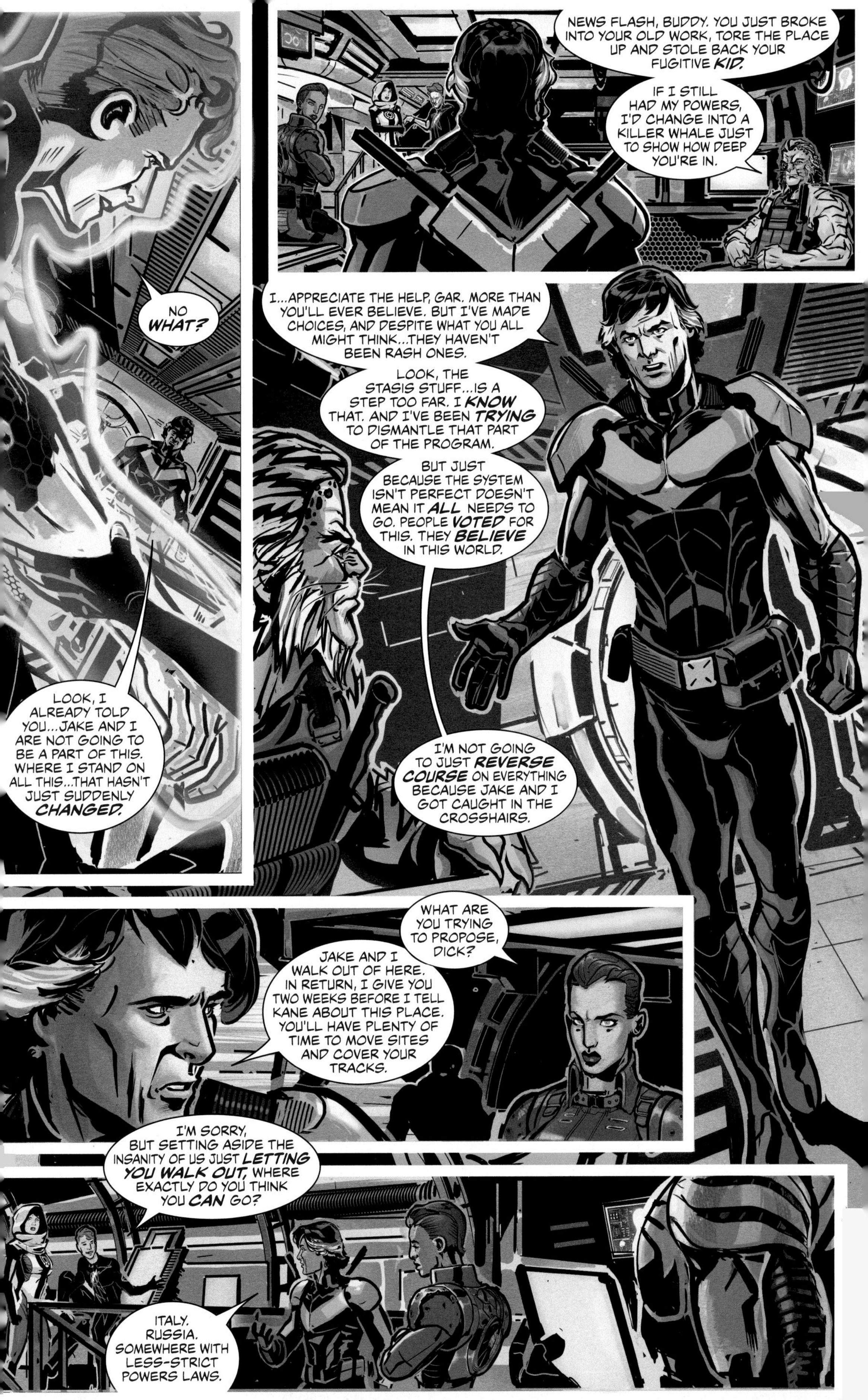
NO *WHAT?*
NEWS FLASH, BUDDY. YOU JUST BROKE INTO YOUR OLD WORK, TORE THE PLACE UP AND STOLE BACK YOUR FUGITIVE *KID.*
IF I STILL HAD MY POWERS, I'D CHANGE INTO A KILLER WHALE JUST TO SHOW HOW DEEP YOU'RE IN.
LOOK, I ALREADY TOLD YOU...JAKE AND I ARE NOT GOING TO BE A PART OF THIS. WHERE I STAND ON ALL THIS...THAT HASN'T JUST SUDDENLY *CHANGED.*
I...APPRECIATE THE HELP, GAR. MORE THAN YOU'LL EVER BELIEVE. BUT I'VE MADE CHOICES, AND DESPITE WHAT YOU ALL MIGHT THINK...THEY HAVEN'T BEEN RASH ONES.
LOOK, THE STASIS STUFF...IS A STEP TOO FAR. I *KNOW* THAT. AND I'VE BEEN *TRYING* TO DISMANTLE THAT PART OF THE PROGRAM.
BUT JUST BECAUSE THE SYSTEM ISN'T PERFECT DOESN'T MEAN IT *ALL* NEEDS TO GO. PEOPLE *VOTED* FOR THIS. THEY *BELIEVE* IN THIS WORLD.
I'M NOT GOING TO JUST *REVERSE COURSE* ON EVERYTHING BECAUSE JAKE AND I GOT CAUGHT IN THE CROSSHAIRS.
WHAT ARE YOU TRYING TO PROPOSE, DICK?
JAKE AND I WALK OUT OF HERE. IN RETURN, I GIVE YOU TWO WEEKS BEFORE I TELL KANE ABOUT THIS PLACE. YOU'LL HAVE PLENTY OF TIME TO MOVE SITES AND COVER YOUR TRACKS.
I'M SORRY, BUT SETTING ASIDE THE INSANITY OF US JUST *LETTING YOU WALK OUT,* WHERE EXACTLY DO YOU THINK YOU *CAN* GO?
ITALY. RUSSIA. SOMEWHERE WITH LESS-STRICT POWERS LAWS.

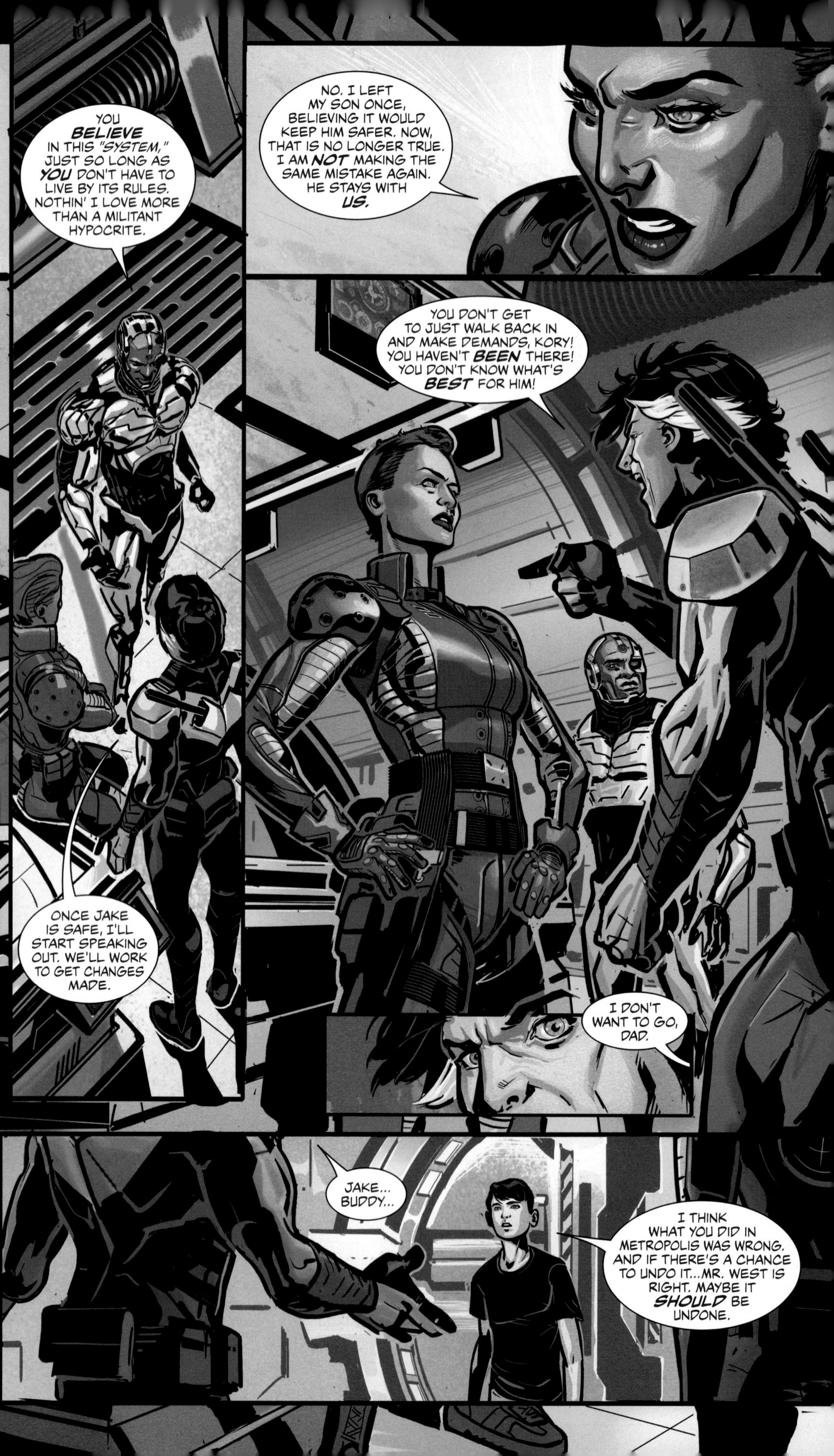

YOU BELIEVE IN THIS "SYSTEM," JUST SO LONG AS YOU DON'T HAVE TO LIVE BY ITS RULES. NOTHIN' I LOVE MORE THAN A MILITANT HYPOCRITE.
NO. I LEFT MY SON ONCE, BELIEVING IT WOULD KEEP HIM SAFER. NOW, THAT IS NO LONGER TRUE. I AM NOT MAKING THE SAME MISTAKE AGAIN. HE STAYS WITH US.
ONCE JAKE IS SAFE, I'LL START SPEAKING OUT. WE'LL WORK TO GET CHANGES MADE.
YOU DON'T GET TO JUST WALK BACK IN AND MAKE DEMANDS, KORY! YOU HAVEN'T BEEN THERE! YOU DON'T KNOW WHAT'S BEST FOR HIM!
I DON'T WANT TO GO, DAD.
JAKE... BUDDY...
I THINK WHAT YOU DID IN METROPOLIS WAS WRONG. AND IF THERE'S A CHANCE TO UNDO IT...MR. WEST IS RIGHT. MAYBE IT SHOULD BE UNDONE.

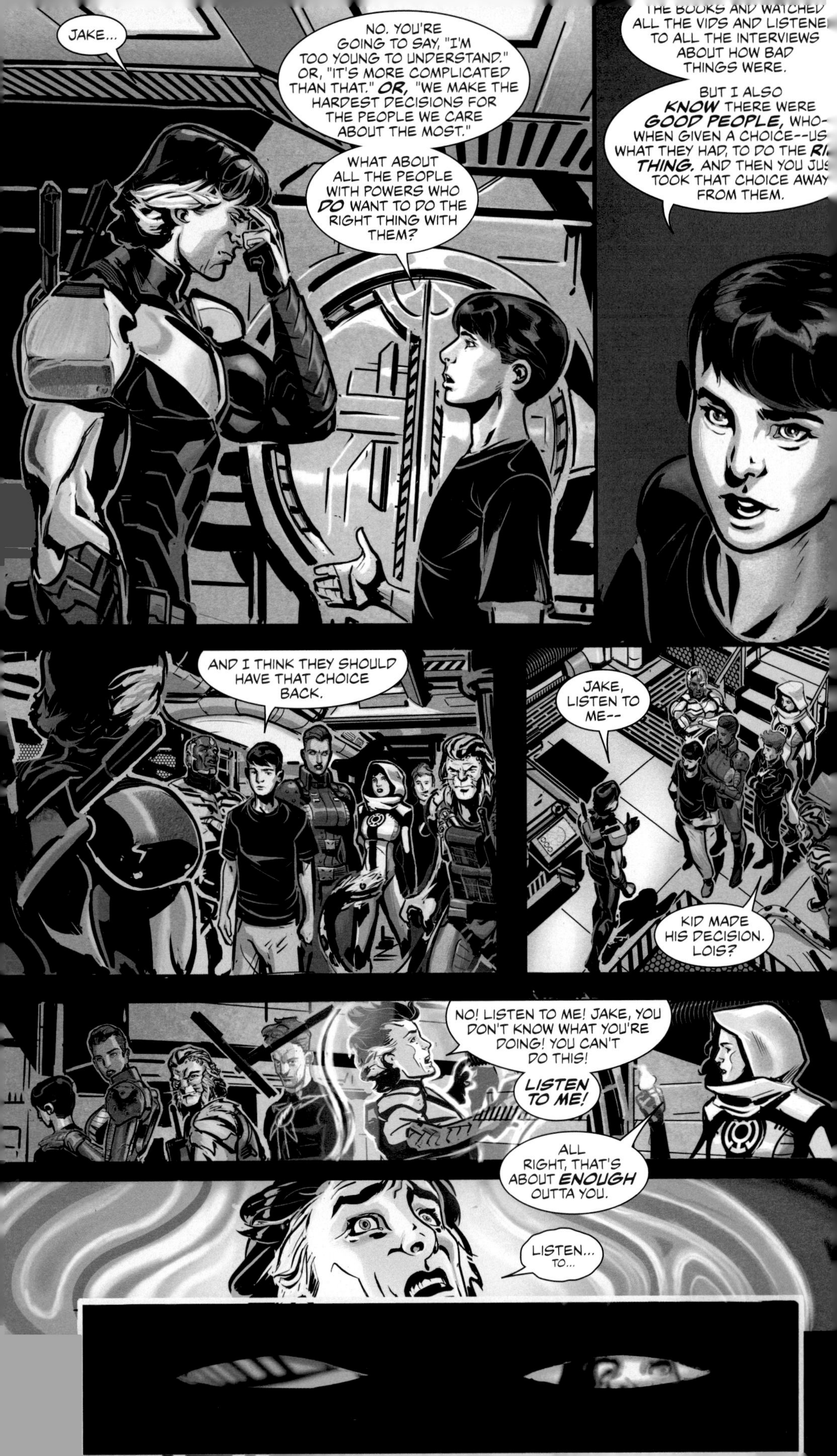
JAKE...
NO. YOU'RE GOING TO SAY, "I'M TOO YOUNG TO UNDERSTAND." OR, "IT'S MORE COMPLICATED THAN THAT." OR, "WE MAKE THE HARDEST DECISIONS FOR THE PEOPLE WE CARE ABOUT THE MOST."
WHAT ABOUT ALL THE PEOPLE WITH POWERS WHO DO WANT TO DO THE RIGHT THING WITH THEM?
THE BOOKS AND WATCHED ALL THE VIDS AND LISTENE TO ALL THE INTERVIEWS ABOUT HOW BAD THINGS WERE.
BUT I ALSO KNOW THERE WERE GOOD PEOPLE, WHO-- WHEN GIVEN A CHOICE--US WHAT THEY HAD, TO DO THE THING. AND THEN YOU JUS TOOK THAT CHOICE AWAY FROM THEM.
AND I THINK THEY SHOULD HAVE THAT CHOICE BACK.
JAKE, LISTEN TO ME--
KID MADE HIS DECISION. LOIS?
NO! LISTEN TO ME! JAKE, YOU DON'T KNOW WHAT YOU'RE DOING! YOU CAN'T DO THIS!
LISTEN TO ME!
ALL RIGHT, THAT'S ABOUT ENOUGH OUTTA YOU.
LISTEN... TO...

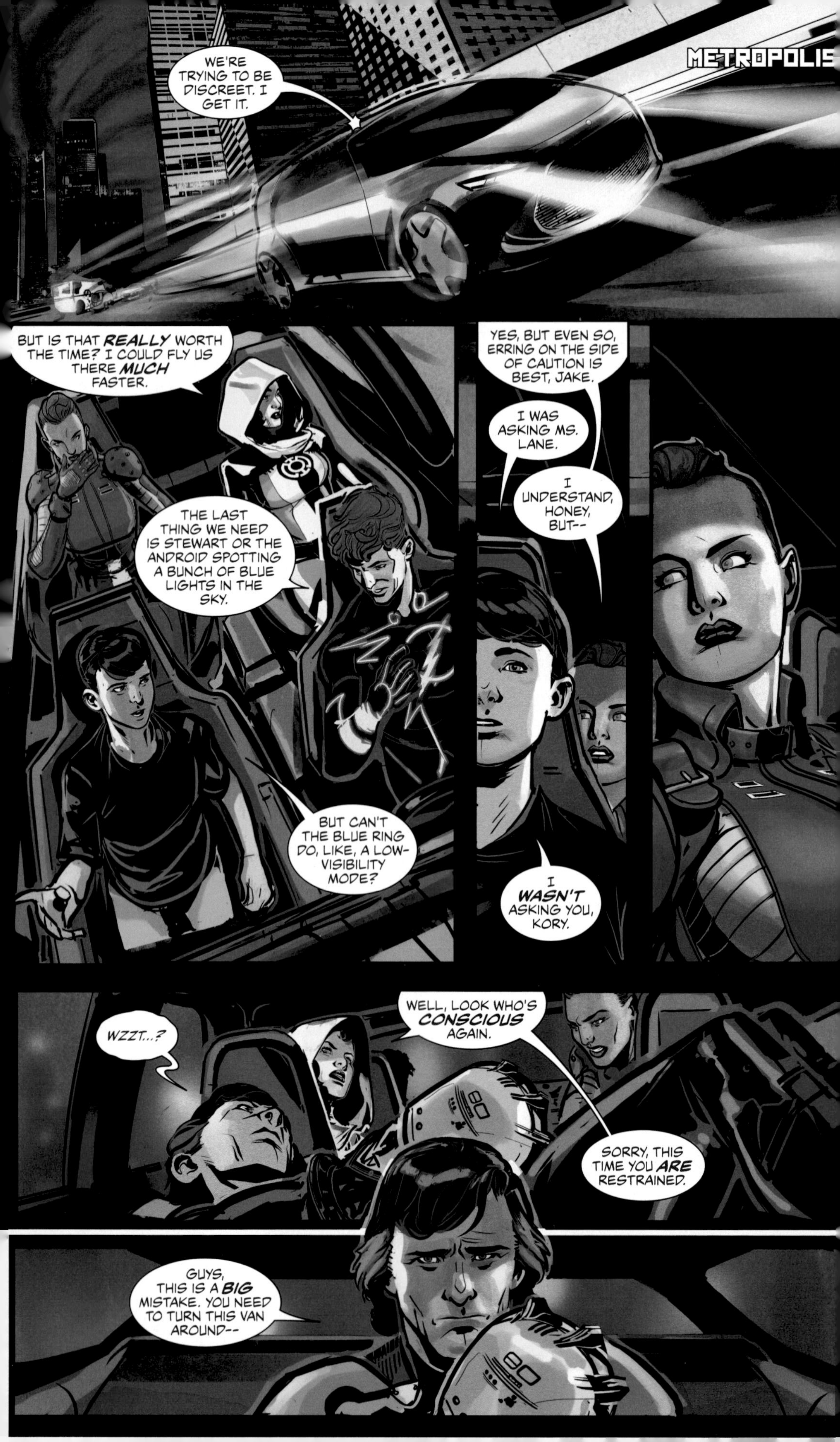
METROPOLIS
WE'RE TRYING TO BE DISCREET. I GET IT.
BUT IS THAT REALLY WORTH THE TIME? I COULD FLY US THERE MUCH FASTER.
THE LAST THING WE NEED IS STEWART OR THE ANDROID SPOTTING A BUNCH OF BLUE LIGHTS IN THE SKY.
BUT CAN'T THE BLUE RING DO, LIKE, A LOW-VISIBILITY MODE?
YES, BUT EVEN SO, ERRING ON THE SIDE OF CAUTION IS BEST, JAKE.
I WAS ASKING MS. LANE.
I UNDERSTAND, HONEY, BUT--
I WASN'T ASKING YOU, KORY.
WZZT...?
WELL, LOOK WHO'S CONSCIOUS AGAIN.
SORRY, THIS TIME YOU ARE RESTRAINED.
GUYS, THIS IS A BIG MISTAKE. YOU NEED TO TURN THIS VAN AROUND--

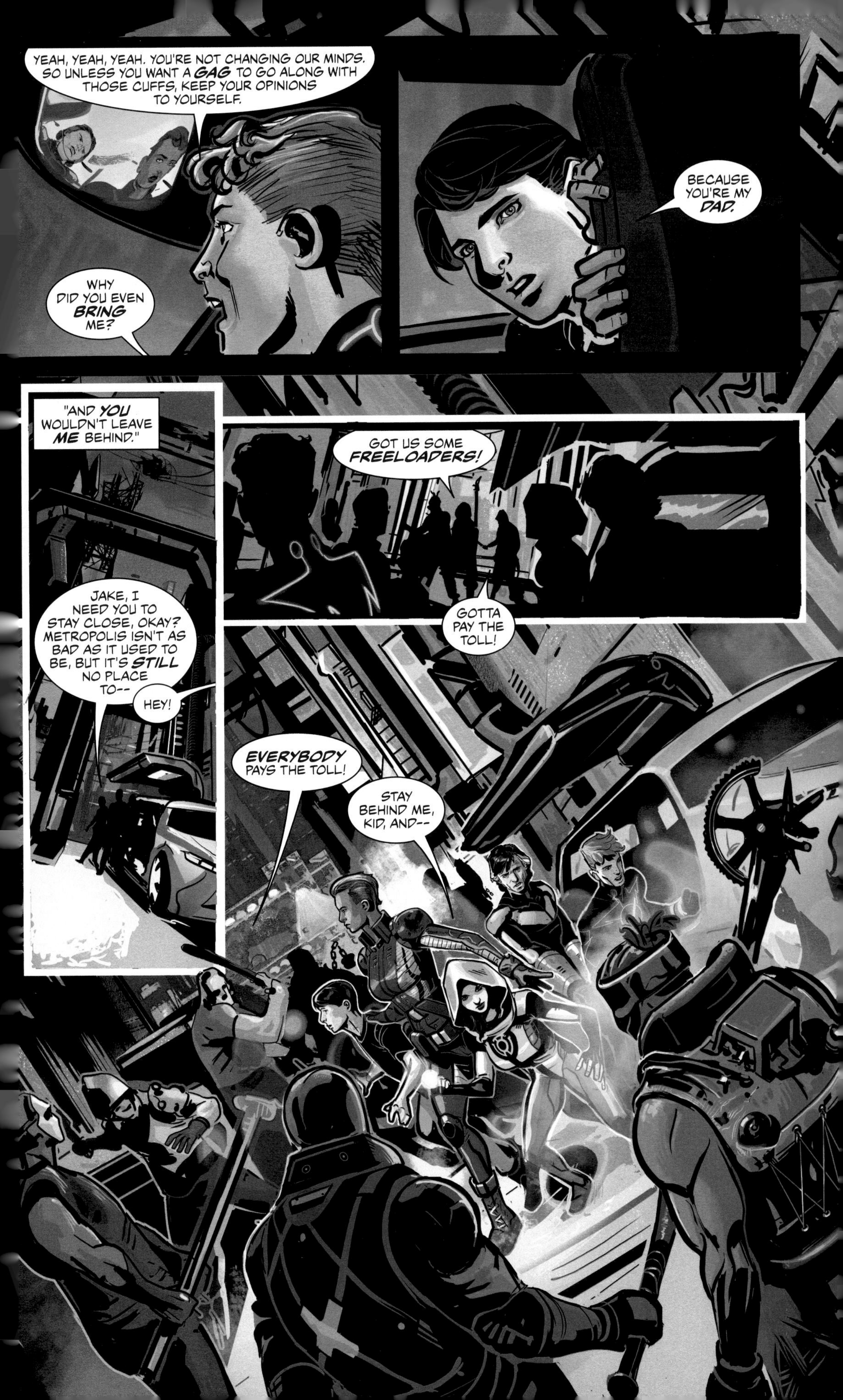
YEAH, YEAH, YEAH. YOU'RE NOT CHANGING OUR MINDS. SO UNLESS YOU WANT A GAG TO GO ALONG WITH THOSE CUFFS, KEEP YOUR OPINIONS TO YOURSELF.
WHY DID YOU EVEN BRING ME?
BECAUSE YOU'RE MY DAD.
"AND YOU WOULDN'T LEAVE ME BEHIND."
JAKE, I NEED YOU TO STAY CLOSE, OKAY? METROPOLIS ISN'T AS BAD AS IT USED TO BE, BUT IT'S STILL NO PLACE TO--
HEY!
GOT US SOME FREELOADERS!
GOTTA PAY THE TOLL!
EVERYBODY PAYS THE TOLL!
STAY BEHIND ME, KID, AND--

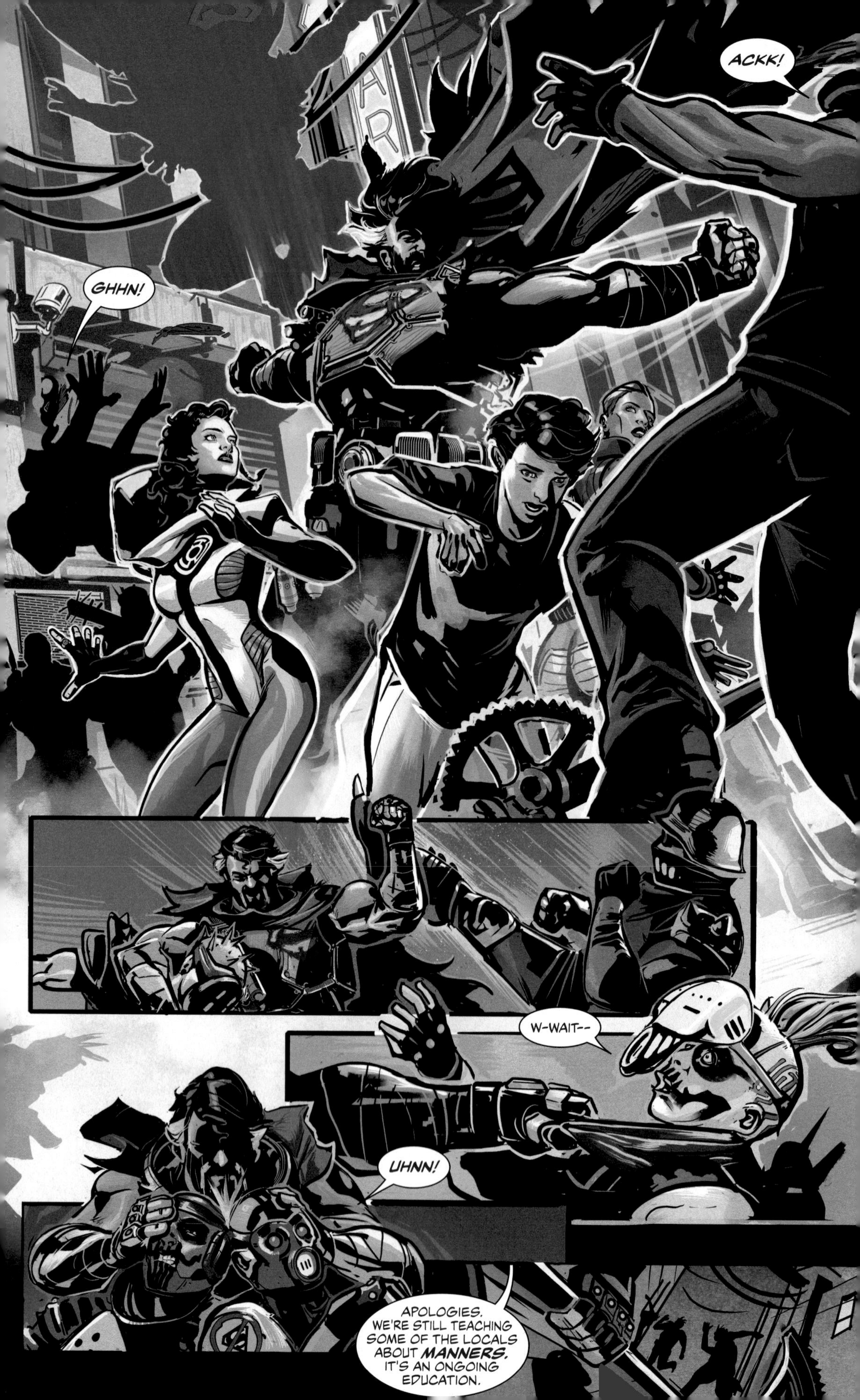
ACKK!
GHHN!
W-WAIT--
UHNN!
APOLOGIES. WE'RE STILL TEACHING SOME OF THE LOCALS ABOUT **MANNERS.** IT'S AN ONGOING EDUCATION.

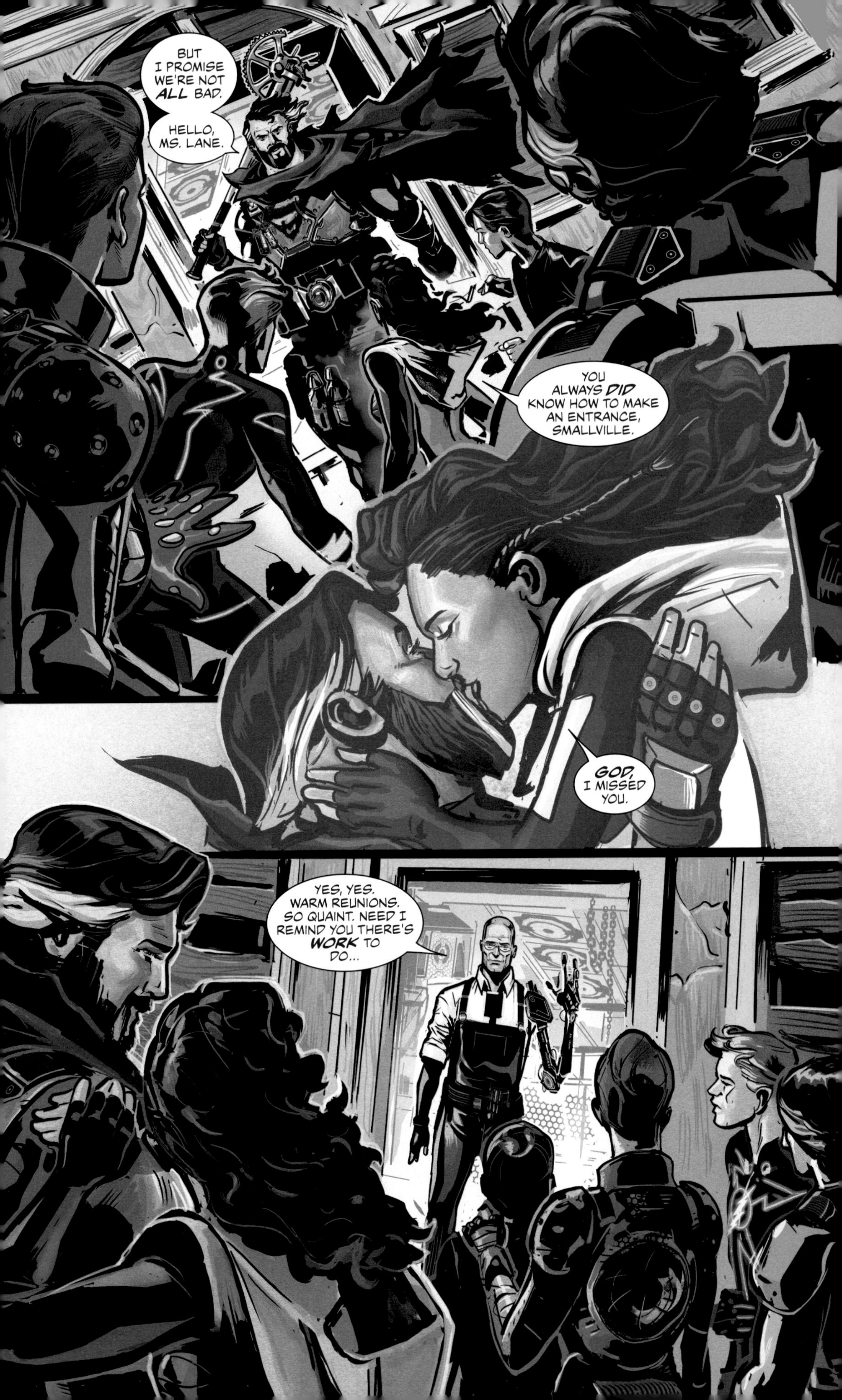
BUT I PROMISE WE'RE NOT ALL BAD.
HELLO, MS. LANE.
YOU ALWAYS DID KNOW HOW TO MAKE AN ENTRANCE, SMALLVILLE.
GOD, I MISSED YOU.
YES, YES. WARM REUNIONS. SO QUAINT. NEED I REMIND YOU THERE'S WORK TO DO...

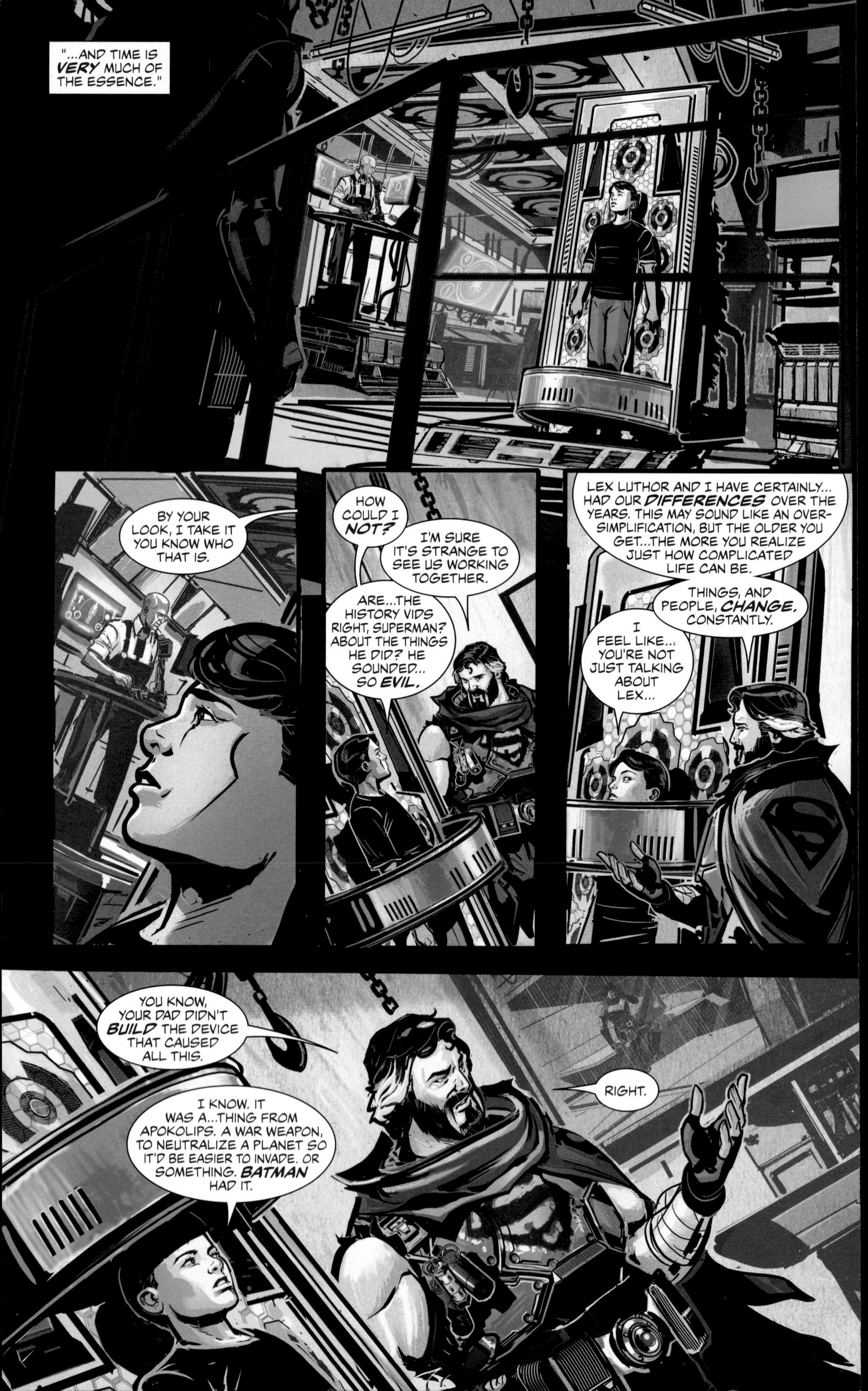
"...AND TIME IS VERY MUCH OF THE ESSENCE."
BY YOUR LOOK, I TAKE IT YOU KNOW WHO THAT IS.
HOW COULD I NOT?
I'M SURE IT'S STRANGE TO SEE US WORKING TOGETHER.
ARE...THE HISTORY VIDS RIGHT, SUPERMAN? ABOUT THE THINGS HE DID? HE SOUNDED... SO EVIL.
LEX LUTHOR AND I HAVE CERTAINLY... HAD OUR DIFFERENCES OVER THE YEARS. THIS MAY SOUND LIKE AN OVER-SIMPLIFICATION, BUT THE OLDER YOU GET...THE MORE YOU REALIZE JUST HOW COMPLICATED LIFE CAN BE.
THINGS, AND PEOPLE, CHANGE. CONSTANTLY.
I FEEL LIKE... YOU'RE NOT JUST TALKING ABOUT LEX...
YOU KNOW, YOUR DAD DIDN'T BUILD THE DEVICE THAT CAUSED ALL THIS.
RIGHT.
I KNOW. IT WAS A...THING FROM APOKOLIPS. A WAR WEAPON, TO NEUTRALIZE A PLANET SO IT'D BE EASIER TO INVADE. OR SOMETHING. BATMAN HAD IT.

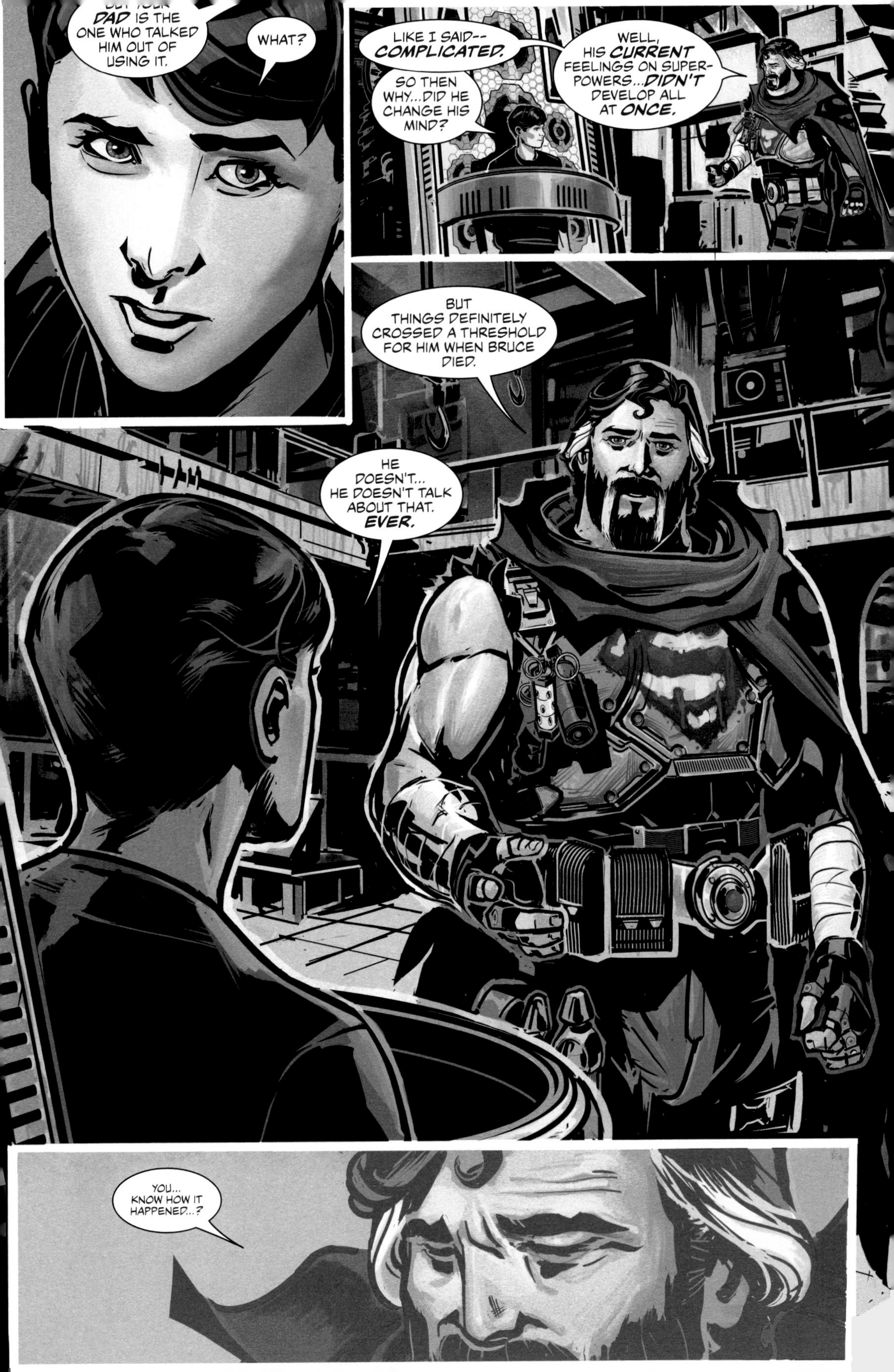
DAD IS THE ONE WHO TALKED HIM OUT OF USING IT.
WHAT?
LIKE I SAID-- COMPLICATED.
SO THEN WHY...DID HE CHANGE HIS MIND?
WELL, HIS CURRENT FEELINGS ON SUPER-POWERS...DIDN'T DEVELOP ALL AT ONCE.
BUT THINGS DEFINITELY CROSSED A THRESHOLD FOR HIM WHEN BRUCE DIED.
HE DOESN'T... HE DOESN'T TALK ABOUT THAT. EVER.
YOU... KNOW HOW IT HAPPENED...?

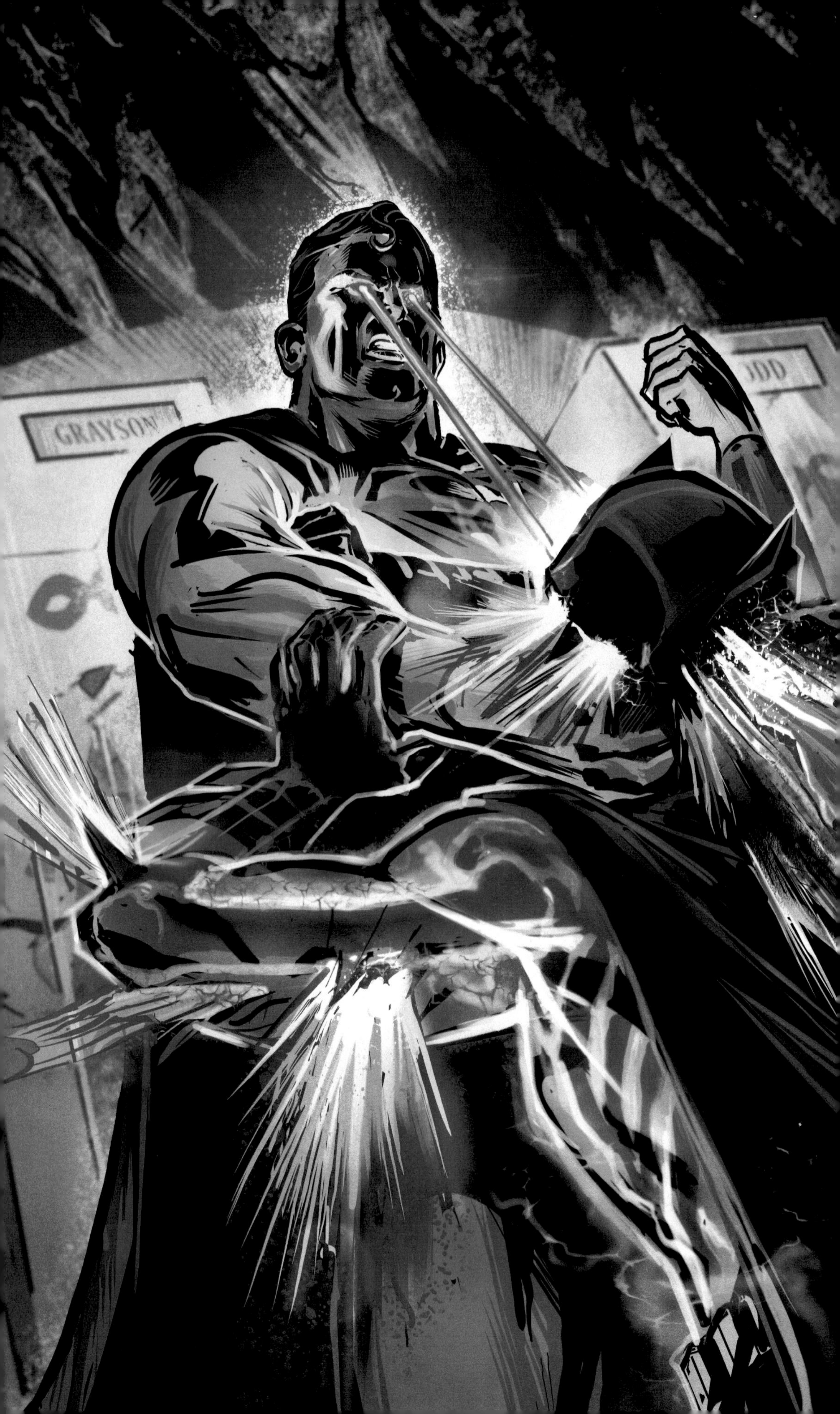
GRAYSON

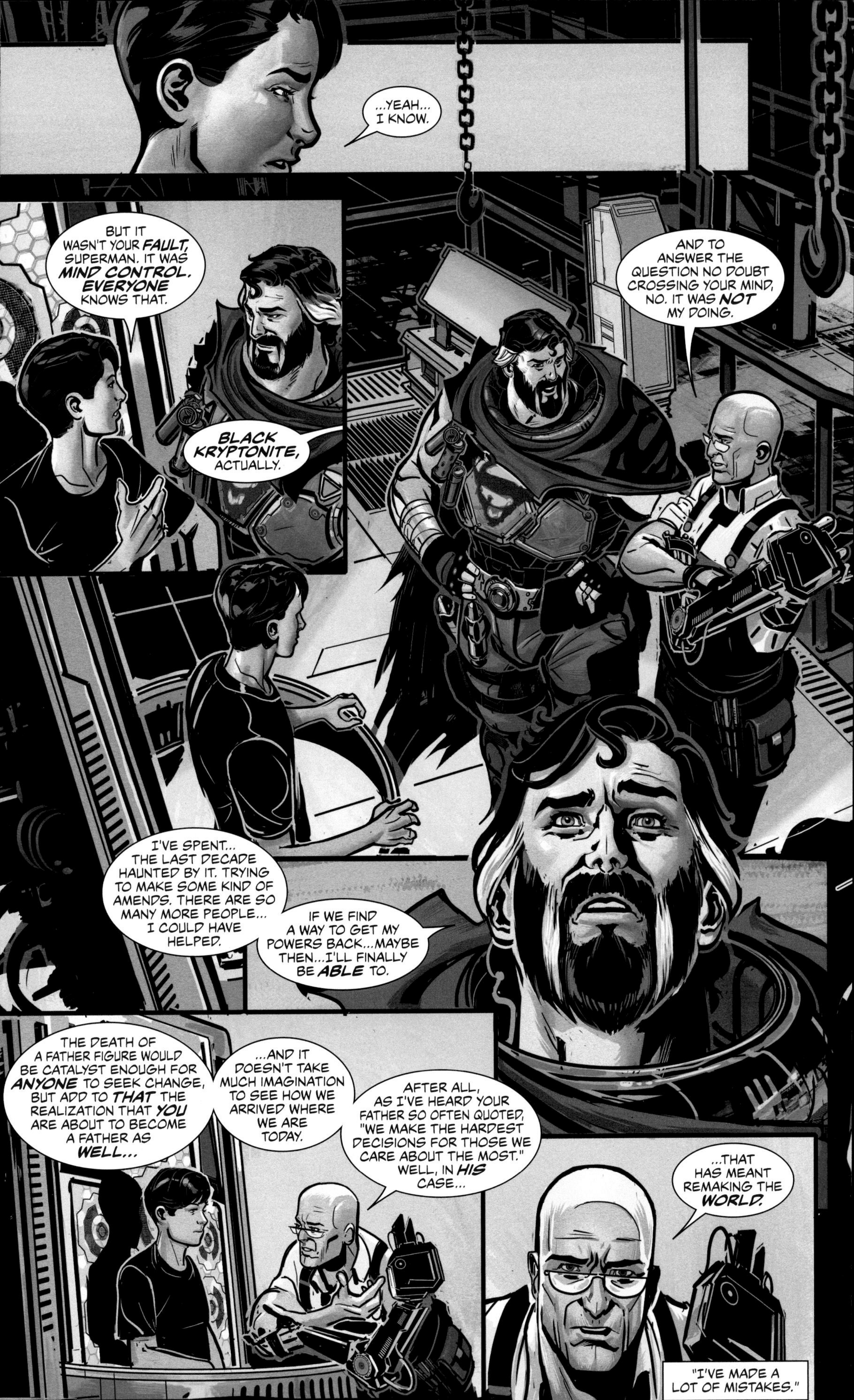
...YEAH... I KNOW.
BUT IT WASN'T YOUR FAULT, SUPERMAN. IT WAS MIND CONTROL. EVERYONE KNOWS THAT.
BLACK KRYPTONITE, ACTUALLY.
AND TO ANSWER THE QUESTION NO DOUBT CROSSING YOUR MIND, NO. IT WAS NOT MY DOING.
I'VE SPENT... THE LAST DECADE HAUNTED BY IT. TRYING TO MAKE SOME KIND OF AMENDS. THERE ARE SO MANY MORE PEOPLE... I COULD HAVE HELPED.
IF WE FIND A WAY TO GET MY POWERS BACK...MAYBE THEN...I'LL FINALLY BE ABLE TO.
THE DEATH OF A FATHER FIGURE WOULD BE CATALYST ENOUGH FOR ANYONE TO SEEK CHANGE, BUT ADD TO THAT THE REALIZATION THAT YOU ARE ABOUT TO BECOME A FATHER AS WELL...
...AND IT DOESN'T TAKE MUCH IMAGINATION TO SEE HOW WE ARRIVED WHERE WE ARE TODAY.
AFTER ALL, AS I'VE HEARD YOUR FATHER SO OFTEN QUOTED, "WE MAKE THE HARDEST DECISIONS FOR THOSE WE CARE ABOUT THE MOST." WELL, IN HIS CASE...
...THAT HAS MEANT REMAKING THE WORLD.
"I'VE MADE A LOT OF MISTAKES."

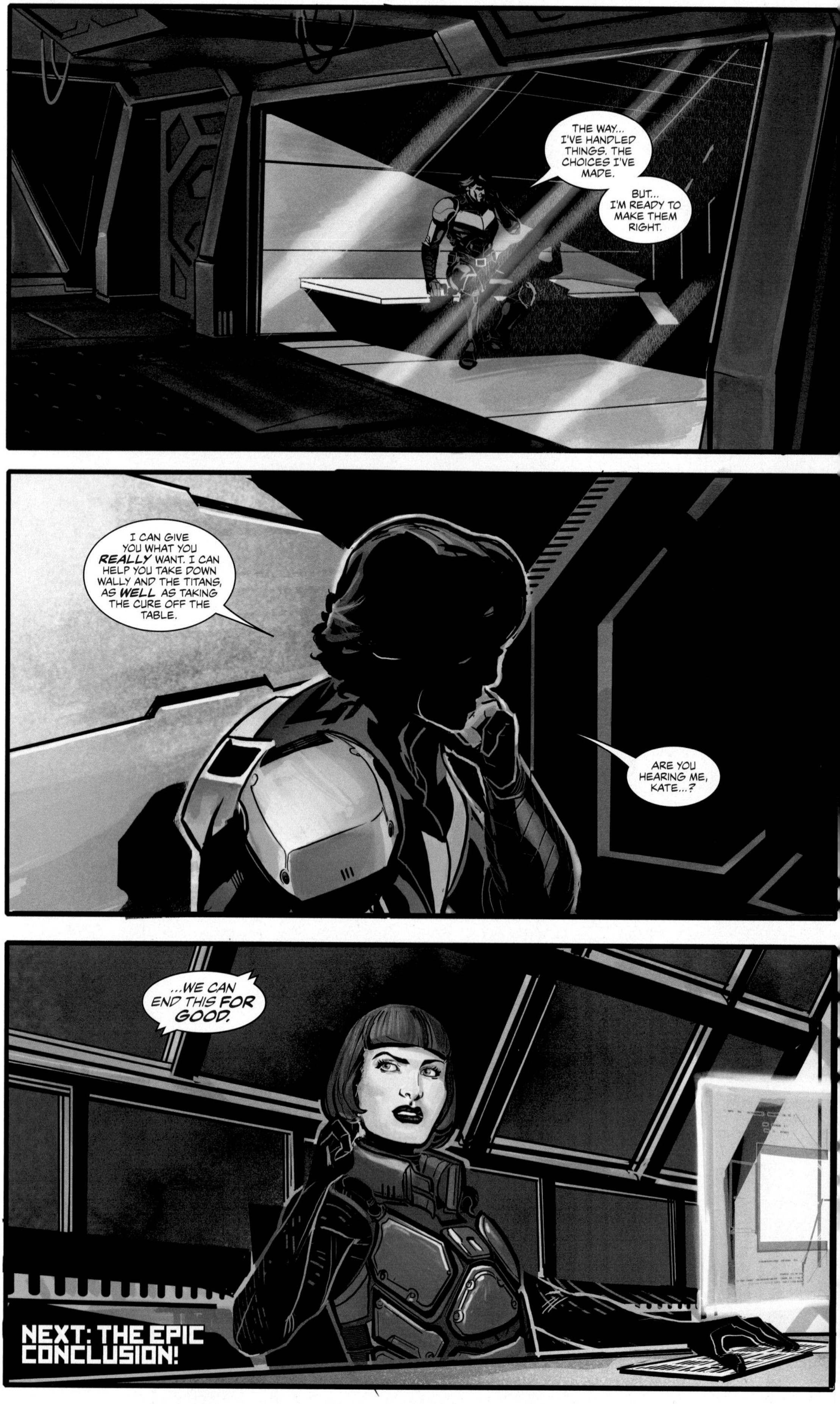
THE WAY... I'VE HANDLED THINGS. THE CHOICES I'VE MADE.
BUT... I'M READY TO MAKE THEM RIGHT.
I CAN GIVE YOU WHAT YOU REALLY WANT. I CAN HELP YOU TAKE DOWN WALLY AND THE TITANS, AS WELL AS TAKING THE CURE OFF THE TABLE.
ARE YOU HEARING ME, KATE...?
...WE CAN END THIS FOR GOOD.
NEXT: THE EPIC CONCLUSION!

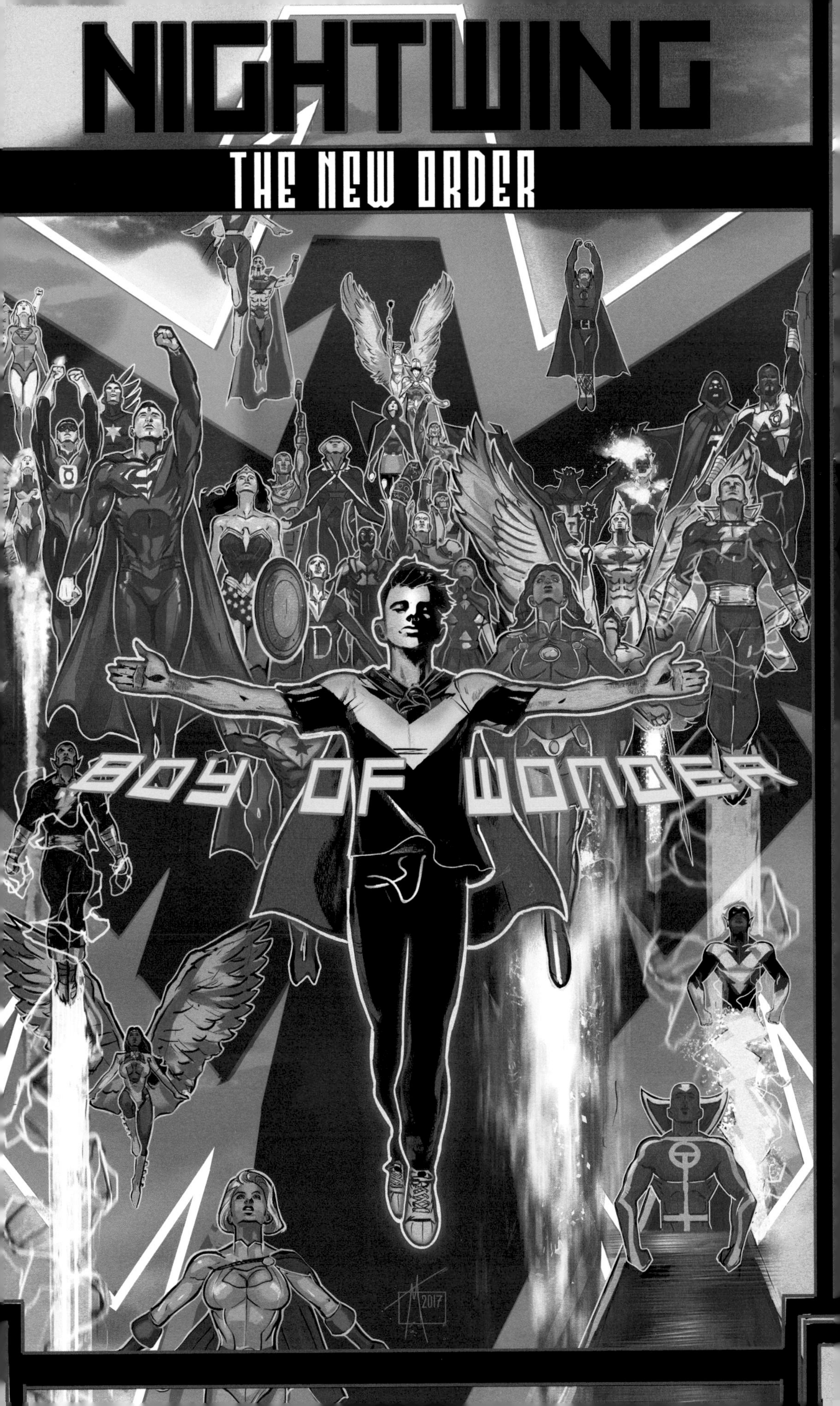
NIGHTWING
THE NEW ORDER
BOY OF WONDER
2017

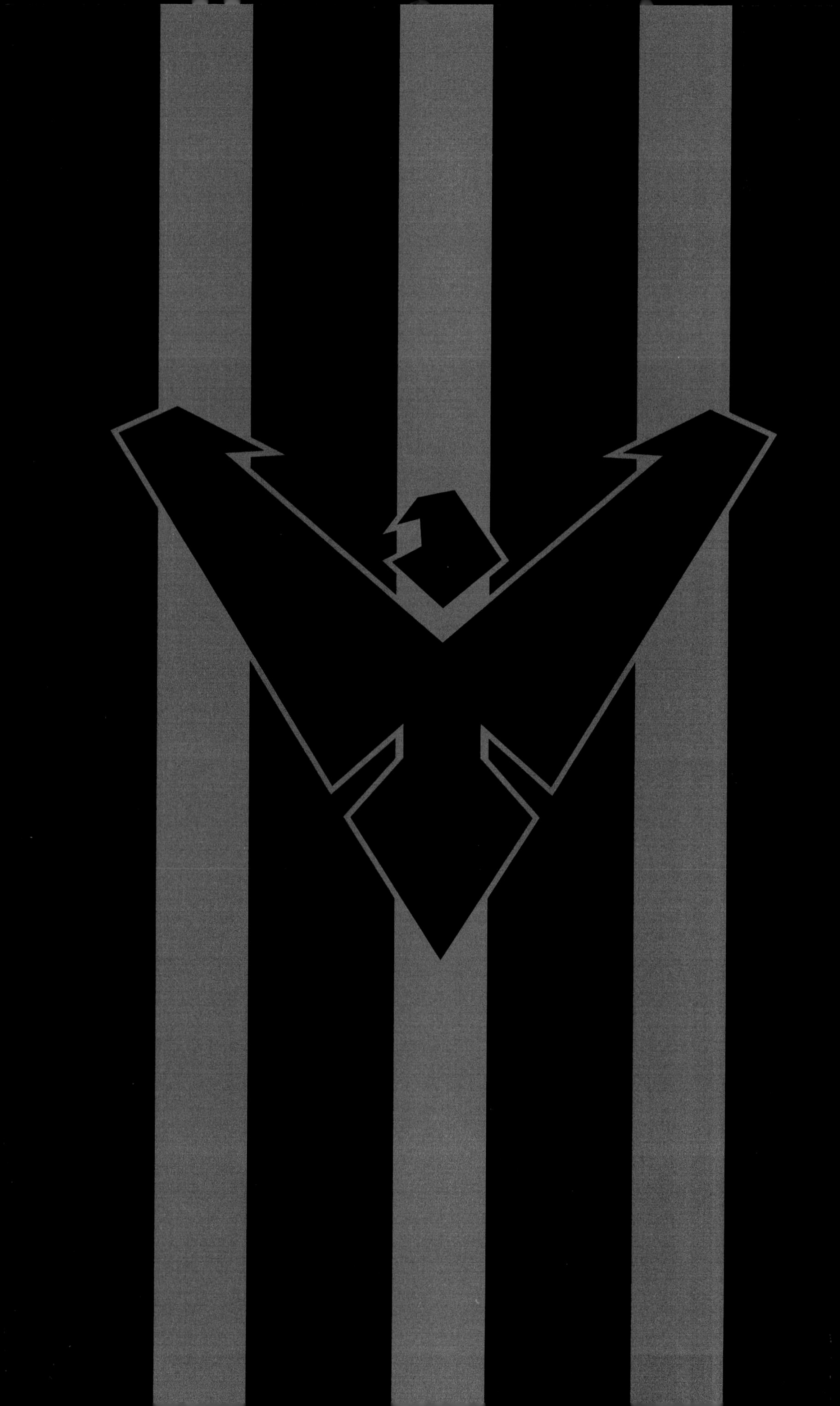

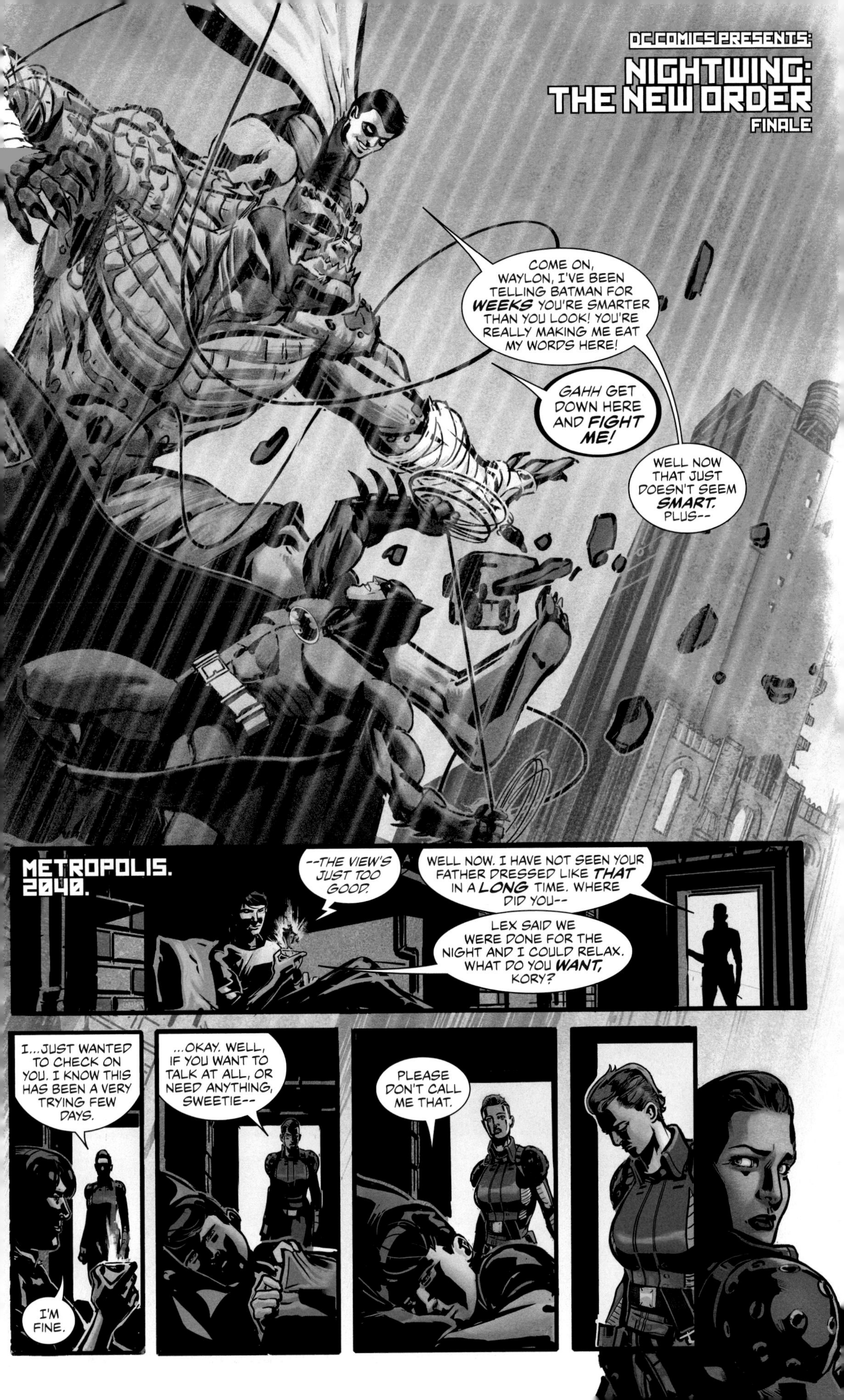
DC COMICS PRESENTS:
NIGHTWING: THE NEW ORDER
FINALE
COME ON, WAYLON, I'VE BEEN TELLING BATMAN FOR WEEKS YOU'RE SMARTER THAN YOU LOOK! YOU'RE REALLY MAKING ME EAT MY WORDS HERE!
GAHH GET DOWN HERE AND FIGHT ME!
WELL NOW THAT JUST DOESN'T SEEM SMART. PLUS--
METROPOLIS. 2040.
--THE VIEW'S JUST TOO GOOD.
WELL NOW. I HAVE NOT SEEN YOUR FATHER DRESSED LIKE THAT IN A LONG TIME. WHERE DID YOU--
LEX SAID WE WERE DONE FOR THE NIGHT AND I COULD RELAX. WHAT DO YOU WANT, KORY?
I...JUST WANTED TO CHECK ON YOU. I KNOW THIS HAS BEEN A VERY TRYING FEW DAYS.
I'M FINE.
...OKAY. WELL, IF YOU WANT TO TALK AT ALL, OR NEED ANYTHING, SWEETIE--
PLEASE DON'T CALL ME THAT.

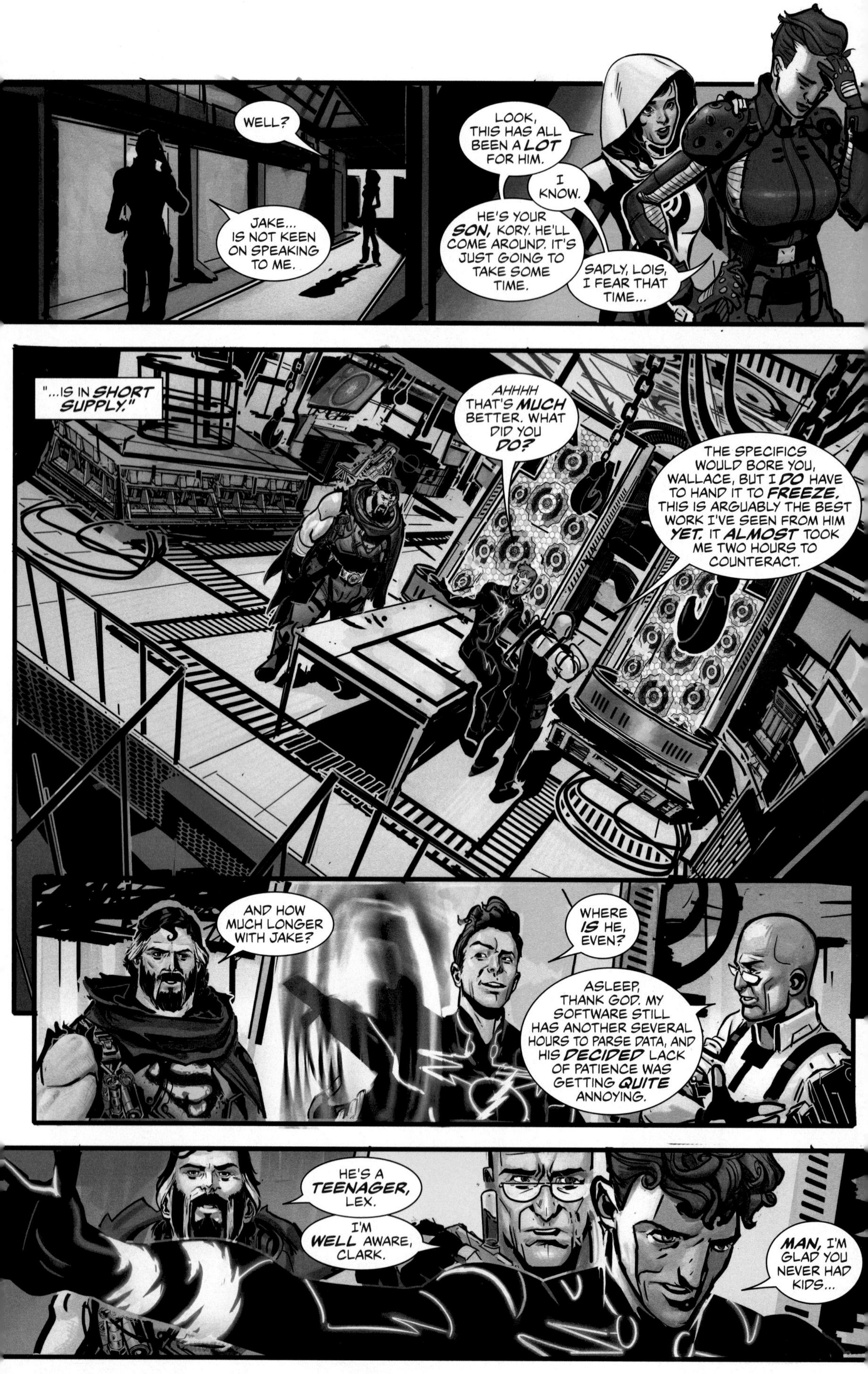
WELL?
JAKE... IS NOT KEEN ON SPEAKING TO ME.
LOOK, THIS HAS ALL BEEN A LOT FOR HIM.
I KNOW.
HE'S YOUR SON, KORY. HE'LL COME AROUND. IT'S JUST GOING TO TAKE SOME TIME.
SADLY, LOIS, I FEAR THAT TIME...
"...IS IN SHORT SUPPLY."
AHHHH THAT'S MUCH BETTER. WHAT DID YOU DO?
THE SPECIFICS WOULD BORE YOU, WALLACE, BUT I DO HAVE TO HAND IT TO FREEZE. THIS IS ARGUABLY THE BEST WORK I'VE SEEN FROM HIM YET. IT ALMOST TOOK ME TWO HOURS TO COUNTERACT.
AND HOW MUCH LONGER WITH JAKE?
WHERE IS HE, EVEN?
ASLEEP, THANK GOD. MY SOFTWARE STILL HAS ANOTHER SEVERAL HOURS TO PARSE DATA, AND HIS DECIDED LACK OF PATIENCE WAS GETTING QUITE ANNOYING.
HE'S A TEENAGER, LEX.
I'M WELL AWARE, CLARK.
MAN, I'M GLAD YOU NEVER HAD KIDS...

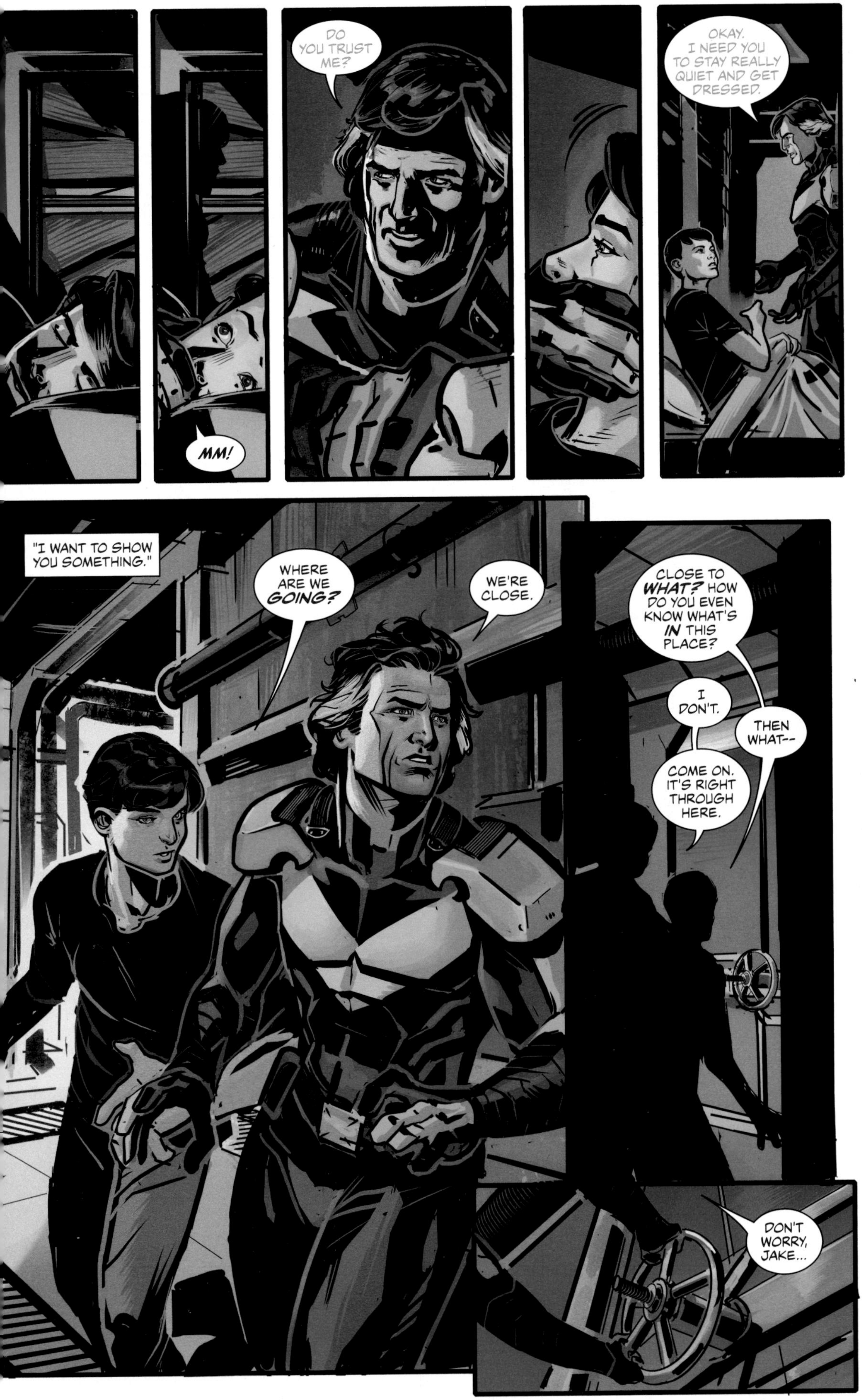
MM!
DO YOU TRUST ME?
OKAY. I NEED YOU TO STAY REALLY QUIET AND GET DRESSED.
"I WANT TO SHOW YOU SOMETHING."
WHERE ARE WE GOING?
WE'RE CLOSE.
CLOSE TO WHAT? HOW DO YOU EVEN KNOW WHAT'S IN THIS PLACE?
I DON'T.
THEN WHAT--
COME ON. IT'S RIGHT THROUGH HERE.
DON'T WORRY, JAKE...

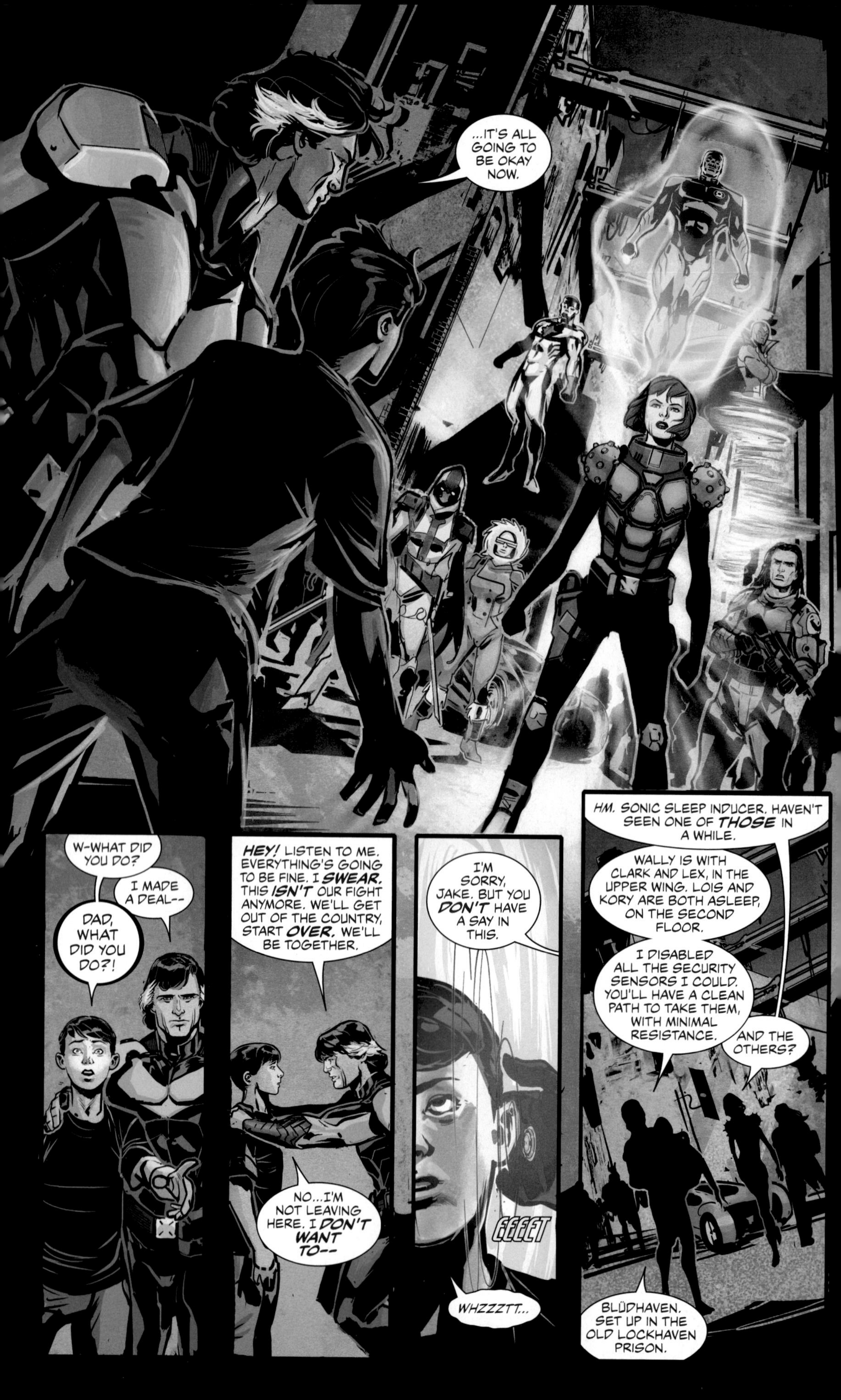

...IT'S ALL GOING TO BE OKAY NOW.
W-WHAT DID YOU DO?
I MADE A DEAL--
DAD, WHAT DID YOU DO?!
HEY! LISTEN TO ME. EVERYTHING'S GOING TO BE FINE. I SWEAR. THIS ISN'T OUR FIGHT ANYMORE. WE'LL GET OUT OF THE COUNTRY, START OVER. WE'LL BE TOGETHER.
NO...I'M NOT LEAVING HERE. I DON'T WANT TO--
I'M SORRY, JAKE. BUT YOU DON'T HAVE A SAY IN THIS.
EEEET
WHZZZTT...
HM. SONIC SLEEP INDUCER. HAVEN'T SEEN ONE OF THOSE IN A WHILE.
WALLY IS WITH CLARK AND LEX, IN THE UPPER WING. LOIS AND KORY ARE BOTH ASLEEP, ON THE SECOND FLOOR.
I DISABLED ALL THE SECURITY SENSORS I COULD. YOU'LL HAVE A CLEAN PATH TO TAKE THEM, WITH MINIMAL RESISTANCE.
AND THE OTHERS?
BLÜDHAVEN. SET UP IN THE OLD LOCKHAVEN PRISON.

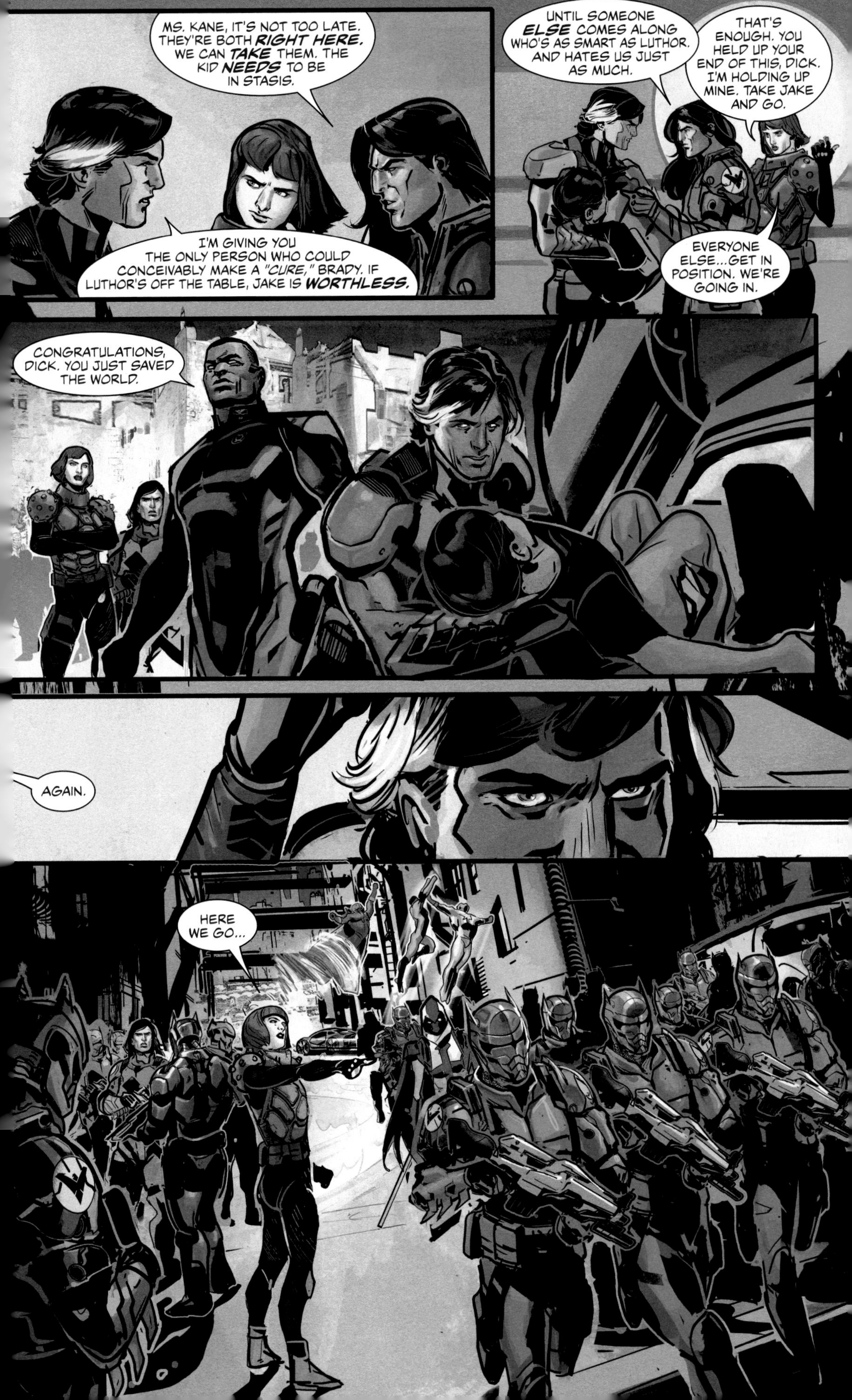

MS. KANE, IT'S NOT TOO LATE. THEY'RE BOTH RIGHT HERE. WE CAN TAKE THEM. THE KID NEEDS TO BE IN STASIS.
I'M GIVING YOU THE ONLY PERSON WHO COULD CONCEIVABLY MAKE A "CURE," BRADY. IF LUTHOR'S OFF THE TABLE, JAKE IS WORTHLESS.
UNTIL SOMEONE ELSE COMES ALONG WHO'S AS SMART AS LUTHOR. AND HATES US JUST AS MUCH.
THAT'S ENOUGH. YOU HELD UP YOUR END OF THIS, DICK. I'M HOLDING UP MINE. TAKE JAKE AND GO.
EVERYONE ELSE...GET IN POSITION. WE'RE GOING IN.
CONGRATULATIONS, DICK. YOU JUST SAVED THE WORLD.
AGAIN.
HERE WE GO...

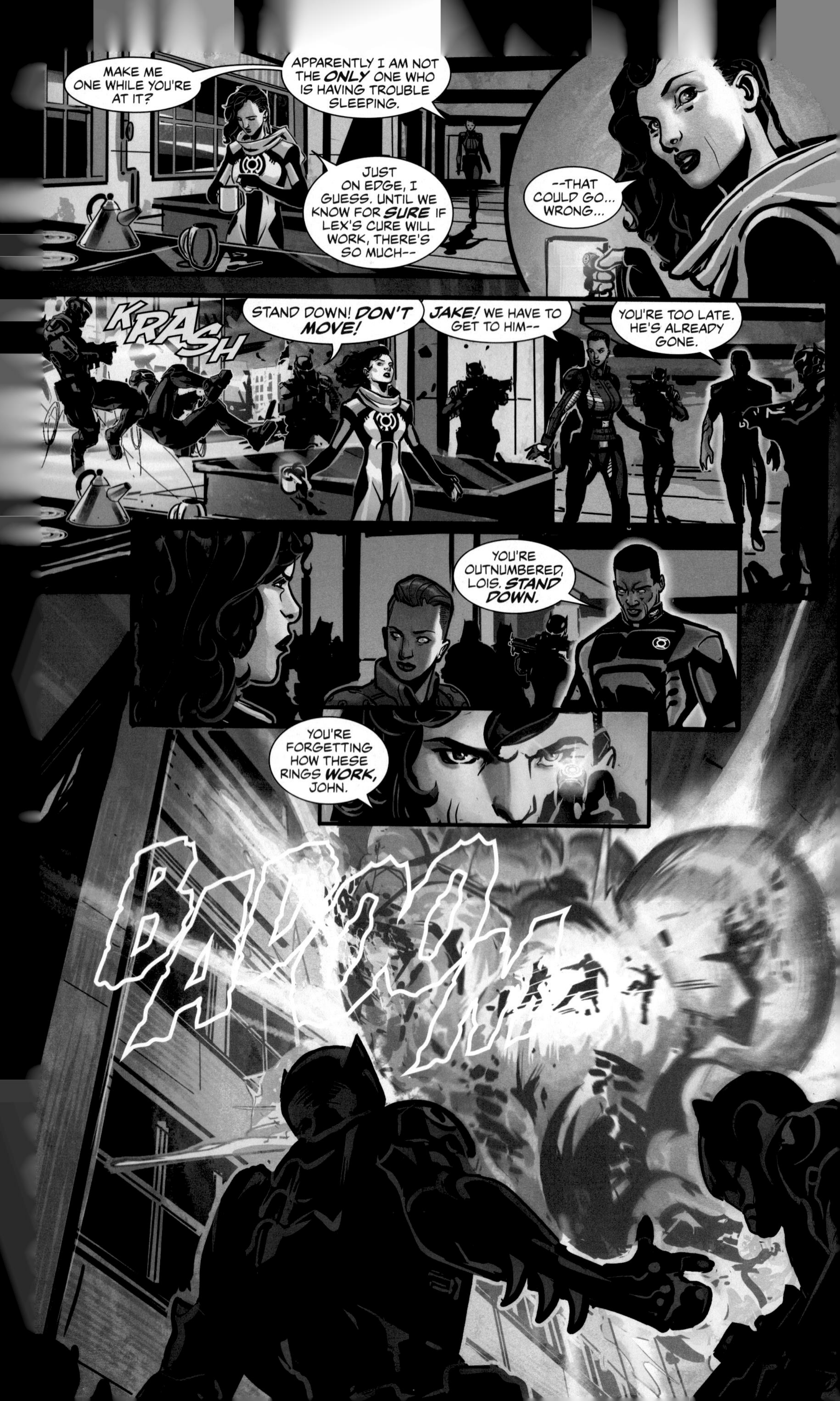
MAKE ME ONE WHILE YOU'RE AT IT?
APPARENTLY I AM NOT THE ONLY ONE WHO IS HAVING TROUBLE SLEEPING.
JUST ON EDGE, I GUESS. UNTIL WE KNOW FOR SURE IF LEX'S CURE WILL WORK, THERE'S SO MUCH--
--THAT COULD GO... WRONG...
KRASH
STAND DOWN! DON'T MOVE!
JAKE! WE HAVE TO GET TO HIM--
YOU'RE TOO LATE. HE'S ALREADY GONE.
YOU'RE OUTNUMBERED, LOIS. STAND DOWN.
YOU'RE FORGETTING HOW THESE RINGS WORK, JOHN.

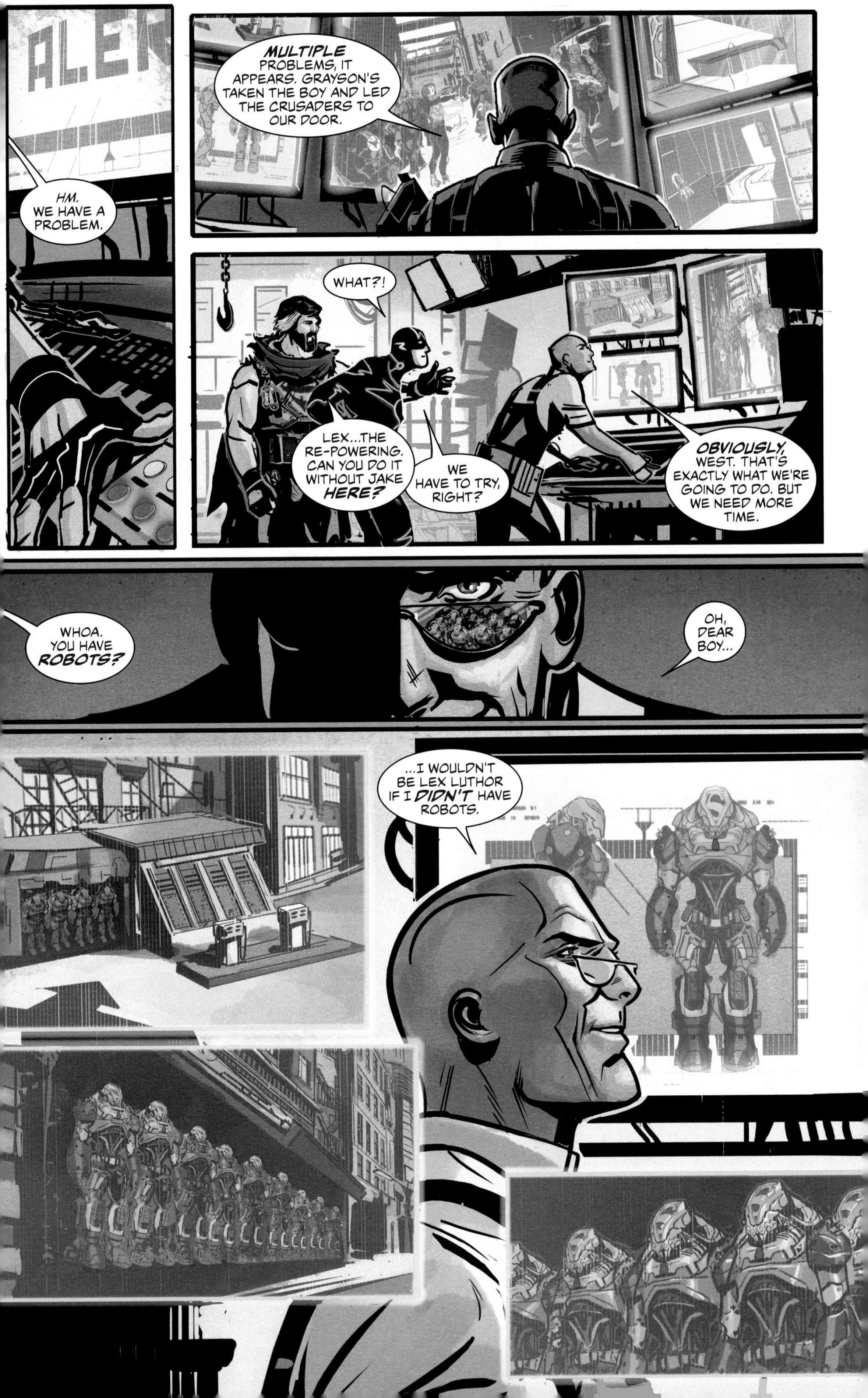
HM. WE HAVE A PROBLEM.
MULTIPLE PROBLEMS, IT APPEARS. GRAYSON'S TAKEN THE BOY AND LED THE CRUSADERS TO OUR DOOR.
WHAT?!
LEX...THE RE-POWERING. CAN YOU DO IT WITHOUT JAKE HERE?
WE HAVE TO TRY, RIGHT?
OBVIOUSLY, WEST. THAT'S EXACTLY WHAT WE'RE GOING TO DO. BUT WE NEED MORE TIME.
WHOA. YOU HAVE ROBOTS?
OH, DEAR BOY...
...I WOULDN'T BE LEX LUTHOR IF I DIDN'T HAVE ROBOTS.
ALE

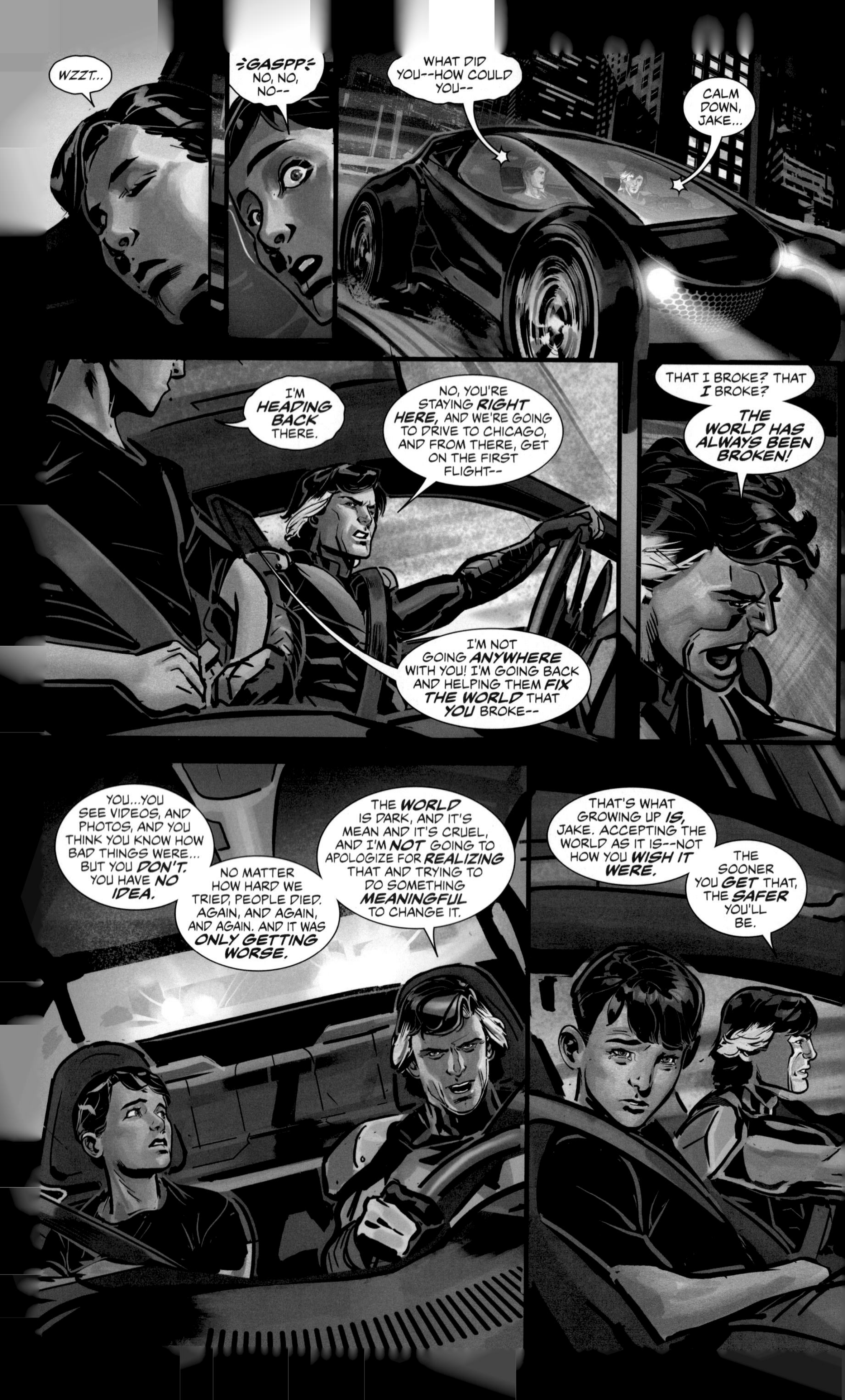
WZZT...
GASPP NO, NO, NO--
WHAT DID YOU--HOW COULD YOU--
CALM DOWN, JAKE...
I'M HEADING BACK THERE.
NO, YOU'RE STAYING RIGHT HERE, AND WE'RE GOING TO DRIVE TO CHICAGO, AND FROM THERE, GET ON THE FIRST FLIGHT--
I'M NOT GOING ANYWHERE WITH YOU! I'M GOING BACK AND HELPING THEM FIX THE WORLD THAT YOU BROKE--
THAT I BROKE? THAT I BROKE?
THE WORLD HAS ALWAYS BEEN BROKEN!
YOU...YOU SEE VIDEOS, AND PHOTOS, AND YOU THINK YOU KNOW HOW BAD THINGS WERE... BUT YOU DON'T. YOU HAVE NO IDEA.
NO MATTER HOW HARD WE TRIED, PEOPLE DIED. AGAIN, AND AGAIN, AND AGAIN. AND IT WAS ONLY GETTING WORSE.
THE WORLD IS DARK, AND IT'S MEAN AND IT'S CRUEL, AND I'M NOT GOING TO APOLOGIZE FOR REALIZING THAT AND TRYING TO DO SOMETHING MEANINGFUL TO CHANGE IT.
THAT'S WHAT GROWING UP IS, JAKE. ACCEPTING THE WORLD AS IT IS--NOT HOW YOU WISH IT WERE.
THE SOONER YOU GET THAT, THE SAFER YOU'LL BE.

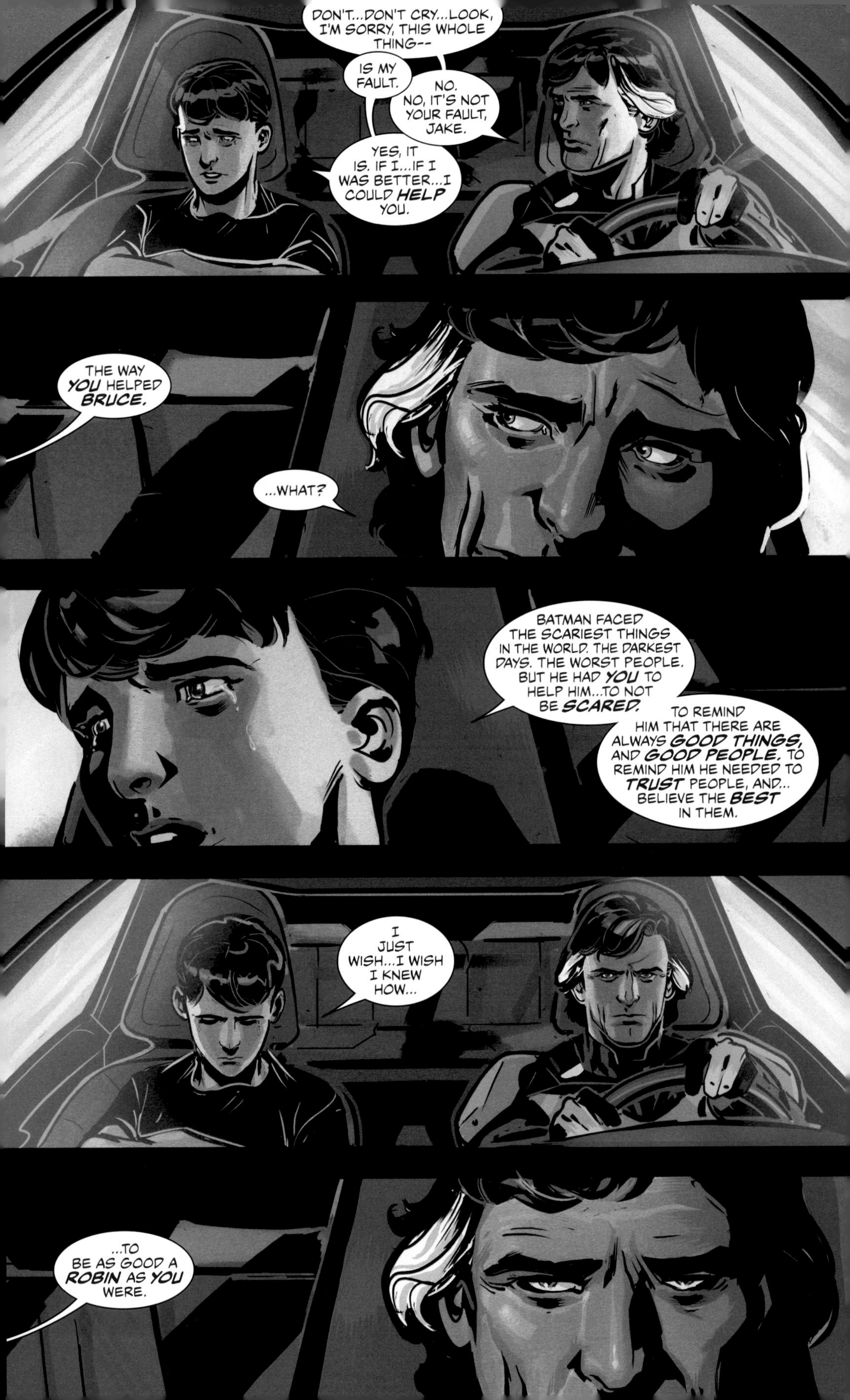
DON'T...DON'T CRY...LOOK, I'M SORRY, THIS WHOLE THING--
IS MY FAULT.
NO. NO, IT'S NOT YOUR FAULT, JAKE.
YES, IT IS. IF I...IF I WAS BETTER...I COULD HELP YOU.
THE WAY YOU HELPED BRUCE.
...WHAT?
BATMAN FACED THE SCARIEST THINGS IN THE WORLD. THE DARKEST DAYS. THE WORST PEOPLE. BUT HE HAD YOU TO HELP HIM...TO NOT BE SCARED.
TO REMIND HIM THAT THERE ARE ALWAYS GOOD THINGS, AND GOOD PEOPLE. TO REMIND HIM HE NEEDED TO TRUST PEOPLE, AND... BELIEVE THE BEST IN THEM.
I JUST WISH...I WISH I KNEW HOW...
...TO BE AS GOOD A ROBIN AS YOU WERE.

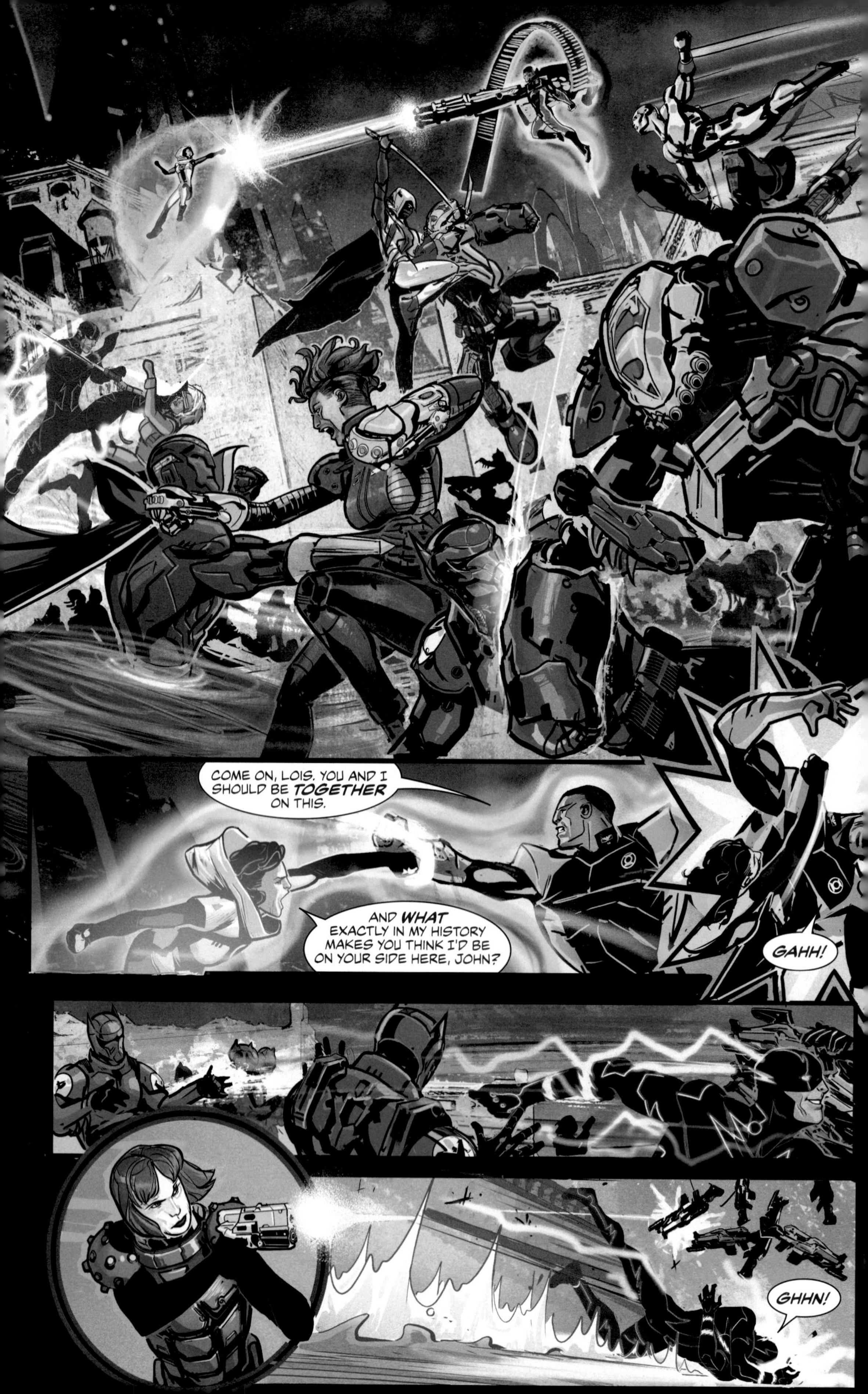
COME ON, LOIS. YOU AND I SHOULD BE TOGETHER ON THIS.
AND WHAT EXACTLY IN MY HISTORY MAKES YOU THINK I'D BE ON YOUR SIDE HERE, JOHN?
GAHH!
GHHN!

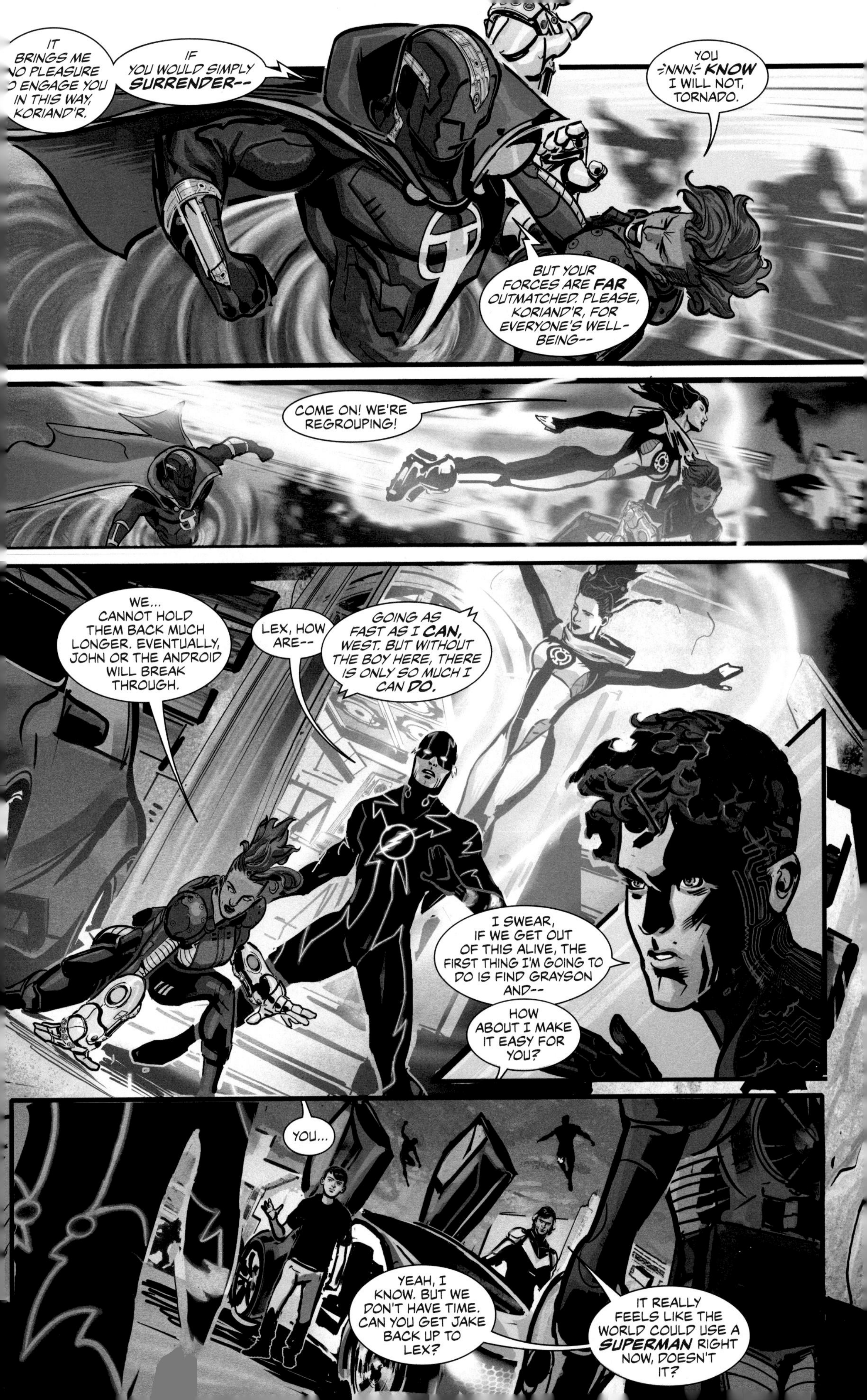

IT BRINGS ME NO PLEASURE TO ENGAGE YOU IN THIS WAY, KORIAND'R.
IF YOU WOULD SIMPLY SURRENDER--
YOU -NNN- KNOW I WILL NOT, TORNADO.
BUT YOUR FORCES ARE FAR OUTMATCHED. PLEASE, KORIAND'R, FOR EVERYONE'S WELL-BEING--
COME ON! WE'RE REGROUPING!
WE... CANNOT HOLD THEM BACK MUCH LONGER. EVENTUALLY, JOHN OR THE ANDROID WILL BREAK THROUGH.
LEX, HOW ARE--
GOING AS FAST AS I CAN, WEST. BUT WITHOUT THE BOY HERE, THERE IS ONLY SO MUCH I CAN DO.
I SWEAR, IF WE GET OUT OF THIS ALIVE, THE FIRST THING I'M GOING TO DO IS FIND GRAYSON AND--
HOW ABOUT I MAKE IT EASY FOR YOU?
YOU...
YEAH, I KNOW. BUT WE DON'T HAVE TIME. CAN YOU GET JAKE BACK UP TO LEX?
IT REALLY FEELS LIKE THE WORLD COULD USE A SUPERMAN RIGHT NOW, DOESN'T IT?

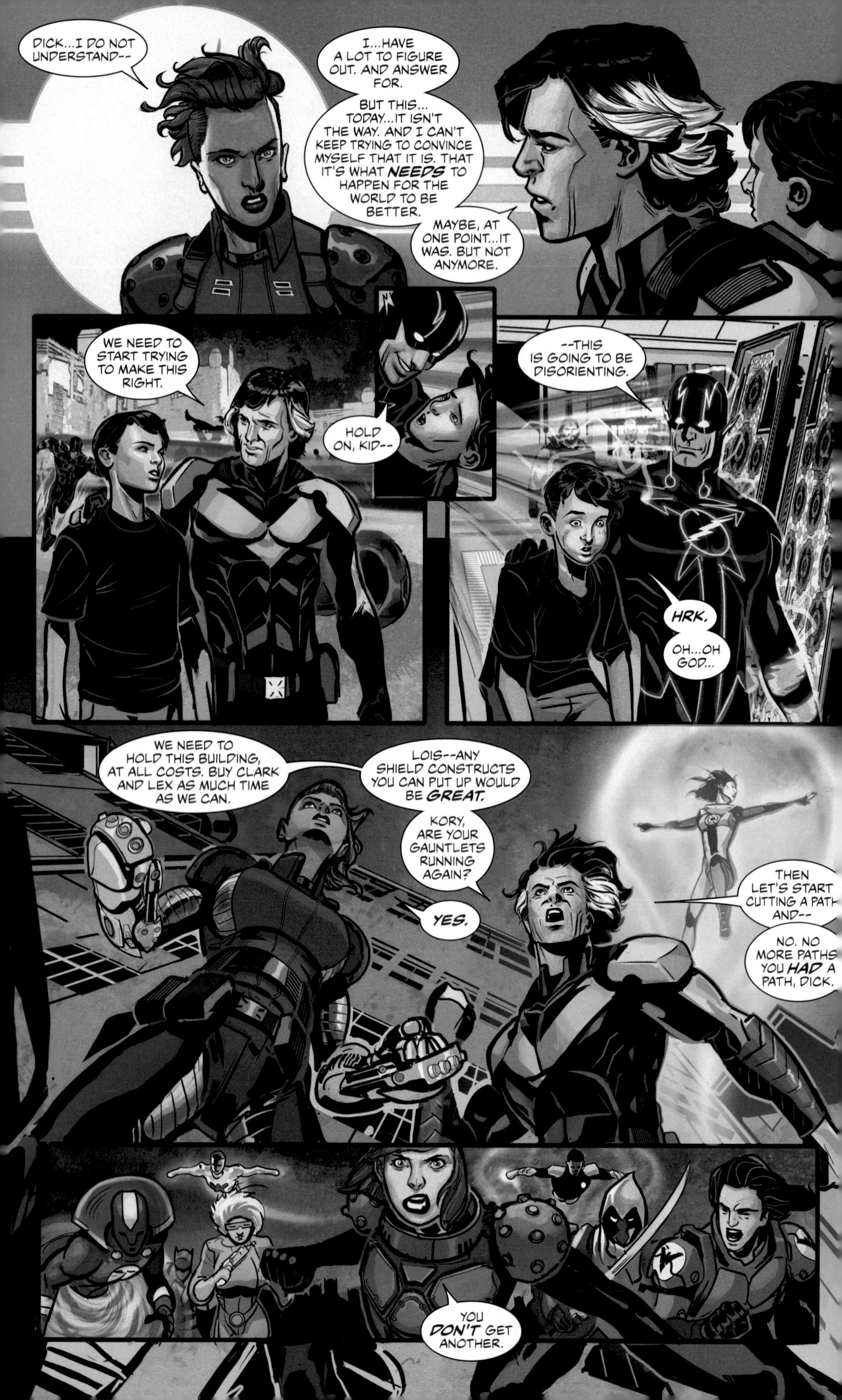
DICK...I DO NOT UNDERSTAND--
I...HAVE A LOT TO FIGURE OUT. AND ANSWER FOR.
BUT THIS... TODAY...IT ISN'T THE WAY. AND I CAN'T KEEP TRYING TO CONVINCE MYSELF THAT IT IS. THAT IT'S WHAT NEEDS TO HAPPEN FOR THE WORLD TO BE BETTER.
MAYBE, AT ONE POINT...IT WAS. BUT NOT ANYMORE.
WE NEED TO START TRYING TO MAKE THIS RIGHT.
HOLD ON, KID--
--THIS IS GOING TO BE DISORIENTING.
HRK.
OH...OH GOD...
WE NEED TO HOLD THIS BUILDING, AT ALL COSTS. BUY CLARK AND LEX AS MUCH TIME AS WE CAN.
LOIS--ANY SHIELD CONSTRUCTS YOU CAN PUT UP WOULD BE GREAT.
KORY, ARE YOUR GAUNTLETS RUNNING AGAIN?
YES.
THEN LET'S START CUTTING A PATH AND--
NO. NO MORE PATHS. YOU HAD A PATH, DICK.
YOU DON'T GET ANOTHER.

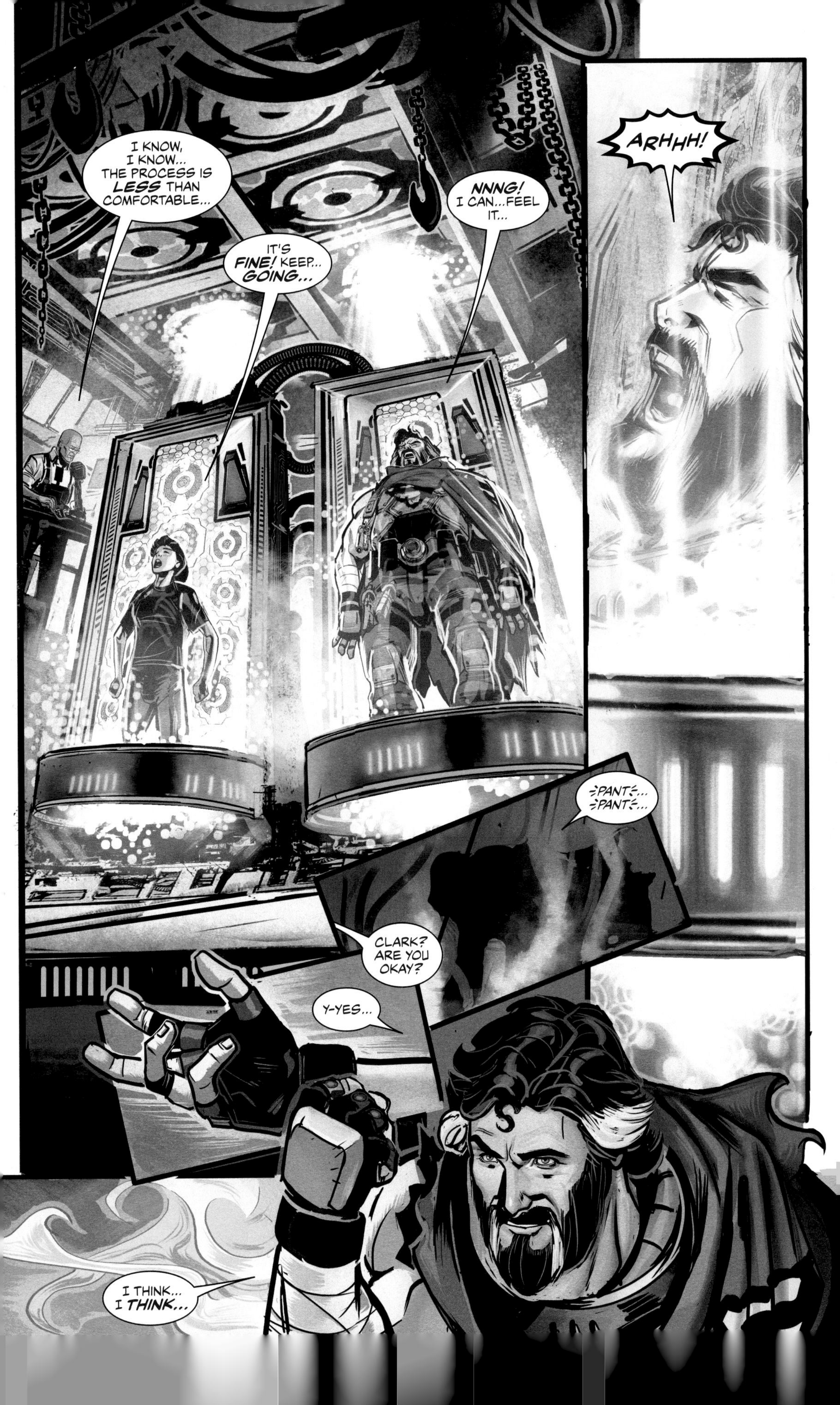

I KNOW, I KNOW... THE PROCESS IS LESS THAN COMFORTABLE...
IT'S FINE! KEEP... GOING...
NNNG! I CAN...FEEL IT...
ARHHH!
PANT... PANT...
CLARK? ARE YOU OKAY?
Y-YES...
I THINK... I THINK...

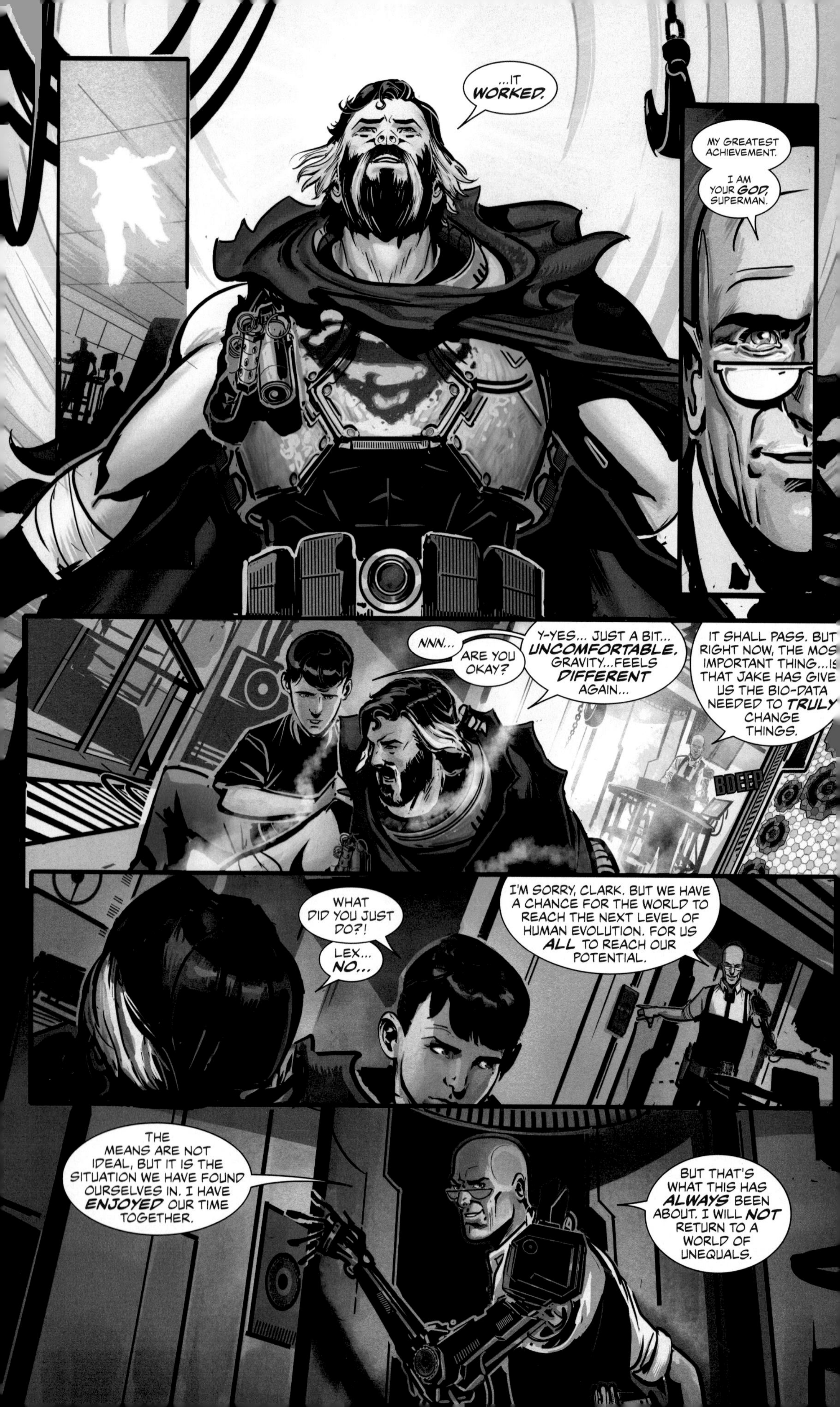
...IT WORKED.
MY GREATEST ACHIEVEMENT.
I AM YOUR GOD, SUPERMAN.
NNN...
ARE YOU OKAY?
Y-YES... JUST A BIT... UNCOMFORTABLE. GRAVITY...FEELS DIFFERENT AGAIN...
IT SHALL PASS. BUT RIGHT NOW, THE MOS IMPORTANT THING...IS THAT JAKE HAS GIVE US THE BIO-DATA NEEDED TO TRULY CHANGE THINGS.
BDEEP
WHAT DID YOU JUST DO?!
LEX... NO...
I'M SORRY, CLARK. BUT WE HAVE A CHANCE FOR THE WORLD TO REACH THE NEXT LEVEL OF HUMAN EVOLUTION. FOR US ALL TO REACH OUR POTENTIAL.
THE MEANS ARE NOT IDEAL, BUT IT IS THE SITUATION WE HAVE FOUND OURSELVES IN. I HAVE ENJOYED OUR TIME TOGETHER.
BUT THAT'S WHAT THIS HAS ALWAYS BEEN ABOUT. I WILL NOT RETURN TO A WORLD OF UNEQUALS.

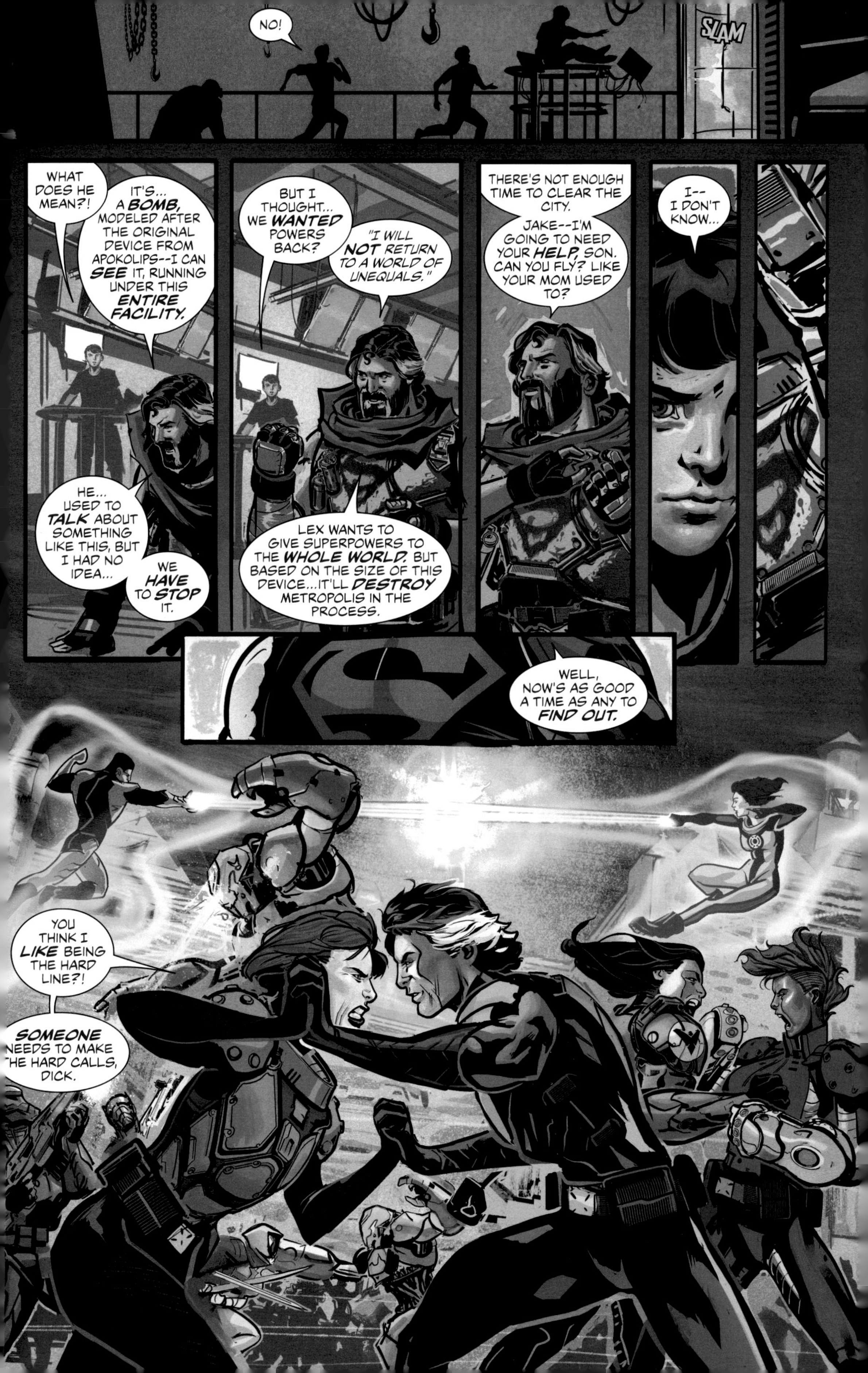
NO!
SLAM
WHAT DOES HE MEAN?!
IT'S... A BOMB, MODELED AFTER THE ORIGINAL DEVICE FROM APOKOLIPS--I CAN SEE IT, RUNNING UNDER THIS ENTIRE FACILITY.
HE... USED TO TALK ABOUT SOMETHING LIKE THIS, BUT I HAD NO IDEA...
WE HAVE TO STOP IT.
BUT I THOUGHT... WE WANTED POWERS BACK?
"I WILL NOT RETURN TO A WORLD OF UNEQUALS."
LEX WANTS TO GIVE SUPERPOWERS TO THE WHOLE WORLD. BUT BASED ON THE SIZE OF THIS DEVICE...IT'LL DESTROY METROPOLIS IN THE PROCESS.
THERE'S NOT ENOUGH TIME TO CLEAR THE CITY.
JAKE--I'M GOING TO NEED YOUR HELP, SON. CAN YOU FLY? LIKE YOUR MOM USED TO?
I-- I DON'T KNOW...
WELL, NOW'S AS GOOD A TIME AS ANY TO FIND OUT.
YOU THINK I LIKE BEING THE HARD LINE?!
SOMEONE NEEDS TO MAKE THE HARD CALLS, DICK.

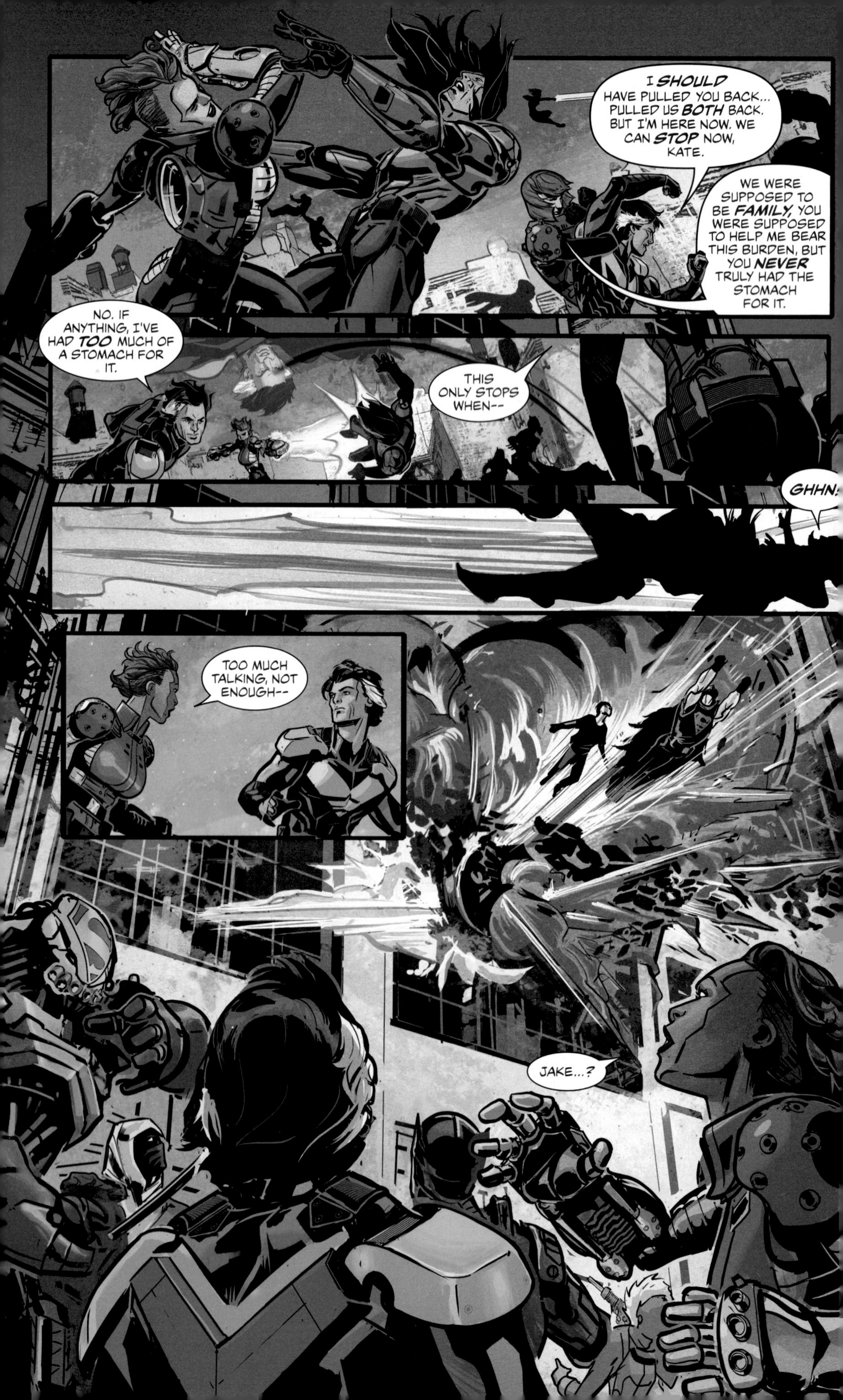
I SHOULD HAVE PULLED YOU BACK... PULLED US BOTH BACK. BUT I'M HERE NOW. WE CAN STOP NOW, KATE.
WE WERE SUPPOSED TO BE FAMILY, YOU WERE SUPPOSED TO HELP ME BEAR THIS BURDEN, BUT YOU NEVER TRULY HAD THE STOMACH FOR IT.
NO. IF ANYTHING, I'VE HAD TOO MUCH OF A STOMACH FOR IT.
THIS ONLY STOPS WHEN--
GHHN!
TOO MUCH TALKING, NOT ENOUGH--
JAKE...?

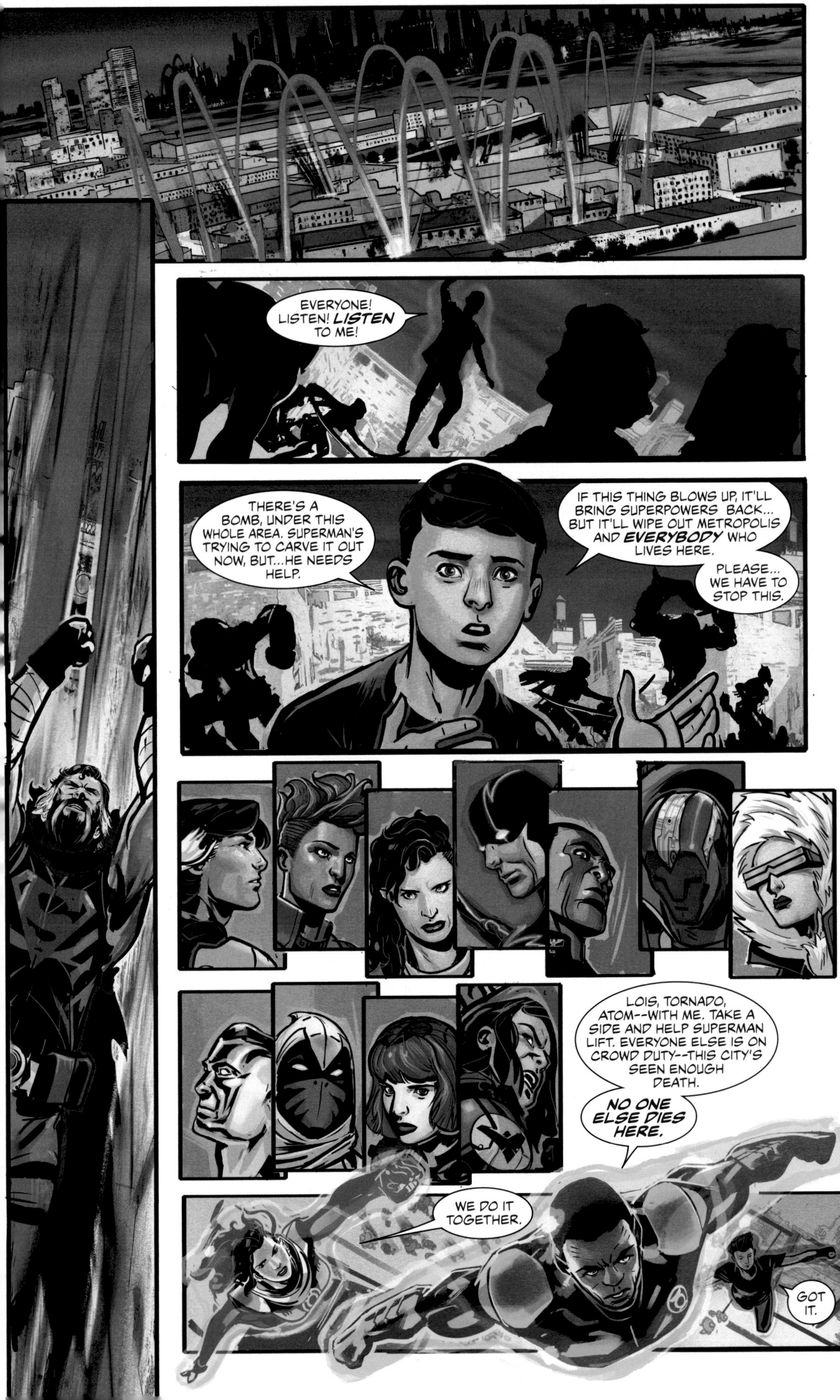
EVERYONE! LISTEN! LISTEN TO ME!
THERE'S A BOMB, UNDER THIS WHOLE AREA. SUPERMAN'S TRYING TO CARVE IT OUT NOW, BUT...HE NEEDS HELP.
IF THIS THING BLOWS UP, IT'LL BRING SUPERPOWERS BACK... BUT IT'LL WIPE OUT METROPOLIS AND EVERYBODY WHO LIVES HERE.
PLEASE... WE HAVE TO STOP THIS.
LOIS, TORNADO, ATOM--WITH ME. TAKE A SIDE AND HELP SUPERMAN LIFT. EVERYONE ELSE IS ON CROWD DUTY--THIS CITY'S SEEN ENOUGH DEATH.
NO ONE ELSE DIES HERE.
WE DO IT TOGETHER.
GOT IT.

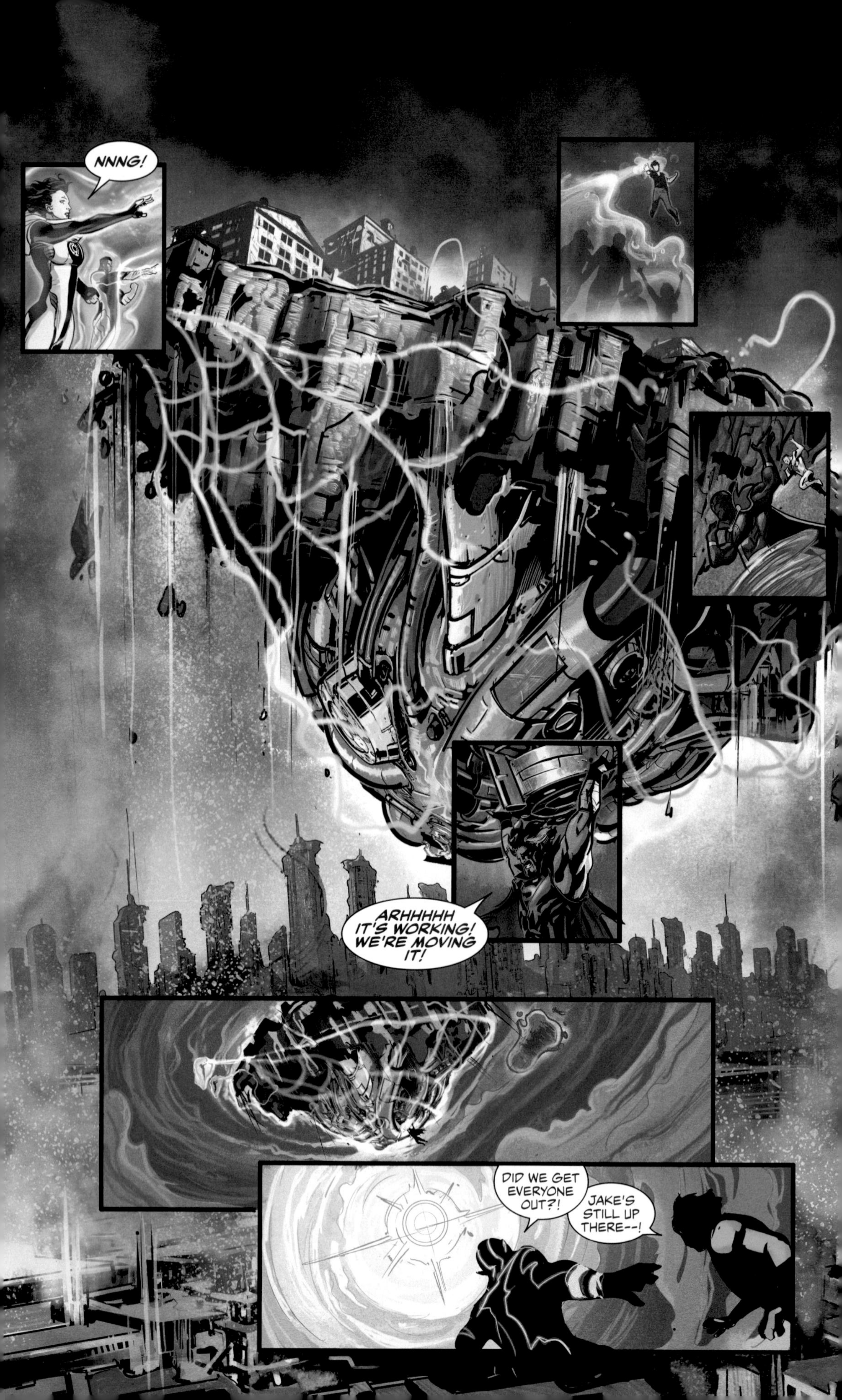
NNNG!
ARHHHHH IT'S WORKING! WE'RE MOVING IT!
DID WE GET EVERYONE OUT?!
JAKE'S STILL UP THERE--!

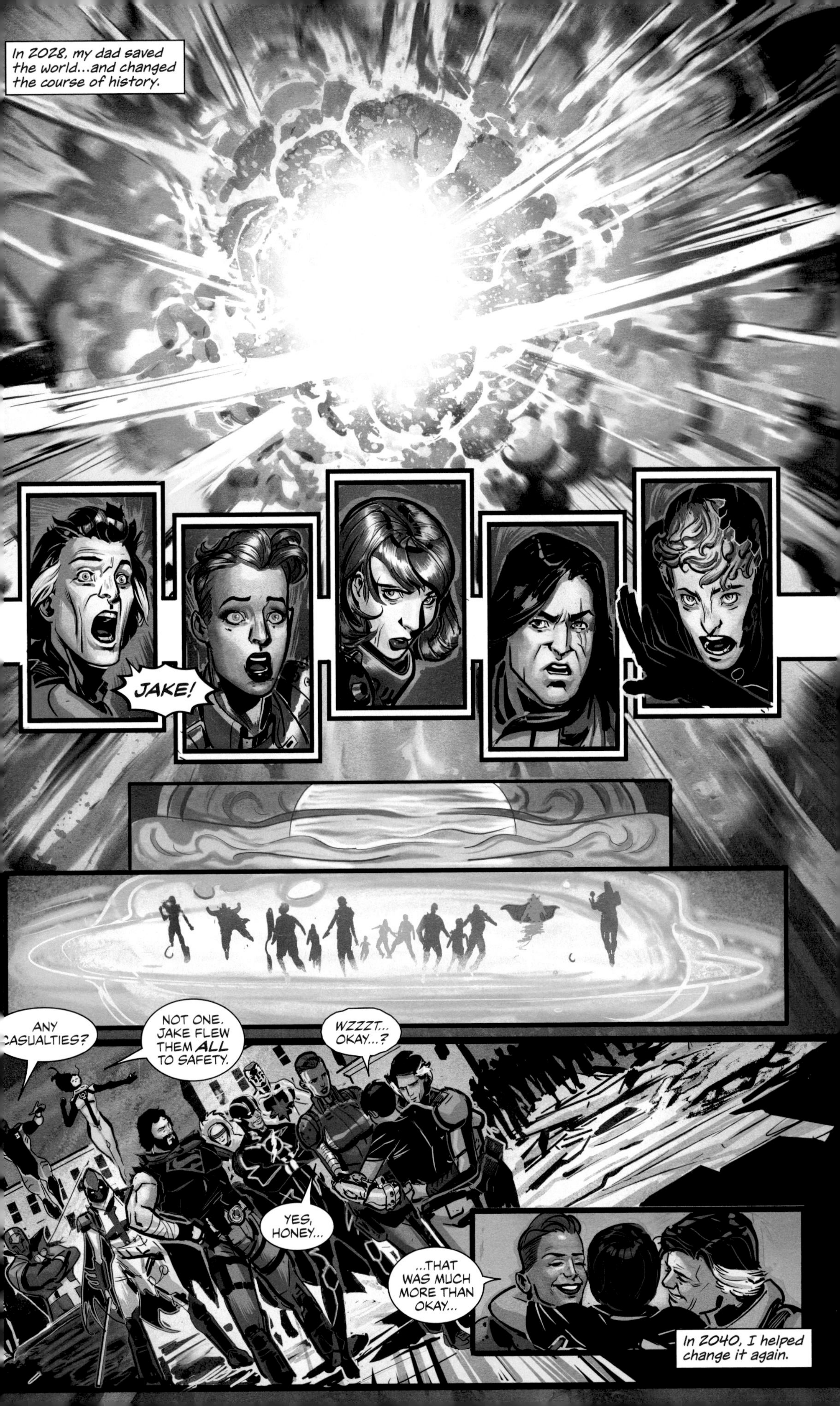
In 2028, my dad saved the world...and changed the course of history.
JAKE!
ANY CASUALTIES?
NOT ONE. JAKE FLEW THEM ALL TO SAFETY.
WZZZT... OKAY...?
YES, HONEY...
...THAT WAS MUCH MORE THAN OKAY...
In 2040, I helped change it again.

With the knowledge that Lex had uncovered, powers started coming back, slowly.

But while they were still illegal for the next five years, thanks to funding initiated by the Alfred Pennyworth Foundation...the legistlation outlawing them was eventually repealed.

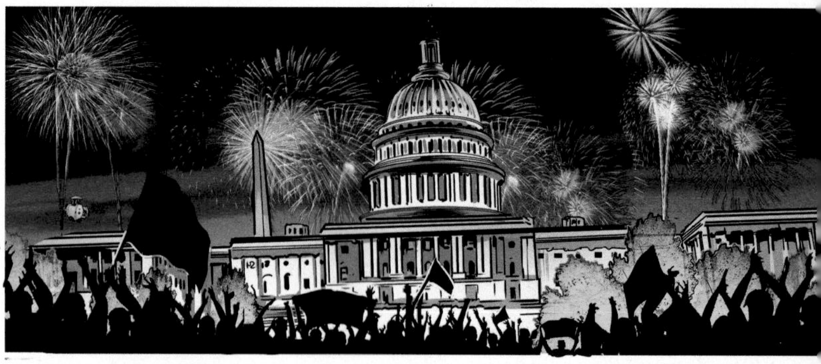

Kate Kane retired shortly after.

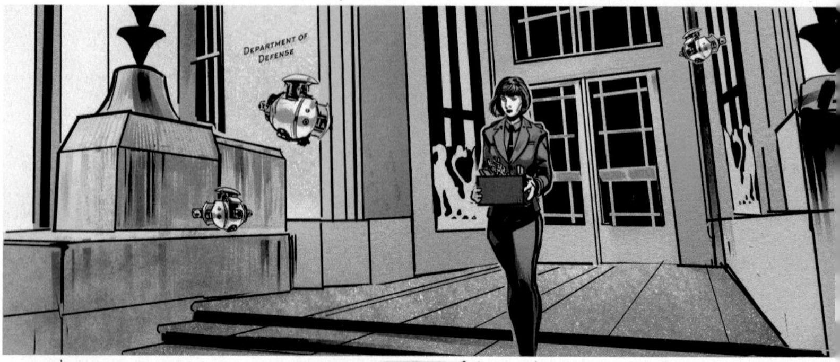
DEPARTMENT OF DEFENSE

The Crusaders still operated--helping to regulate powers--but without my dad. It was the start of a new era and a new generation.

Liz finally getting "promoted" reflected that.

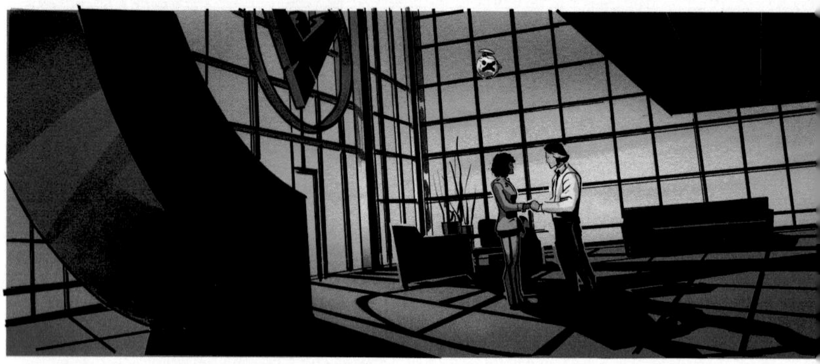

Mom and Dad stayed friends, as best they could. For all their differences, they both loved me unconditionally. And they were **there** for me. Always.

In fact, after I graduated... it was Dad who had the idea for us to work together.

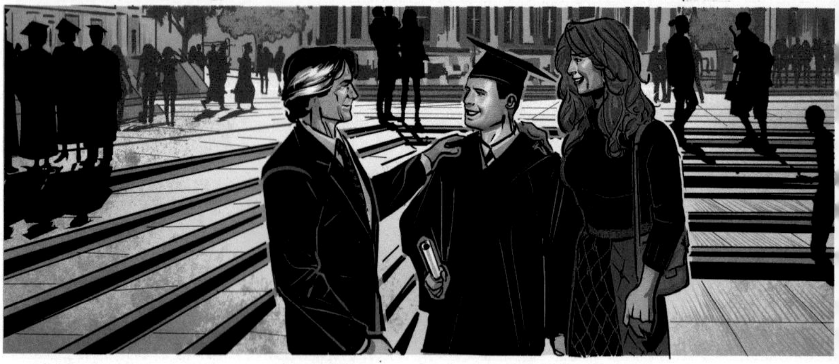

He spent his remaining days teaching kids with powers how to control them.

It was, in a lot of ways, how he tried to atone for the things he'd done.

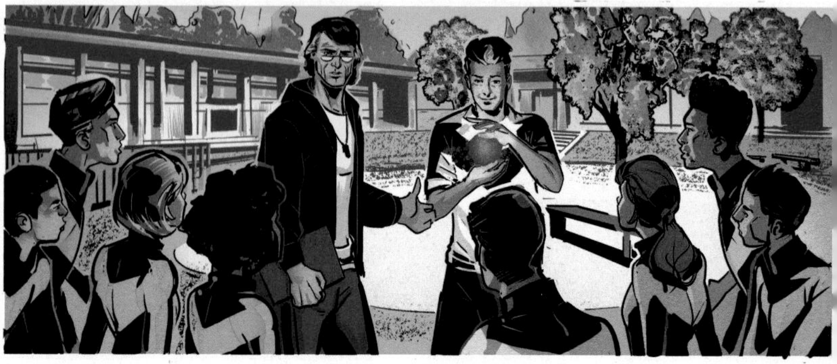

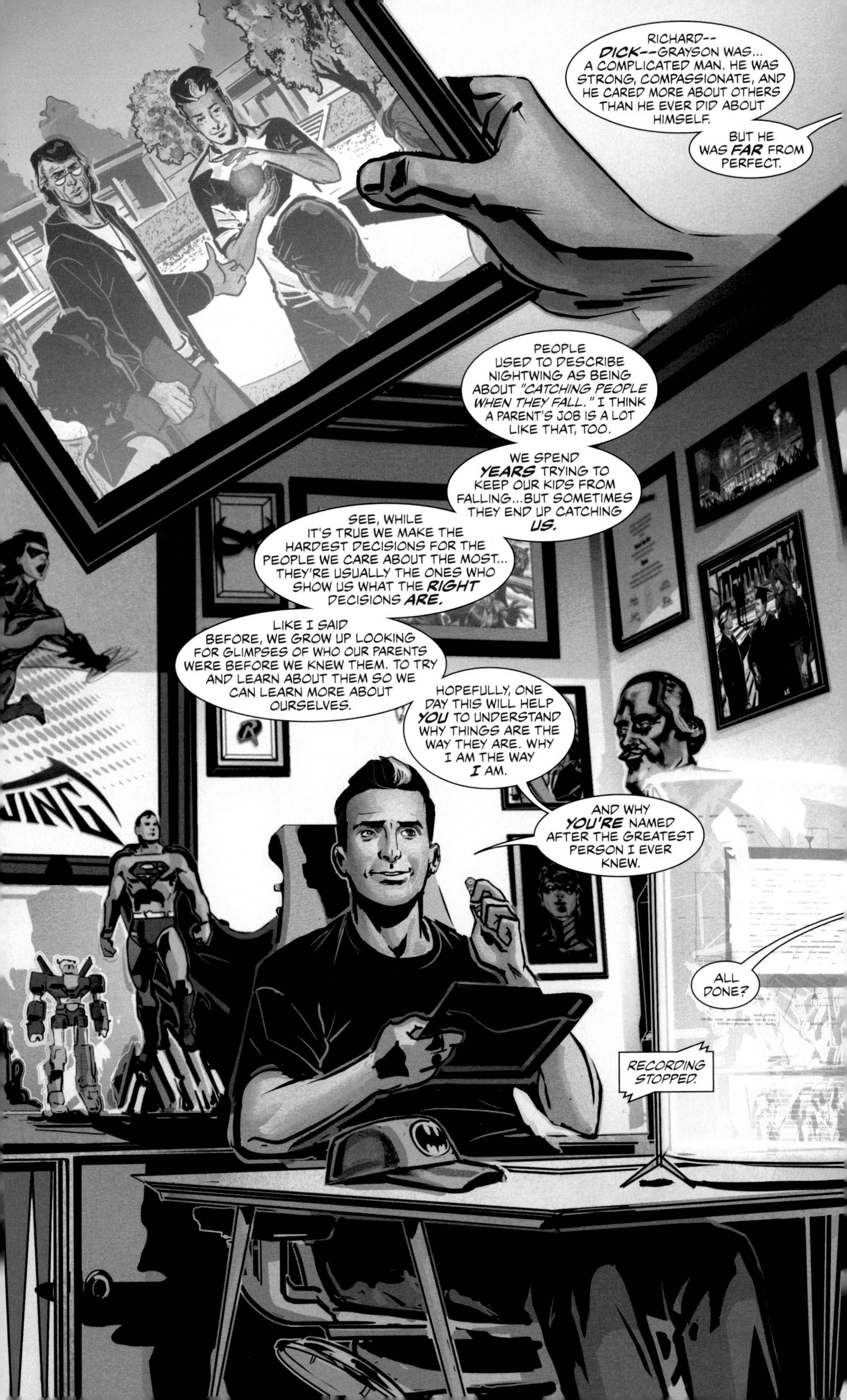
RICHARD--DICK--GRAYSON WAS... A COMPLICATED MAN. HE WAS STRONG, COMPASSIONATE, AND HE CARED MORE ABOUT OTHERS THAN HE EVER DID ABOUT HIMSELF.
BUT HE WAS FAR FROM PERFECT.
PEOPLE USED TO DESCRIBE NIGHTWING AS BEING ABOUT "CATCHING PEOPLE WHEN THEY FALL." I THINK A PARENT'S JOB IS A LOT LIKE THAT, TOO.
WE SPEND YEARS TRYING TO KEEP OUR KIDS FROM FALLING...BUT SOMETIMES THEY END UP CATCHING US.
SEE, WHILE IT'S TRUE WE MAKE THE HARDEST DECISIONS FOR THE PEOPLE WE CARE ABOUT THE MOST... THEY'RE USUALLY THE ONES WHO SHOW US WHAT THE RIGHT DECISIONS ARE.
LIKE I SAID BEFORE, WE GROW UP LOOKING FOR GLIMPSES OF WHO OUR PARENTS WERE BEFORE WE KNEW THEM. TO TRY AND LEARN ABOUT THEM SO WE CAN LEARN MORE ABOUT OURSELVES.
HOPEFULLY, ONE DAY THIS WILL HELP YOU TO UNDERSTAND WHY THINGS ARE THE WAY THEY ARE. WHY I AM THE WAY I AM.
AND WHY YOU'RE NAMED AFTER THE GREATEST PERSON I EVER KNEW.
ALL DONE?
RECORDING STOPPED.

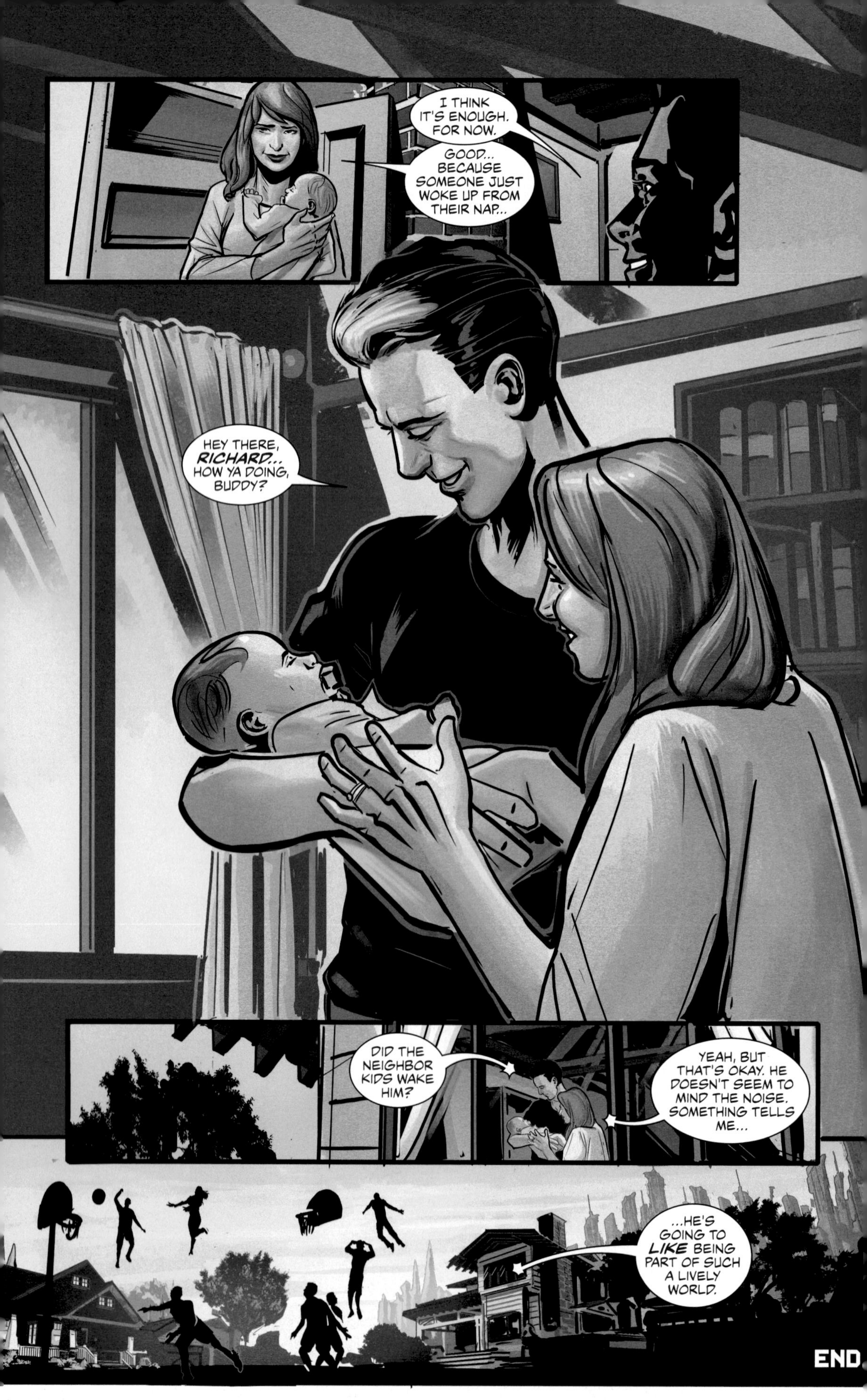
I THINK IT'S ENOUGH. FOR NOW.
GOOD... BECAUSE SOMEONE JUST WOKE UP FROM THEIR NAP...
HEY THERE, RICHARD... HOW YA DOING, BUDDY?
DID THE NEIGHBOR KIDS WAKE HIM?
YEAH, BUT THAT'S OKAY. HE DOESN'T SEEM TO MIND THE NOISE. SOMETHING TELLS ME...
...HE'S GOING TO LIKE BEING PART OF SUCH A LIVELY WORLD.
END

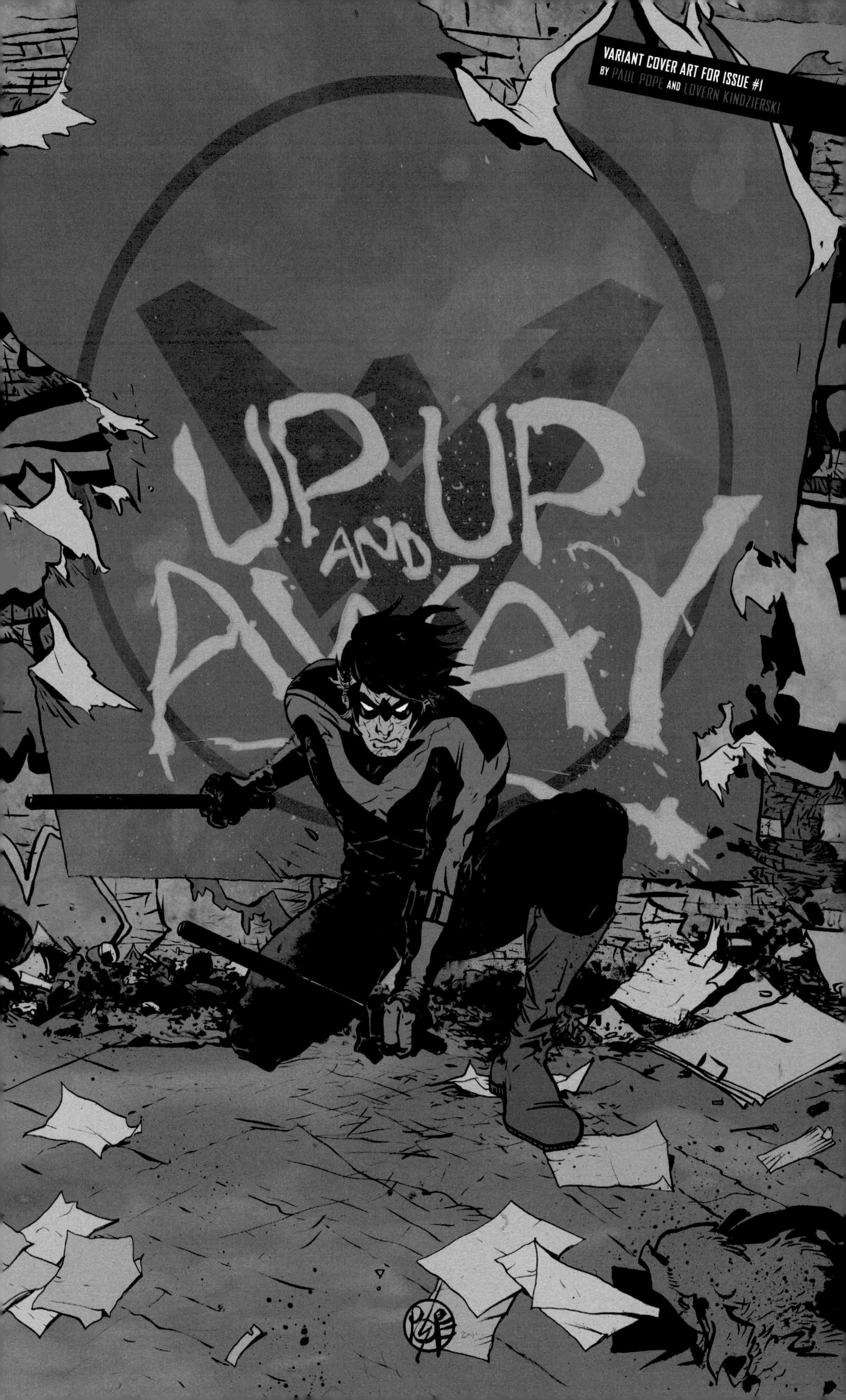
UP UP AND AWAY

VARIANT COVER ART FOR ISSUE #1
BY PAUL POPE AND LOVERN KINDZIERSKI

DC UNIVERSE REBIRTH

NIGHTWING

VOL. 1: BETTER THAN BATMAN

TIM SEELEY
with JAVIER FERNANDEZ

VOL. 1 BETTER THAN BATMAN
TIM SEELEY ★ JAVIER FERNÁNDEZ ★ CHRIS SOTOMAYOR

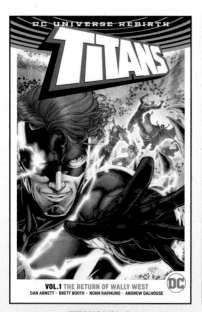

TITANS VOL. 1:
THE RETURN OF WALLY WEST

BATGIRL VOL. 1:
BEYOND BURNSIDE

BATMAN VOL. 1:
I AM GOTHAM

NIGHTWING
VOL. 1: TRAPS AND TRAPEZES
KYLE HIGGINS
with EDDY BARROWS

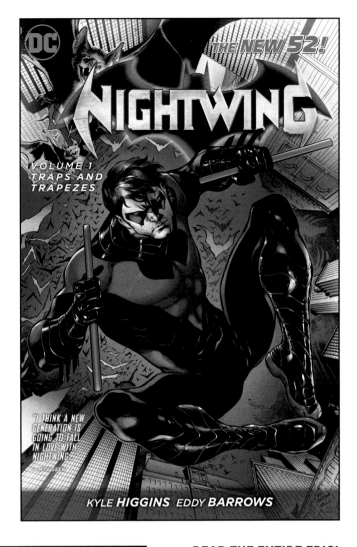

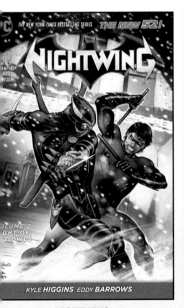

**NIGHTWING
VOL. 2: NIGHT OF THE OWLS**

**NIGHTWING
VOL. 3: DEATH OF THE FAMILY**

READ THE ENTIRE EPIC!

NIGHTWING VOL. 4:
SECOND CITY

NIGHTWING VOL. 5:
SETTING SON

"A new generation is going to
fall in love with Nightwing."
– MTV GEEK

SUPERMAN: UNCHAINED
with JIM LEE and others

BATMAN: GATES OF GOTHAM
with TREVOR MCCARTHY and others

BATMAN: ETERNAL
with JASON FABOK and others